1

Can Pay Be Strategic?

Can Pay Be Strategic?

A Critical Exploration of Strategic Pay in Practice

Jonathan Trevor

First published 2011 by
PALGRAVE MACMILLAN

Palgrave Macmillan in the UK is an imprint of Macmillan Publishers Limited, registered in England, company number 785998, of Houndmills, Basingstoke, Hampshire RG21 6XS.

Palgrave Macmillan in the US is a division of St Martin's Press LLC, 175 Fifth Avenue, New York, NY 10010.

Palgrave Macmillan is the global academic imprint of the above companies and has companies and representatives throughout the world.

Palgrave® and Macmillan® are registered trademarks in the United States, the United Kingdom, Europe and other countries.

ISBN 978–0–230–22354–7   hardback

This book is printed on paper suitable for recycling and made from fully managed and sustained forest sources. Logging, pulping and manufacturing processes are expected to conform to the environmental regulations of the country of origin.

A catalogue record for this book is available from the British Library.

Library of Congress Cataloging-in-Publication Data

Trevor, Jonathan.
  Can pay be strategic? : a critical exploration of strategic pay in practice/by Jonathan Trevor.
      p. cm.
  ISBN 978–0–230–22354–7 (hardback)
1. Compensation management.   2. Compensation management—Case studies.   3. Wage payment systems.   4. Wage payment systems—Case studies.   I. Title.
  HF5549.5.C67T74 2010
  658.3'2—dc22   2010027589

10   9   8   7   6   5   4   3   2   1
20   19   18   17   16   15   14   13   12   11

Printed and bound in Great Britain by
CPI Antony Rowe, Chippenham and Eastbourne

To my parents, Gareth and Gillian

Contents

List of Figures and Tables

Figures

Tables

Confidentiality Agreement

The study has benefited greatly from the generous access secured by each of the sponsors within the case study firms. Pay is a highly emotive aspect of employment and it is incumbent upon the researcher to observe appropriate discretion when interviewing and discussing matters of pay management. In the interests of confidentiality, all material has been anonymized and no reference is made to any unique characteristics that might identify any of the case study companies. The research was conducted very much on the basis of mutual interest in the subject, goodwill between parties and a spirit of openness and honesty.

Acknowledgements

I am indebted to each of the case study companies for their agreement to having the data and findings published and thus reach a wider audience. To the individuals in each of the companies concerned I offer my sincere thanks for their valued contributions. Their enthusiastic participation throughout has made it a stimulating and exciting project to undertake on my part. Not only were they generous with their time as participants but their unstinting interest in the research was both stimulating and encouraging. My thanks also go to the people in the professional organizations and consultancies who provided professional insight and generous access to sensitive and pay trend data and relevant information.

Special recognition goes to Dr Philip Stiles, Judge Business School, and Professor William Brown, University of Cambridge, for their guidance, encouragement and moral support, both professionally and personally. And finally, very special thanks are owed to my parents for their unfaltering support, and this book is dedicated to them.

List of Abbreviations and Acronyms

ABI	Association of British Insurers
AESOP	All employee share ownership programme
CAGR	Compound annual growth rate
CIPD	Chartered Institute of Personnel & Development
Company1–7	Case study companies coded 1 to 7
Consult1–3	Consultancy companies coded 1 to 3
EPS	Earnings per share
FMCG	Fast moving consumer goods
HIWS	High involvement work systems
HR	Human resources
HRA	Human resource accounting
HRIS	Human resource information systems
HRM	Human resource management
IR	Industrial relations
LTI	Long-term incentives
MIP	Management incentive plan
NAPF	National Association of Pension Funds
NDA	Non-disclosure agreements
PRP	Performance-related pay
R&D	Research and development
RBV	Resource-based view
ROI	Return on investment
ROTA	Return on total assets
SHRM	Strategic human resource management
STI	Short-term incentives
TSR	Total shareholder return
WERS	Workplace Employment Relations Series

1
Introduction

Pay is a key element of the employment relationship. In addition to being the largest single operating cost for many firms, pay has been advocated more recently as a means through which organizations can achieve enhanced performance and sustained competitive advantage. Contemporary theories of pay highlight the role of pay as a management tool for the achievement of managerial ends and underline the importance of aligning employee behaviours to the strategic direction of the organization. This is a departure from established patterns of pay management, which emphasized the collective determination of pay and tenure-based pay progression. Pay remains a powerful means of attracting and retaining valued talent, but it is in relation to eliciting behavioural outcomes, discretionary behaviours for example, and performance (individual, team and organizational) that pay offers the greatest organizational advantage. Referred to under a variety of different terms (including new pay, reward management, strategic rewards, dynamic pay and strategic compensation management) but referred to here as *strategic pay*, these strategic theories of pay reflect a fundamental shift in the philosophy of pay and employment more broadly. Strategic pay has very rapidly come to represent the 'received wisdom' within practice, mirroring an equally rapid ascendancy in theory as the 'new orthodoxy'. Available pay trend data suggests that organizations in the private sector especially are attempting to use pay systems to deliver outcomes of strategic value.

Our understanding of strategic pay, however, is limited in practice, despite the volume of prescriptive academic and practitioner commentary available on the subject. In particular, it is not clear how companies are managing strategic pay systems and how well these systems fulfil the potential promised by its advocates. The challenges associated with attempts to use pay strategically are well documented in practitioner circles, for example with performance-related pay. A small but vocal body of critical human resource commentary from the academic community points to failings in strategic employment theories of a conceptual, normative and prescriptive nature. The implication is that what has come to represent 'standard' theory is not without some major shortcomings. Furthermore, this criticism is made without a strong empirical base that would give these claims some grounded credibility.

This book seeks to review recent theoretical developments within the context of an empirically grounded exploration of the pay practices of leading companies. The relevant literature on the conceptual nature of strategic pay was reviewed. A research design and methodology was developed to investigate strategic pay in practice, with the aim of collecting rich primary data that would enable grounded theory to emerge to illustrate (a) *what* firms are doing in relation to pay, (b) *how* they are managing pay and, finally, (c) *how well*.

Some of the key research questions that needed to be addressed in this context included whether firms use pay strategically. If not, on what basis are pay systems being managed? If firms *are* attempting to use pay strategically: what is this in response to and for what purpose? More specifically, is pay being used purposefully to attract and retain valued talent? Is pay being used as a tool through which companies' and individuals' performances might be enhanced? Is pay being used as a means of eliciting desired employee behaviours such as commitment, loyalty and motivation? Are pay systems being used for the expressed purpose of securing sustained competitive advantage?

To address the dearth in the published literature on the subject of strategic pay in practice, it was important to understand better how firms are attempting to manage their strategic pay systems. How is the process of pay determination configured and who does it involve? What are the outcomes of the pay determination process and what form do they take organizationally?

In terms of effectiveness, do the pay systems used yield outcomes of strategic value, for the individual and the organization? Are strategic pay systems integral to the ability of firms to attract and retain valued talent? Do they, indeed, foster commitment, loyalty and motivation, among other desired behaviours? In short, do strategic pay systems do what they are supposed to do in practice? If this was found to be the case, it would provide important and independent confirmation of the value of strategic pay in practice and provide a counterclaim to much of the critical commentary of those who label the perceived benefits of strategic pay as mere rhetoric. If strategic pay systems do not yield outcomes of strategic value in practice, we need to understand better why this is the case, and investigate what implications this would have for current theory and practice and what alternative approaches might exist that would warrant further investigation.

Chapter 2 reviews the relevant literature on the transition from 'old pay' to 'new pay' and the emergence of strategic pay as the new orthodoxy. A brief outline of the basis upon which strategic pay decisions are made is included, together with the critical commentary of what has fast become standard theory. This provides the backdrop against which the emerging findings of the empirical investigation are framed.

Chapter 3 describes the study and some of the key methodological issues. An exploratory approach is adopted, which takes advantage of both quantitative and qualitative methods, including in-depth case study research. Results from the quantitative and qualitative data analyses are reviewed.

Chapter 4 is the first of the four primary findings chapters and presents the quantitative findings of the review of *industry*-level pay trends within the fast moving consumer goods (FMCG) sector. Chapter 5, the *approach*-level findings, brings analysis down to the level of the firm and discusses the approach that the case study firms have adopted to pay practice. Chapter 6, the *design*-level findings, explores case study company pay practice at the design level of the pay determination process, and provides the policy context for the final level of analysis: an operational review of case study company pay practice. This is set out in Chapter 7, the *pay operation*-level findings.

Chapter 8 draws upon the empirical findings of all levels of the study to form an overall portrait of case study company pay practice and highlights the key findings. Chapter 9 addresses many of the themes to emerge from the findings overall, and attempts to explain their significance for pay theory and practice. The final chapter, Chapter 10, addresses the implications of the research for theory, practice and future research. The study concludes by suggesting an alternative conception of pay management that seeks to reconcile the manifest theoretical tensions and to draw attention to the grounded experience of pay in practice.

2
From Old Pay to New Pay

The first section of this chapter reviews post-war developments to pay within the UK and multinational firms. It highlights a transition from collectively determined pay arrangements to more recent models of managerially determined pay. A review of empirical data and contemporary theory reveals the pervasiveness of strategic theories of pay, which emphasize the managerial determination of pay for the achievement, primarily, of the managerial ends of enhanced company performance and competitive advantage. Such theories have come to the fore within both theory and practice, and represent the 'new orthodoxy' of theory and the 'received wisdom' of practice.

There is a dearth of understanding in the relevant literature about the use of strategic systems pay in practice. Themes common to all strategic theories of pay, such as strategic choice, the alignment of pay practice to company strategy and the linkage to company performance, are not well understood in the context of contemporary company practice. In addition, there is a small but vocal body of critical commentary that challenges many of the assumptions – normative, prescriptive and conceptual – upon which strategic theories of pay are founded. Such criticism, however, is lacking an empirical base with which to ground its assertions. A pressing need exists, therefore, for a grounded exploration of strategic pay in practice.

From 'old pay' to 'new pay'

Broadly defined, pay is the means by which employees are financially rewarded in the workplace (Brown and Walsh, 1994). It is a central element of the employment relationship, constituting 'one side of the coin that makes up the effort and reward bargain' (Kessler, 2000, 2001). The basis

4

upon which pay and related employment measures are determined has undergone profound change throughout the post-war period in Britain, as a result of far-reaching political and economic change (Cully et al., 1999; Brown, 2001). The Workplace Employment Relations Series (WERS) of workplace-level surveys – Britain's largest and most comprehensive longitudinal survey of employment patterns – portrays a dramatic decline in the determination of pay by multi-employer collective bargaining (Cully et al., 1999; Brown, 2001).

These surveys demonstrate that multi-employer collective bargaining as a means of determining pay, in the private sector especially, has been replaced by unilateral employer discretion (Cully et al., 1999). Figure 2.1 illustrates that within the period 1984–2004 collective bargaining over pay declined dramatically, to be replaced by managerial pay determination at the company or workplace level.

WERS data reveals a portrait of management at the level of the workplace and above determining pay unilaterally for employees across multiple sites (Milward et al., 2000). The collective laissez-faire ethos of pay determination through collective bargaining at the industry level has been replaced by unilateral pay determination by employers acting alone and increasingly centralizing pay decisions at the level of the organization. The most recent in the WERS series, the 2004 survey *Inside*

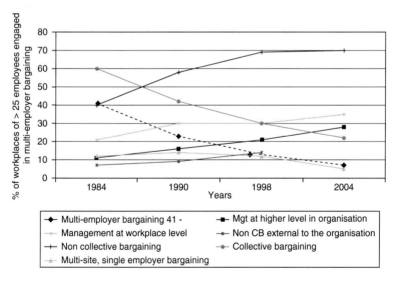

Figure 2.1 Economy-wide workplace level trends in pay determination 1984/ 1990/1998/2004

the Workplace, reveals that the overall trend towards employer discretion over the determination of pay, terms and conditions has continued, with around just one quarter of workplaces (27%) setting pay by means of collective bargaining and 70 per cent by means of unilateral employer discretion. The picture is even more marked within the private sector, with just 14 per cent of workplaces setting their pay through collective bargaining. The most recent data suggests that the progressive trend towards unilateral employer discretion over pay determination continues unabated.

Never before in post-war Britain have employers enjoyed as much freedom to determine the basis of employee pay unilaterally and in the interests of achieving purely managerial ends. The external labour market is credited, in large part, with replacing collective bargaining as the primary determinant of pay levels and practice, but Brown (2001) notes that employers, employing the same labour, do pay their employees different rates for the job. There are clearly other forces at work that labour market theory does not adequately account for. A number of factors prevent employers from being the 'passive recipients' of labour market rates of pay, including imperfect competition within both the product market and the labour market as a result of imperfect market information; the permissive nature of product market conditions; the type of labour employed; and, finally, that pay is rarely used in isolation, being one of a series of complementary interventions aimed at eliciting workforce productivity (ibid.).

What are management doing with their new-found freedom to determine pay unilaterally? Drawing again upon the WERS series, the longitudinal data indicates that an increasing proportion of organizations are using performance as the basis for pay awards (Milward et al., 2000). Results from the WERS 1998 survey reveal that *performance* was cited as a factor of pay determination in 25 per cent of firms, or 33 per cent of employees, a relatively low proportion by comparison to higher-order factors, including job grade/classification and skills/core competencies (Cully et al., 1999). Further analysis of the data, however, taking into account company size reveals a positive relationship between establishment size and the use of incentive-based pay. Larger establishments are using performance-based pay systems to a greater degree (Nash, 2003). The 2004 WERS survey reveals that performance-related pay arrangements were used in 40 per cent of workplaces overall and 44 per cent in the private sector (Kersley et al., 2006), a marked increase over previous years. Additional 'strategic pay' measures also feature more than in previous years, including profit-related payments or bonuses (37%) and employee share schemes (21%) (ibid.).

Additional survey data reveals an even starker portrait of strategic pay adoption. The Chartered Institute of Personnel and Development, for the last seven years, has conducted a survey of reward management practices in organizations operating in the UK across industry and in both the public and private sectors. Across all sectors, but especially in private sector services, data reveals the seemingly inexorable rise of 'new pay' practices as the norm. In the most recent series of their survey reviewing pay arrangements in the UK,[1] the Reward Management Annual Survey Report 2007, the CIPD reports that 35 per cent of respondents have a formal reward (pay) strategy, with a further 40 per cent planning to introduce one in 2007. Large organizations are far more likely to have adopted a formal reward strategy, with 49 per cent of organizations employing between 1000 and 4999 employees, having had one for the past four years or more, and 57 per cent of organizations employing in excess of 5000 employees having had one for the past four years or more (CIPD, 2007). Short-term, cash-based and incentive schemes are common across the private sector and are most typically linked to individual performance (64%), business results overall (53%), or a combination of the two (47%) (ibid.).

These developments in pay are not solely confined to the UK. Proprietary consultancy data gathered from a sample of over one hundred Fortune 500 firms operating globally reveal that all (100%) have had a global reward strategy in place for four or more years (Mercer Human Resource Consulting, 2004). Global pay strategies are put in place for a number of reasons, the most important, however, being in support of global expansion. The main reasons for introducing global pay strategies include global expansion (29%), improved governance structures (17%), cost management (15%), compliance and reporting (12%) and mergers and acquisitions (5%) (ibid.). On a domestic, regional and global level, the survey data indicates that firms are embracing strategic pay for the achievement of competitive advantage.

Additional data from Watson Wyatt Worldwide, a remuneration consultancy, reports a trend towards the increasing centralization of pay management (determination). Within their sample, 56 per cent of multinational firms[2] currently without a centralized pay structure, were planning to implement one over the next two years, compared to 42 per cent in 2004. Two-thirds of multinational firms surveyed (66%) report that they have adopted a globally consistent human resources (HR) strategy, including provision for standardized pay arrangements. Over half of the sample organizations (51%) have a formal or informal global total rewards strategy, with another 20 per cent planning to introduce a strategy within the next 12 to 24 months.

Overall, data from a range of sources indicates that employers enjoy more freedom than ever before to determine pay unilaterally, in the interests of achieving managerial ends. Having abandoned collective structures of pay determination, management has embraced new pay practice – performance-based pay systems in particular – with their new-found freedom. Large private sector firms in particular have been at the vanguard of the transition from old pay to new pay, but the rest of the field – private and public – is not lagging far behind. These developments are not confined solely to the UK. Large multinational firms, also, have embraced strategic pay practices and are no doubt a powerful force encouraging others to do the same.

The promise of strategic pay – a managerialist account

Why are firms embracing strategic pay so enthusiastically? Pay programmes characteristic of 'old pay' and 'traditional pay', focused on job-evaluated grade structures, payment by time, salary progression as the basis of seniority, internal labour markets and service-related benefits, and were developed to suit hierarchical organizations, operating in predictable environments. A great deal of managerial time and effort was devoted to managing pay structures to ensure internal relativity between roles, grades and functions. The internal labour market was the primary determinant of wage setting, in place of, or in combination with, trade union representation. Such stable structures went hand in hand with the implicit promise of job security and other protections, including generous retirement and ill-health benefits. The philosophy underpinning pay was one of 'hygiene' and equity (Herzberg, 1975; Gerhart and Rynes, 2003). Provided that perceived needs around equity were satisfied, pay as a motivator was taken out of the equation and, while linked to productivity, was not the behavioural lever that more recent pay interventions are purported to be.

New pay – or *strategic pay* – on the other hand, is positioned as a means of enhancing company performance and securing competitive advantage, through the alignment of pay strategies, systems, practices and processes to the organizational strategy.

As a management tool, pay is no longer purely a cost of hiring necessary labour, but a means of aligning a company's unique and inimitable asset – their employees – to the strategic direction of the organization: 'The starting point for any reward system design process needs to be the strategic

Table 2.1 Traditional versus strategic pay systems

Item	Traditional	Strategic
Reward basis	Job	Person
Market position	High	Based on skills and knowledge
Equity focus	Internal and external	External
Hierarchy	Significant-level differences	Minimal-level differences
Contract	Loyalty and entitlement	Employability and performance

Source: Lawler (2000).

agenda of the organization. The first step in designing the reward system for an organization is to focus on the individual and organizational behaviours that are needed in order for the organization to be successful' (Lawler et al., 1995). Once aligned, pay becomes a powerful means through which firms may attract and retain desired talent, and elicit desired behaviour outcomes in the form of employee motivation, commitment and loyalty, all of which are conducive to enhanced company performance. With a particular focus on performance, new pay incorporates considerably more scope for pay 'at risk', with employees' pay potentially being contingent upon one of, or a combination of, company performance, team/division performance and individual performance.

Under strategic pay (and performance-based rewards more broadly), collective and individual failure and success are reflected in the pay of each employee. Designed to encourage *mutuality* of interest, new pay is 'implemented with a high degree of employee involvement and results in both parties "winning"' (Schuster and Zingheim, 1992). To be most effective, strategic pay systems need to support the business strategy in terms of maintaining the consistency of internal wage differentials; ensuring the competitiveness of wage rates in relation to local labour markets; reflecting relative employee contributions; representing a centralized, or decentralized, administrative style, as appropriate to the organization (Milkovich and Newman, 1999). 'The [reward] design must be congruent with the basic organization design and management style of the organization which, in turn, needs to be strongly influenced by the organization's strategy' (Lawler, 2000).

Central to the new pay movement is a belief that rewards can, and do, make a difference to organizational performance (Gerhart and Rynes, 2003). Rewards, if managed effectively, profoundly benefit the organization by attracting and retaining key talent, motivating staff and encouraging objective, supporting behaviours and directing their efforts in such a way as to achieve stated corporate goals: 'Compensation

Table 2.2   Administrative versus strategic pay systems

Administrative Focus	Strategic Focus
Job	Person
Individual	Team
Time	Output
Lag system	Lead system
Top-down	Bottom-up
Centralized	Decentralized
Static	Dynamic
Internal equity	External equity
Fixed	Variable

Source: Rynes and Gerhart (2000).

consultants and researchers increasingly argue for basing rewards partly on organizational performance as a way to assure that employees are involved in, and care about, their organization. Employee stock owner-ship plans, profit sharing, stock options, and gain sharing are examples of plans that can link employees to the success of the business and reward them for it' (Lawler et al., 1995).

For Bergman and Scarpello (2002), the primary goal of compensation systems is to 'elicit desired behaviours from employees'. For Armstrong and Murlis (1998), the aims of strategic pay are to:

- Support the achievement of the organization's strategic and shorter-term objectives
- Assist with the communication of organizational values and per-formance expectations
- Promote the organization's culture and support change
- Drive and support desired behaviours
- Encourage value-added performance
- Promote continuous development
- Compete in the employment market
- Motivate all members of the organization from the shop floor to the board room
- Promote teamwork
- Promote flexibility
- Provide value for money
- Achieve fairness and equity.

Armstrong and Brown (2001) remark that the rationale for a strate-gic approach to rewards is to 'ensure that the results and behaviours (of employees) are consistent with key organizational goals and behavioural standards'. It is an important tool for communicating and reinforcing new values and behaviours, supporting accountability for results and rewarding the achievement of new performance goals (Flannery et al., 2004; Armstrong and Murlis, 2004). The introduction of measures such as performance-related pay is expected to confer economically advantageous benefits for the organization, including the following (adapted from Gilman, 1999):

- Signals a change in organizational culture (Kessler and Purcell, 1992; Lewis, 1991; Fowler, 1988; Pendleton, 1992).
- Can be used to bring about a restructuring of the employment relationship (Kessler and Purcell, 1992; Currie and Procter, 2001; Fowler, 1988).
- Allows companies to reward selectively without an increase in the pay bill (Goodhart, 1993).
- Decentralises collective bargaining (Walsh, 1992).
- Marginalizes the role of trade unions (Kessler and Purcell, 1992; Currie and Procter, 2001; Fowler, 1988).
- Permits closer corporate financial control (Kessler and Purcell, 1992; Currie and Procter, 2001; Pendleton, 1992).
- As organizations become flatter, it becomes more difficult to reward through promotion.
- Performance-related pay (PRP) enables selected rewarding, combined with development programmes, such as performance management systems, to dilute employee dissatisfaction. (Goodhart, 1993).

The CIPD (2007) reward management survey indicates that organizations have embraced such aspirations. By far the most common goal for strategic pay is that of supporting the achievement of business goals (84%), closely followed by rewarding high performers through performance differentiation (77%) and the recruitment and retention of value talent (68%) (see Table 2.3). The emphasis on supporting business goals, through attracting and retaining the necessary calibre of employee, but more importantly through rewarding high performance, is indicative of the shift away from old pay to strategic pay. Arguably, supporting the achievement of strategic goals and performance differentiation represent the two outcomes of pay most valued strategically, which is reflected in the relative importance attached to them.

By what terms might 'new' pay be judged strategic? Firstly, strategic theories of pay emphasize the right of management to unilaterally

Table 2.3   Reward strategy goals

Reward Strategy Goals (in rank order)	%
Support business goals	84
Reward high performers	77
Recruit and retain high performers	68
Achieve/maintain market competitiveness	67
Link pay to market	65
Support career development and progression	53
Manage pay costs	49
Ensure internal equity	43

Source: Chartered Institute of Personnel and Development (2007).

determine pay – crucially – free from interference, in the interests of promoting organizational performance and, thereby, securing and sustaining competitive advantage. Managerial decisions over pay are becoming increasingly centralized, as indicated by the longitudinal WERS dataset (see Figure 2.1), with control being exercised at the organizational level and not at the workplace level, which was characteristic of pay determination in the past. Secondly, theories of strategic pay all share the assumption that, given the right, management are *capable* of exercising such choice for the betterment of the organization through enhanced performance. Innately rational decision makers are able, through strategic planning, to deploy those pay systems that represent optimal interventions for achieving optimal pay outcomes, contributing to performance and value maximization (in terms of employee behaviours and levels of productivity, for example). The primacy of managerial choice as *the* determinant of pay practice is characteristic of all theories of strategic pay.

The literature on strategic human resource management is fraught with tension between so-called universalistic best practices and context-specific contingent practices. On the one hand much empirical data supports the notion that there exist certain practices that have universal application which, when used, result in positive additive outcomes (Pfeffer, 1994, 1998). Often termed best practice, the notion of universality has gained much currency within the management literature and is pervasive in corporate discourse despite manifest differences between organizations (for example strategic orientation, characteristics of the internal and external operating environment). Conversely, contingency theory argues that value resulting from company practice is only realized when the elements of the organizational design, such as human capital practice, are aligned to the organization's strategy, which is itself aligned to market opportunities in the external environment. Emphasizing the importance of 'fit' between strategy, systems, practice(s) and processes, the firm's human capital practices are used as a means of aligning employees to the goals and values of the organizations.

Fit requires that firm practice is necessarily contingent upon the technical and social properties of the context into which it is introduced and operated, therefore rendering firm practice idiosyncratic. Indeed, it is the unique qualities of the firm's human capital that permits sustained competitive advantage. While intuitively appealing, the notion of fit and alignment is not on the whole well supported by existing empirical data that has focused largely on establishing correlations between firm performance and crude measures of firm practice using large-scale quantitative datasets. Strategic pay theory is beset by the same tension, being characterized both by prescriptions advocating those best practices deemed to have universal application and by prescriptions promoting the choice of pay practices that best fit the unique goals and contextual characteristics – commercial, institutional and technical – of the organization. Nevertheless both represent a departure from the philosophical underpinnings of old pay and are characteristic of notions of strategic pay.

Finally, perhaps one of the most notable differences between old pay and new pay is the emphasis placed on the individualization of the employment relationship over collective agreements and associated structures for the collective determination of pay. The prevalence of performance-based pay systems is the most obvious example of the individualization of pay. Differentiating between the relative performance of individuals, and differentiating pay concomitantly, represents the antithesis of collectively determined pay where performance gives way to the importance attached to common equity between roles.

Strategic theories of pay differ substantially, therefore, in a number of significant ways. The emergence of strategic pay theory now as standard theory has redefined the role and perceived contribution of pay organizationally and economically. No longer a 'cost of doing business' pay is, itself, when used strategically, a source of value creation and, along with other human capital measures, the means by which firms can secure sustained competitive advantage. Strategic pay is a compelling concept that has been aggressively and persuasively promoted by academics and practitioners alike. To understand the conceptual nature of strategic pay, and the promise of the benefits it confers upon organizations, its emergence must be placed in the context of broader developments.

Human resource management and the pedigree of strategic pay

The rise of strategic pay is linked to reform in the management of the employment relationship overall and in particular to the advent of human resource management (HRM). Replacing industrial relations and personnel management as the 'dominant logic', HRM represents a significant departure ideologically from past theory (Storey, 2001). HRM emerged during the mid-1980s with the publication of two, now 'classic' texts by academics at Michigan (Frombrun et al., 1984) and Harvard (Beer et al., 1984). The 'Michigan' model emphasized the importance of linking the firm's HR strategy to the business strategy. Employees, theory holds, are a *resource* to be maximized, and business strategy should be the first order determinant defining the type of labour employed and the way in which it is managed. Employee development, employee performance and remuneration are informed by the business strategy above all else (Frombrun et al., 1984). The 'Harvard' model differed by arguing that employees are not a resource in the conventional sense of the term and should not be managed as such. Engaging employees' understanding and commitment is a key contributor to company performance, with the HR strategy and the business strategy going hand in hand (Beer et al., 1984). Both models stress the same desired outcomes, however, of enhanced organizational performance and sustained competitive advantage.

A core assumption of both models is that management within employing organizations can, and should, exercise considerable discretion over the management of their employees (Guest, 1997). In many cases, discretion equates to freedom – the freedom of management to deploy performance-based pay systems, the freedom to manage employment with minimal (or the complete absence of) interference from trade unions and employee representatives, and other such constraints characteristic of 'traditional employment management'. HRM empowers employers to manage free from constraint (Guest, 1997).

The advent of HRM coincided with developments in related disciplines and offered an intuitively appealing, managerially orientated, agenda on employment (Storey, 1995). In particular, HRM has found traction with the persuasive argument that market value depends less on tangible resources in highly competitive market environments than on the ability of the firm to mobilize intangible assets – their HR. The traditional role of recruiting and retaining employees, alone, is not sufficient, however, to ensure competitive advantage. To achieve success,

Table 2.4 A prototypical human resource management model

Beliefs and assumptions

- That it is the human resource that gives competitive edge
- That the aim should be not mere compliance with rules, but employee commitment
- That, therefore, employees should, for example, be very carefully selected and developed

Strategic qualities

- Because of the above factors, HR decisions are of strategic importance
- Top management involvement is necessary
- HR policies should be integrated into the business strategy – stemming from it and even contributing to it

Critical role for managers

- Because HR practice is critical to the core activities of the business, it is too important to be left to personnel specialists alone
- Line managers are (or need to be) closely involved as both deliverers and drivers of the HR policies
- Much greater attention is paid to the management of managers themselves

Key levers

- Managing culture is more important than managing procedures and systems
- Integrated action on selection, communication, training, reward and development
- Restructuring and job redesign to allow devolved responsibility and empowerment

---

Source: Storey (2001).

organizations must also leverage the skills and capabilities of their employees by encouraging individual and organizational learning, and creating a supportive environment and culture in which knowledge can be created, shared and applied (Wright and Snell, 1998). The linkage between HR and company performance is a compelling one. A great deal of empirical work has sought to understand better the linkage between HRM and company performance. The highly influential theory and commentary to emerge from such work, representing the backdrop to developments in pay, is discussed later.

The resource-based view and the value of human capital

Commentary on the determinants of corporate competitive advantage has undergone a profound shift in the recent past. Within mainstream strategy literature there has been growing recognition that investment in and the mobilization of internal resources – HR in this case – is equally important to sustained competitiveness as the traditional emphasis of positioning within the external product market (Wright et al., 2001; Stiles and Kulvisaechana, 2003). The resource-based view (RBV) of the organization, the most prominent of these developments, establishes the importance of building valuable resources and bundling them together in unique and dynamic ways (Penrose, 1959; Rumelt, 1984; Barney, 1991). Competitive advantage is thus dependent not solely on the capitalization of traditional assets, such as natural resources, fixed assets or technologies, all of which are increasingly easy to imitate with the transparency of corporate activity and the speed with which information is made available, but on the valuable, rare, unique and hard-to-imitate resources that comprise the organization's human capital and intellectual capital – its people (Boxall, 1999).

Human capital can be defined as comprising the 'experience, judgement and intelligence of the individual managers and workers in the firm' (Wright et al., 2001; Jackson and Schuler, 1995). The value derived from human capital is only fully realized when combined with the organization's physical and capital assets (Boxall, 1999).

Human capital, unlike fixed assets, is an 'invisible asset' but, being intangible, is difficult to define and measure in conventional value terms (Itami, 1987). A firm's human capital is a source of sustainable competitive advantage, because: 'If the types and levels of skills are not equally distributed, such that some firms can acquire the talent they need and others cannot, then *ceteris paribus* that form of human capital can be a source of sustained competitive advantage' (Snell et al., 1996). Unlike traditional or tangible assets, such as technology or fixed assets, human capital is inimitable because of causal ambiguity and the effects of path dependency upon decisions (Becker and Gerhart, 1996; Barney, 1991). 'First, it is difficult to grasp the precise mechanism by which the interplay of human resource practice and policies generates value; second, these HR systems are path dependent. They consist of policies that are developed over time and cannot be simply purchased in the market by competitors' (Becker and Gerhart, 1996). The interdependency and linkages between HR practices combined with the unique external and internal contextual characteristics of individual companies create barriers to imitation thus sustaining their competitive advantage (Boxall, 1999).

The increasing importance of the RBV is in part responsible for the rise in the perceived importance of HRM, and human capital theory in particular, and bringing about a 'convergence between the fields of strategy and HRM' (Wright et al., 2001; Stiles and Kulvisaechana, 2003). The RBV of the firm lends credence to the oft-abused and much-maligned platitude 'people are our most important asset', which, despite being labelled 'the biggest lie in contemporary American business', is manifest of the perceived value of people to organizational success (Hammer and Champy, 1993).

Best practice, configurations and human resource management

Consistent with the principles of the 'Harvard' model of HRM, a highly compelling perspective on the linkage between HRM and performance is the idea of 'best practices' (Pfeffer, 1998). Universalists, such as Pfeffer (1994, 1998), contend that there exist best practices with universal application, which benefit firms in performance terms irrespective of context (ibid.). Quite simply, the more high-performance HRM best practices, the greater the performance returns. A number of influential studies have attempted to establish demonstrably the linkage between HR practices and performance using single measures, for example compensation, recruitment and so on (Storey, 2001). Bartel (1994) sought to establish a link between the level of the use of training programmes and productivity growth. Terpstra and Rozell (1993) reviewed the size of the 'talent pool' from which potential employees are selected, the basis of selection (for example testing) and the use of formal selection procedures, and found a positive relationship between financial firm performance and multi-input selection procedures when recruiting new employees (Becker and Huselid, 1992; Schmidt et al., 1979). Gerhart and Milkovich (1990) and Weitzman and Kruse (1990) have identified compelling linkages between the use of financial incentives and workplace productivity. Similarly, linking objective setting and performance management to compensation is also widely credited with contributing to increased profitability (Schuster and Zingheim, 1992, 2000).

Such reliance on single HR practices, however, may not achieve the promised returns. Increasingly, it is being recognized that individual HR practices 'have the limited ability to generate competitive advantage in isolation' but 'in combination ... they can enable a firm to realise its full competitive advantage' (Barney, 1995). In other words, relying on single HR practices to predict performance may not prove to be fruitful. More recent commentary has emphasized the importance of patterns or configurations of HR practice (Delery and Doty, 1996; Brewster et al., 2005). Individual HR practices, when aligned horizontally or integrated, yield superior performance (Delery and Doty, 1996). MacDuffie (1995) argues that 'implicit in the notion of a "bundle" (of HR practices) is the

Table 2.5 Summary of human resource best practices (identified within extant literature)

Freund and Epstein (1984)	Arthur (1992)	Pfeffer (1994)	Delany, Lewin & Ichiowski (1989), Huselid (1995)	MacDuffie (1995)
Job enlargement	Broadly defined jobs	Employment security	Personnel selection	Work teams
Job rotation	Employee participation	Selective recruiting	Performance appraisal	Problem-solving groups
Job design	Formal dispute resolution	High wages	Incentive compensation	Employee suggestions
Formal training	Information sharing	Incentive compensation	Job design	Job rotation
Personalized work hours	Highly skilled workers	Employee ownership	Grievance procedures	Decentralization
Suggestion systems	Self-managed teams	Information sharing	Information sharing	Recruitment and hiring
Quality circles	Extensive skills training	Participation	Attitude assessment	Contingent compensation
Salary for blue collar workers	Extensive benefits	Empowerment	Labour/management participation	Status differentiation
Attitude surveys	High wages	Job redesign/teams	Recruiting intensity	Training of new employees
Production teams	Salaried workers	Training and skill development	Training intensity	Training of experienced employees
Labour/management committees	Stock ownership	Cross-utilization	Training hours	
Group productivity incentives			Cross-training	Promotion criteria (seniority v merit)
Profit sharing		Symbolic egalitarianism		
Stock purchase plan		Wage compression		
		Promotion from within		

Source: Youndt et al. (1996), referenced in Stiles and Kulvisaechana (2003).

lvement systems, traditional systems, identification systems and none
ms. Comprehensive systems are defined by the use of a full range
IR practices. Involvement systems emphasize the use of certain
tices over others, as a means of achieving desired outcomes, such
mployee involvement and participation. Traditional systems focus
e on the maintenance of bureaucratic control and structure, through
prehensive and inflexible processes and systems. Identification
ems stress the use of practices promoting organizational identifica-
and commitment, but little else. Finally, none systems involved
little use of HR practices and systems (Bowen and Ostroff, 2004;
ght and Boswell, 2002). Purcell and Ahlstrand (1994) similarly
eloped three magnitudes of organizational strategy to encompass
various elements of the strategic management value chain. 'First
er' organizational strategies are those that seek to define the long-
n direction and scope of activities of the organization. 'Second order'
egies are those that, in support of first order strategies, seek to
ne the internal structure, connections and reporting relationships.
rd order' strategies include the functional management of activities,
a as the management of HR and finance.

ithin the context of these developments to SHRM, pay is a strategic
iagement tool for engaging and retaining organizations' human
tal (Lawler et al., 1995). Firms pursuing an innovation-based com-
tive strategy, for example, seek to create conditions whereby they
ome a unique provider in the product market (Schuler and Jackson,
7). The profile of desired employee behaviours is characterized by
wish for a high degree of creative behaviour; a longer-term focus;
atively high level of cooperative, independent behaviour; a moderate
ree of concern for quality; a moderate concern for quantity; an equal
ree of concern for process and results; a greater degree of risk-taking;
a high tolerance of ambiguity and unpredictability (ibid.). This
iires companies to formulate and implement clear policies, centred
ecruiting key talent, developing core competencies, both technical
behavioural, and appraising and rewarding long-term performance
hart and Rynes, 2003). Firms pursuing a market-focused strategy,
he other hand, require relatively repetitive and predictable behav-
s; a more medium-term focus; a modest amount of cooperative
ependent behaviour; a high concern for quality; a modest concern
quantity of output; a very high regard for process management
improvement; low emphasis on risk and task uncertainty; and a
t deal of commitment to the goals of the organization (Schuler and
son, 1987).

idea that practices within it are interrelated and internally consistent, and that "more is better" with respect to the impact on performance, because of the overlapping and mutually reinforcing effect of multiple practices'. This view emphasizes the need for strong consistency among HR practices (internal fit) in order to achieve effective performance, for which there is much empirical support (Huselid, 1995; Delaney and Huselid, 1996; Arthur, 1994; Pfeffer, 1994; MacDuffie, 1995). HR practices that attempt to promote employee engagement and partici-pation, autonomy, recruitment from a wide talent pool, high levels of training and integrated compensation measures are all associated with enhanced organizational performance (Arthur, 1994; Pfeffer, 1998). High performance work systems that include a high occurrence of *com-mitment* HR interventions such as pay for performance systems, highly selective recruitment, comprehensive and frequent communication and employee engagement also correlate positively with lower rates of employee attrition, enhanced productivity and quality, and enhance-ments to organizational performance overall (Wood, 1996). On the other hand, HR practices that concentrate on 'control, efficiency and the reduction of employee skills and discretion are associated with increased turnover and poorer manufacturing performance' (Stiles and Kulvisaechana, 2003).

Both *bundles* of best practices and *configurations* share an 'architectural state' and have therefore 'generalizable qualities' (Becker and Gerhart, 1996; Stiles and Kulvisaechana, 2003). In practice, defined best practices reflect not specific HR interventions with universal application, but perhaps *principles*, which, architecturally, have universal application: 'best practices might be more appropriate for identifying the principles underlying the choice of practices, as opposed to the practices them-selves' (Guest, 1997; Guest et al., 2000).

Configurational theory posits that there are combinations of HR practices suited to different organizational strategies. Unlike either universalistic or contingency theories, configurational theories of HRM emphasize alignment that is *both* horizontal and vertical. Huselid and Becker (1995) and Delery and Doty (1996) in particu-lar provide support for the notion of horizontal alignment in their respective studies. In summary, while some promote the value of vertical fit, other commentators, such as Pfeffer (1998), in influential work promote instead an array of employment 'best practices' that have universally a value-added effect on organizational performance. Others maintain, however, that these two approaches – vertical and horizontal integration – often viewed as conflicting within the literature, are in fact complementary and not mutually exclusive (Stiles and Kulvisaechana, 2003).

Strategic human resource management

In a development to the work of the Michigan model, an additional powerful body of recent theory, that of strategic human resource management (SHRM), emphasizes the importance of the *alignment* or *contingency* of HRM practices vertically with the business strategy (Delery and Doty, 1996). Rynes and Gerhart (2000) illustrate a top- down model of alignment between corporate strategy, business strategy and functional strategies, including HR and reward strategies. Corporate strategic decisions are choices concerning product strategies, industries in which the organization is to compete, and the choice of what to offer to market. Business strategy, taking a lead from the corporate strategy, is the means by which the organization differentiates itself from competitors. While two companies may compete within the same product market, each may pursue a different business strategy as a means of enhancing their competitiveness and extracting maximum rents from the finite financial capacity of the market. Functional strategies refer to the means by which both corporate and business strategies are 'successfully implemented or executed' (Gerhart and Rynes, 2003), including HR and reward strategies. The relationship between the business strategy, HR strategy, pay strategy and company performance is therefore assumed to be linear (Becker and Huselid, 1998; Stiles and Kulvisaechana, 2003).

Thus, the approach adopted to the management of HR is contingent upon the organization's strategy. Strategies between firms vary, as noted, and the majority of recent commentary on HRM has attempted to investigate how HR practices vary accordingly, using established strategy typologies such as the framework of prospector, analyser and defender put forward by Miles and Snow, or Porter's model of competitive advantage through differentiation on cost, market-focus or quality (Porter, 1980; Miles and Snow, 1978; Delery and Doty, 1996; Jackson and Schuler, 1995). The emphasis here is on alignment, or fit, between the external environment, organizational strategy and HR systems and practices. The high-profile and much-referenced study by Huselid (1995) indicated that the most successful organizations tie HRM practice to strategy, resulting in higher than average performance outcomes (ibid.). The study of the alignment of industrial relations (IR) systems in steel mini-mills by Arthur (1992, 1994) highlighted the high degree of fit between business strategy and the IR strategy employed by the organization. Arthur found that 90 per cent of those organizations pursuing

a low-cost competitive strategy employed some form of IR system, whereas 60 per cent of those organizatic ferentiation competitive strategy used a commitmei (Arthur, 1992, 1994). The relationship between comp IR system is evidence, Arthur (1994) argues, of organi to maximize vertical fit.

More recent research on *control-based* theories of HF Arthur's findings on cost reduction IR strategies, part IR strategy (Snell, 1992). *Control theory* views HRM which managers control employee behaviours for the ing organizational goals. Control HRM is characte defined jobs, specialization of employees, close supe toring of employees by management, hierarchical stri tion of power and a focus on cost reduction strateg 2003). Not dissimilar to Dyer and Holder's (1988) *ir* HRM, the involver IR system, identified by Arthur, p performance and commitment, through a recipro investment in training, communication and socializ bined with above-industry median wages and empl participation in decision making (Arthur, 1992). Th consistent with high-commitment management prac

Bowen and Ostroff (2004), in conducting cluster a ing firms, identified five distinct HR systems – *com*

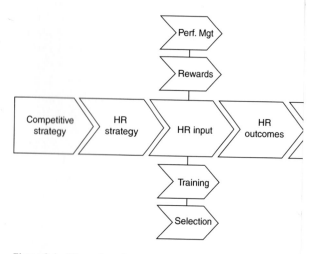

Figure 2.2   The value chain and strategic human resource n

Conversely, the use of people management practices associated with cost management-orientated HRM reflects the belief that overall corporate performance is enhanced through the reduction of costs, notably labour, and the associated wage bill: 'the characteristics of a firm pursuing the cost-reduction strategy are tight controls, overhead minimization and pursuit of scale' (Schuler and Jackson, 1987). Principally, human resources are costs to be minimized. The management of costs, particularly for those organizations operating in competitive product markets, is often viewed as a primary, if not the only, means of securing financial performance in the interest of shareholder value. As such, the emphasis placed upon cost management within the overall business model of the organization will dictate and inform the choice and management of pay systems. Work conducted by Coase (1937), later developed by Robertson and Langlois (1994), and more recently by McKelvey and Page (1999), reveals that the model is driven by the management of 'transaction costs', by which the firm operates within the boundaries of cost and quantity. Organizations act as *functions of production*, and are primarily concerned with the 'transformation of homogeneous inputs into homogeneous outputs'. As a result, they are typically bound by cost and highly sensitive to external economic factors. Ultimately, these boundaries define the company's composition and governance, and with it internal controls and processes such as HRM (Robertson and Langlois, 1994). Youndt et al. (1996) note that organizations pursuing cost management strategies typically employ 'administrative' HR systems, 'reducing cost and eliminating uncontrollable behaviour', and that the practice of high involvement work systems (HIWS) in such circumstances would not be 'cost effective' and would not therefore be typically used within cost-sensitive firms.

The basis of strategic pay choices

What is the basis upon which management use pay systems strategically? The dominant paradigm is that of the 'classical' or 'rational' school of strategic management (Whittington, 1997; Okuno-fujiwara, 2002). *Rationalists* contend that in seeking to maximize profit, pay managers choose from an array of strategic options, selecting strategies, systems, technologies and practices that best suit the interests of the firm (Becker and Gerhart, 1996). 'A fundamental assumption of much of the literature on compensation is that organizations have considerable discretion in the design of pay policies and that choice may have consequences for organizational performance' (Gerhart and

Milkovich, 1990). Like rational accounts of strategic management, strategic pay emphasizes the importance of the managerial choice within pay system formulation/selection, the choice of the 'right' or optimal strategy being the critical factor for success (success expressed in relation to financial performance) (Lawler et al., 1995). The task of the manager in the strategy process is to screen the internal and external environment for opportunities (Beckert, 1999).

Parallels may be drawn between military theory and conduct, and much classical strategic management theory is rooted in classical economics. Eschewing social, political and cultural paradigms, the classical school is best understood through transaction cost economics (Coase, 1937; Williamson, 1986), industry structure analysis (Porter, 1980) and the ideal of rational economic man (Von Newmann and Morgenstern, 1944). The theory of rational economic man defines strategy as the necessary means of a single entrepreneurial individual, or an entrepreneurial group, singular in vision, acting with perfect rationality to maximize 'his' or 'their' economic advantage. Translated into modern commercial endeavour, shareholders, investors and managers are united and unanimous in their desire to extract maximum profits from commercial activity (Reid, 1987).

Rational man (Simon, 1957) makes optimal decisions in environments that are 'highly specified and clearly defined'. Within a decision-making situation, rational man is already in possession of a whole range of possible alternatives, from which the optimal course of action may be chosen (Reid, 1987). Each alternative carries within it a set of consequences. Existing rational decision theories broadly group classifications of consequence into one of three categories: certainty, risk and uncertainty. Certainty theories assume that the agent, as decision maker, has comprehensive and accurate knowledge of the consequences of his decision: 'in this paradigm [the rational paradigm approach] an individual is always assumed to be perfectly rational and to be calculating how to maximize her own exogenously given utility, independently of any social context she may be in, and independently of any psychological feeling she has' (Okuno-fujiwara, 2002). Risk theories assume accurate knowledge of a probability distribution of each of the alternatives. Uncertainty theories assume that the consequences of each alternative belong to some subset of all possible consequences, and that the decision maker cannot allocate definite probabilities to the occurrence of particular consequences (Simon, 1959). Options with certain or known outcomes are considered to be more preferable to rational man than those options with uncertain outcomes.

Drawing upon his capability for 'preference ordering', rational man ranks all sets of consequences from most to least preferred – preference ordering: 'those (economic and decision theory) models assume that preferences are defined over outcomes, that those outcomes are known and fixed, and that decision makers maximize their net benefits, or utilities, by choosing the alternative that yields the highest levels of benefit (discounted by costs)' (Jones, 1999). Based upon the ranking of the consequences, the decision maker selects the option leading to the most preferred set of consequences. This is considered rational decision making. Where the consequences fall under the category of risk, because there is probable but not complete certainty of outcome, the rational choice is defined as that for which the greatest utility is expected. Where the consequences fall under the category of uncertainty, the definition of what is rational becomes much less clear. One approach is to view rational decisions, in the face of uncertainty, as those that seek to minimize risk, as opposed to maximizing opportunity. Nevertheless in the same way that consequences, advantageous or disadvantageous, are not known, neither is it possible to accurately forecast the risk inherent within any given option.

The classical conception of rational economic man, defined by Adam Smith, viewed 'each individual continually exerting himself to find out the most advantageous employment of whatever capital he can command' (Okuno-fujiwara, 2002). Applied to a contemporary example, one might say that each and any company, as an economic entity, is continually exerting itself to maximize return on investment (ROI). According to Smith, the promotion of self-interest is governed according to the principles of prudence (Reid, 1987). Prudence, like rationality, 'embodies the dual principle of reason (the ability to foresee consequences and to discern advantage) and self-command (the readiness to abstain from short-term opportunism in order to benefit more fully in the long term)' (Whittington, 1997). These values are the essence of modern long-term strategic business planning.

Mintzberg (1990) identified three basic premises of the 'classical school'. Firstly, the control of strategy formulation by a conscious process of thought, derived directly from notions of rational economic man. Secondly, ultimate responsibility for control of the 'conscious process' must rest with the chief executive officer, the *strategist*, reflecting the individualism of economics and the military notion of the detached general objectively planning and dispassionately marshalling resources. Finally, implementation is a phase of activity distinct and wholly separate from the strategy formulation process. It assumes that the enactment of the strategy is straightforward and unproblematic, the relevant contingencies having been identified within a formulation process, and reflected within the strategy itself: 'classical strategic management has become the dominant paradigm for the organization of commercial activity for the purpose of achieving fixed ends' (Whittington, 1997). For classicists, financial company performance, in the form of profit, is the unifying goal of business, and rational planning by leadership is the best means of achieving it. Key features of the classical approach include the emphasis placed upon the power of rational analysis and planning; the separation of conception (planning) from execution; and the commitment to the unifying goal of profit maximization (Whittington, 1997).

Reward specialists choose reward strategies or make reward-related decisions on the basis of economic considerations aimed at achieving optimal outcomes. Optimal outcomes are, typically, financial outcomes achieved through an overall corporate strategy, centrally agreed by the finance function and senior management acting in the interests of shareholders. Reward specialists are imbued with the ability to choose the necessary reward inputs (practices) from an array of 'strategic' options in order to affect the desired optimal outcomes. Within most SHRM and new pay theories, 'optimal' reward management is defined in terms of fit with the overall corporate strategy. Thus, the optimal reward strategy is one, out of an array of strategic options, that aligns most closely with the overall corporate strategy.

The nature of action being based upon economic imperatives renders the reward specialist, as would be the case with any other actor, rational. Moreover, optimization implies several attributes of actors, the environment and action. The first attribute is a capacity for the actor to comprehensively and accurately capture all information salient to a decision pertaining to the management of rewards. This assumes that all salient information is readily available to the actor and of such a nature that it can be objectively scrutinized for the purposes of informing reward management decisions. Secondly, the actor is able to compute and process all salient information, thereby being able to make decisions or formulate courses of action leading to the achievement of optimal outcomes. Thirdly, optimization, being absolute, is not open to interpretation – the right decision is the *right* decision, irrespective of actor.

While neoclassical economics, and transaction cost economics by extension, incorporate provision for uncertainty, strategic management – much of which is founded upon neoclassical assumptions – neglects the effect of uncertainty on decisions. The presumption of choice, and by definition, the right choice resulting from careful analysis of salient information, is a key facet of much of the prescriptive strategic management literature. As such, the literature, and commonly held perceptions that influence and are, in turn, influenced by the literature, stress the autonomy of management. Organizational behaviour, more than anything else – or in the extreme, as a result of nothing else – is purely a condition of managerial agency. The manager, as agent, reigns supreme. The manager decides in the context of economic goals, choosing the most appropriate methods from an array of options, with the power and resources to ensure enactment, thereby promoting value for the organization.

Classical strategic management emphasizes profitability as the 'supreme goal of business' and rational planning as the best means of achieving it (Whittington, 1997). Rooted in classical economics of the eighteenth-century Scottish enlightenment, classical strategic management is very much part of the neoclassical management-led revolution in organizational determination and governance (Chandler, 1962; Ansoff, 1965; Sloan, 1963). At the heart of classical theories of strategic management is an attachment to rational analysis and planning, the separation of conception and execution, and the commitment to profit maximization as the universal goal. The concept of profit maximization, or optimization, reflecting rational decision making by management, establishes a platform from which one might adopt a *unitarist* view of the organization. In the unitarist organization there is a common rationale for organizational planning, policy, practice and action shared by all.

The unitarist perspective of united economic interest is at the heart of much of the strategic management literature that has gained much currency in contemporary organizational and business studies. Not unlike military planning, the classicists view the corporate leadership as detached from the organization: 'these preconceived plans are executed according to the commands transmitted through obedient hierarchies to officers and men at the front: it is not for them to reason why, but simply to execute their orders' (Whittington, 1997). Such distance permits a necessary degree of objectivity and, when combined with knowledge, ability and conviction, enables decision makers comprehensively to prescribe rational courses of organizational action for the purpose of maximizing financial outcomes. Defined, classical strategic management amounts to: 'the determination of the basic long term goals and objectives of an enterprise, and the adoption of courses of action and the allocation of resources necessary for those goals' (Chandler, 1962). The detached planning process is supported by rigid hierarchies, through which the strategy is executed in line with the expectations of those who designed it. The supporting hierarchical organizational structure is not cooperative or inclusive, but rather a controlling mechanism through which conflict is managed and the compliance of those lower down in the organizational hierarchy is ensured.

Some perceived shortcomings of standard theory

Developments within pay theory and practice have resulted, arguably, in strategic pay becoming the dominant paradigm in contemporary approaches to pay, which is now reflected in the mainstream as standard theory. Its ascendancy as standard theory has not gone unchallenged, however. Strategic pay (and HRM more broadly) has attracted critical commentary. Its conceptual, empirical and prescriptive underpinnings have been questioned, and despite the volume of prescriptive and normative commentary available, there is a dearth of grounded commentary on the nature, form and effectiveness of strategic pay in practice. What research has been conducted reveals a perspective on practice that does not sit easily with theory (see Kessler, 1994; Smith, 1993; Cannell and Wood, 1992; Kessler and Purcell, 1992). Such studies have had a limited impact, however, upon the popularity and pervasiveness of strategic pay, both theoretically and practically. Additional commentary that is critical of the broader strategic basis of pay and related HR interventions highlights some fundamental weaknesses that merit greater exploration.

Despite the compelling evidence for a linkage between the use of HRM practices and enhanced performance, there are currently no generally accepted accounting procedures for measuring human resources (Cascio, 1991; Armstrong, 1995). At best, progress has been mixed, with one major review concluding: 'as tempting as it is to try to establish a balance sheet value for a firm's human assets, such attempts are probably doomed; at this point it is not possible to calculate a figure that is both objective and meaningful' (Ferguson and Berger, 1985).

Empirical evidence does not universally provide support for either best practice or SHRM. Delery and Doty (1996), using methods similar to mainstream studies of the HRM practice and performance linkage, find modest support for a fit with the Miles and Snow's (1978) typology. Youndt et al. (1996) find limited evidence of the alignment principle in their study of employment patterns in manufacturing plants. MacDuffie (1995) explicitly rejects the strategy alignment hypothesis on the basis that there is little or no evidence for a demonstrable difference between HRM practices in mass production and those in flexible production.

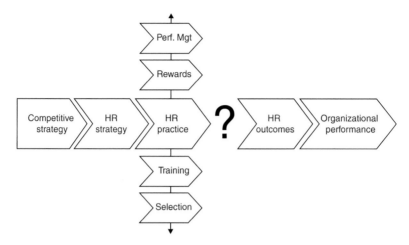

Figure 2.3 A gap in our understanding of the relationship between practice and performance

In addition, there are a number of problems with asserting a linkage between human capital and human resource initiatives and organizational performance (Becker and Huselid, 1998; Guest, 1997; Legge, 2001). A key challenge to the dominant model of the human capital value chain, which implicitly assumes linearity, is the problem of reverse causality. Are companies successful because of the way they manage their people (the deployment of human capital/HRM practices), or is it simply the case that successful firms deploy those human resource practices perceived to be of value? Moreover, SHRM that emphasizes the alignment of human resources to organizational strategies (for example, a cost leadership strategy and a differentiation strategy) oversimplifies, or wholly discounts, the influence of context on the shape and formation of HR practices, including pay (Donaldson, 2001). The specific context of each organization renders the alignment of pay and strategy very complex as a result of idiosyncrasies, thereby making generalizations about HR and human capital problematic (Kessler, 2001).

Furthermore, conceptual classifications of competitive strategy are not mutually exclusive (Stacey, 1993). Rather, it is apparent that those organizations, primarily competing on the basis of low cost, are also able to compete on the basis of quality: in effect minimizing cost while maximizing quality (Legge, 2001). This reflects, perhaps, some of the conceptual 'fuzziness' of dominant strategic management theories used as the nodes to which HRM strategies should be matched

(Legge, 1995). Models espoused by the strategic management theorists at the normative level ascribe prescriptions that have received little empirical verification (Legge, 2001). It is not clear that these higher order features of the organization are any more tenable conceptually than the belief and aspiration for control (Legge, 1995).

Similarly, much of the rhetoric of normative models of HRM emphasize the maximization of employee contribution through 'soft' HRM practices, high commitment work systems and high involvement work systems of the sort discussed already. However, these configurations of HR practice may not suit all modes of strategic management. High commitment HR systems require an extensive investment of time and finance, and appear contrary to a competitive strategy emphasizing cost minimization as the primary means of competitive advantage. Accordingly, one might envisage a multi-divisional structured organization, with each division competing in a distinct product market/ functional area that requires (according to the orthodox doctrine of SHRM) the practice of different modes of HRM. The complexity of a large, diversified multi-divisional organization must, by necessity, be reflected in its employment structures. This added emphasis on matching, vertically and horizontally, gives those that have responsibility for people management a not insignificant challenge.

Finally, a number of prescriptive criticisms might be levelled at SHRM. Discounting the conceptual criticisms that the achievement of SHRM is a 'lengthy, complex and iterative process' and that empirically there is little evidence to support such claims, is the matching of strategy and HRM policies even desirable? (Legge, 1995). Integration and matching is acknowledged to be a highly problematic area. Matching, or the 'vertical' alignment of HRM policies to strategy, and the 'internal' (Baird and Meshoulam, 1988) and 'horizontal' (Delery and Doty, 1996) integration of HR practices with themselves and other elements of the organization's design become even more problematic. This is particularly the case when the organization competes in a highly diversified product market, necessitating a highly diversified divisional form of organizational structure. The greater the scope and scale of the organization, the greater the challenge of attempting to encompass the additional complexity within a matching exercise.

Summary

A review of the relevant literature reveals the progressive emergence of strategic pay in theory and practice. Strategic pay has arguably come to represent the new orthodoxy of pay theory and the received wisdom in practice. Evidence reveals the widespread adoption of strategic pay in practice, consistent with the prescriptions of strategic theories of pay. As part of broader developments in the management of the employment relationship overall, strategic theories of pay emphasize the value of pay organizationally as a means of leveraging performance outcomes, resulting in enhanced company performance and sustainable competitive advantage.

A limited but vocal element of critical theory casts doubts, however, on the efficacy of strategic theories of pay. The implication made by critical commentators is that strategic theories of pay are more rhetorical than substantial, and point to a number of serious conceptual, prescriptive and normative shortcomings of 'standard theory'. While providing valuable insights, critical HRM theorists offer little by way of alternatives to the orthodoxy. Their critique of standard theory also suffers from a lack of empirical grounding and lacks credibility, therefore, in the eyes of strategic pay advocates. Their concerns have also found little traction with practitioners.

The review of the literature highlights an opportunity for an important contribution to the subject, by redressing the gap in knowledge left void by both standard and critical commentary. It is to this end that this book seeks to make a contribution.

3
The Study

How is a study of strategic pay in practice best approached? What methods are most appropriate given the research question and the subject under investigation? This chapter, firstly, considers established approaches to the subject and proposes an alternative research agenda considered better suited to the exploration of strategic pay in practice. Drawing upon conceptual and empirical perspectives, from multiple disciplines, a multi-level exploratory approach to the research of strategic pay practice is proposed, incorporating quantitative and qualitative methods, together with a detailed description of the data gathered.

A multi-level approach to an exploratory study of strategic pay in practice

The subject of pay has traditionally been approached through a variety of independent disciplines, including economics, sociology, psychology and management. The result is a highly fragmented corpus of theory, with little consensus between disciplines on subjects of shared interest and importance (Kessler, 2001). Each discipline has brought to the subject a particular style and methodological approach, and because some disciplines are dominant in the field (economics for example), there is a bias towards the use of specific methods with implications for our current understanding (Marsden, 1986).

The most recent commentary on pay is rooted firmly in the tradition of neoclassical economics and shares many of its assumptions and proclivity for positivist approaches to the subject (Purcell, 1999). Strategic theories of pay, in particular, contend that outcomes of the greatest strategic value are realized when pay is aligned closely with the strategic direction of the organization. Standard theory assumes causality. However, the causal relationships underpinning the notion of alignment between pay and strategy, expressed often in terms of a 'value chain', remain problematic conceptually, as discussed, despite having received the lion's share of academic and practitioner attention (Wright et al., 2001). Empirical work in the area relies typically on data collected through large-scale, cross-sectional quantitative surveys of company-level practice, attempting to establish correlations between high performance and specific HR practices (Shenkar and Zeira, 1987). Correlation is not causality, however, and establishing firmly and conclusively the causal linkages between practice and performance, and thereby empowering theorist and practitioner with tools of probabilistic and/or predictive utility, remains the 'holy grail' of HRM research (Keenoy, 1999; Storey, 2001).

Critical commentary highlights inherent weaknesses in standard conceptualizations of practice, performance and the relationship between the two, but offers little in the way of robust alternatives either theoretically or methodologically (Guest, 1997). The weaknesses inherent in standard conceptualizations inevitably frustrate past, current and future attempts to codify the practice and performance linkage empirically, and bring into question the value of such studies (Keenoy, 1999; Legge, 1995, 2001; Storey, 2001). Despite the pessimism with which critical commentators approach mainstream research efforts, issues of pay system effectiveness and related pay outcomes, and their impact on competitive advantage, are clearly important and merit further development. Given the shortcomings of both conventional and critical treatment of strategic pay, this study makes an important academic and practitioner contribution by developing a grounded perspective of strategic pay in practice.

How are the issues raised in the research question best investigated? In the context of largely positivist approaches to the subject, with their perceived advantages and disadvantages, this study adopts an exploratory approach to the phenomenological investigation of *professional, technical and managerial* (strategic) pay in practice. Such an approach is considered better suited to addressing the dearth of understanding on the subject than purely descriptive, illustrative, experimental and explanatory approaches (Scapens, 1990).

Professional, technical and managerial grades are defined as the non-manual, and non-board-level, population of managerial employees. The phenomenon of strategic pay occurs at multiple levels, and a multi-level perspective is adopted accordingly, which, when combined with the exploratory approach, permits the development of 'holistic' insights

(Gummerson, 1991). As Becker and Gerhart (1996) note in direct reference to pay: 'More effort should be devoted to finding out what managers are thinking when they make the decisions they do. This suggests a need for deeper qualitative research to complement the large scale, multiple firm studies that are available.'

Using both quantitative and qualitative methods to draw upon primary and secondary data, this study permits a robust rounded investigation of the many facets of pay in practice. Quantitative methods are used primarily to review and compare trends in pay determination and pay practice, with broader economy-wide developments. Comprising the bulk of the research, qualitative methods are used primarily to develop a multi-level perspective of strategic pay practice. Building upon the strengths of existing research, but representing a novel departure to standard approaches, this study *explores* the issues of strategic pay practice and performance through a series of case studies using organizations purposefully selected as market leaders. So instead of seeking to establish correlations, this research *explores* strategic pay practice in high-performing firms and qualitatively *assesses* the perceived effectiveness of pay practice from the perspective of the multiple stakeholders involved in the pay determination process. By conventional standards, therefore, the case studies have been selected on the basis of the dependent variable, namely their performance.

Using a multi-level framework

Existing research investigating strategic pay and related HRM practice does so on the basis of assumptions about the causal linkages between practice and performance. As illustrated in Chapter 2, standard theory assumes a value chain in which *cause*, the independent variable, results in the *effect*, the dependent variable. Thus, practice results in performance – cause and effect. Implicit within the highly pervasive notion of the value chain model is the one-dimensional nature of the causal linkage between the elements comprising the chain. The value chain model does not incorporate sufficient provision to recognize the array of mediating variables that influence performance, the dependent variable, nor the complex interactions that occur at different *levels* between the elements of the value chain (Wright and Nishii, 2004). Strategic pay interventions are, for example, necessarily formulated at the level of the organization. The behavioural outcomes elicited by strategic pay systems are exhibited at the level of the individual, however (ibid.). Such variation in level is not sufficiently accommodated by the standard conception of the value chain and related theory: 'One of the reasons this three-tier framework is useful is that it helps identify an important development that existing industrial relations systems theory does not specifically address: the apparent inconsistencies and internal contradictions in strategies occurring at different levels of industrial relations within the firm' (Kochan et al., 1986).

The approach adopted here is not to view pay practice in such 'one-dimensional' terms. Consistent with other multi-level approaches (see Kochan et al., 1986 for example), this study has purposefully created a multi-level framework for the grounded exploration of companies' attempts to manage managerial, professional and technical pay strategically in practice. Based upon primary observations of pay in practice, and piloted within one of the case study companies, it is argued here that the subject of pay practice is most usefully approached through a framework comprising three levels. The first level, *the pay approach*, reflects the implicit or espoused values, principles and aspirations that underpin pay practice. The second level, *the pay design*, reflects the technical content of the intended pay policy. The third and final level, *the pay operation*, reflects what is achieved operationally as pay practice.

These three levels of pay practice are not mutually exclusive. Rather, they reflect three states of pay practice as they are *experienced* organizationally. By recognizing three states of the same pay practice, or system comprising individual pay practices, it is possible to differentiate between the three levels: between the principles underpinning pay, expressed in the form of pay strategies; between the technical design of pay practice, expressed in the form of policy; and between achieved pay practice. In being able to differentiate between the three states of the *same* pay practice, or system, it is therefore possible to assess any potential disconnection. What is desired (approach), and what is intended (design), may not be reflected in what is achieved (operation). Such a nuance in the *management* of pay practice, as an example, is neglected by standard theories of strategic pay that assume linearity. It also affords the flexibility to review multiple and varying aspects of the pay determination process and pay practice within an overall exploratory approach to the subject. While applied here specifically to pay practice, this framework has broader application and constitutes, it is hoped, a valuable contribution to the multi-level approach to company practice.

The fast moving consumer goods sector as a unit of analysis

A single industry was chosen from which case studies were selected. The fast moving consumer goods (FMCG) sector was chosen because, firstly, as a sector, FMCG[1] represents a distinct group of companies, competing for both product and labour. Secondly, by virtue of being closely aligned with consumers, FMCG organizations are characterized by relatively rapid responses to contextual change. Product development, marketing and corporate positioning in the FMCG sector are necessarily dynamic, providing an interesting subject of change, with appreciable time-related events.

Global food products' market growth since 2003 has accelerated, reflecting higher consumer spending on premium food products, and the recovery of the global economy.

The global food products' market was worth $2708.6 billion in 2004, reflecting a 3 per cent year-on-year increase since 2000. The global beverages sector was valued at $927.9 billion in 2004, having expanded at a slower compound annual growth rate (CAGR) of 2.1 per cent when compared to food. Tobacco performed worse still, experiencing a CAGR growth of 1.8 per cent since 2000, being valued at $338.1 billion in 2004. Tobacco growth is credited with price increases and not an increase in tobacco consumption, which has increased only marginally at a rate of 0.3 per cent since 2000 (Datamonitor, 2005). The expectation is that the global food, beverage and tobacco markets will experience uniform growth rates over the next five years. Industry forecasts predict that total market value in 2009 will be $4570.6 billion, a 2.8 per cent

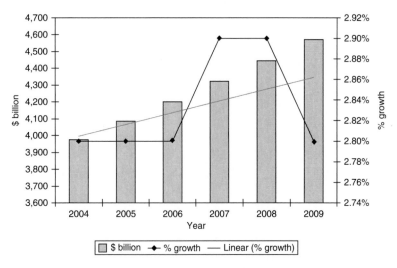

Figure 3.1   Global food, beverage and tobacco industry group value forecast: $billion 2004–9

CAGR increase in the period 2004–9. The strongest-performing industry is expected to be the food industry, which will continue its steady growth, owing to continuing strength in the global economy and the increasing global population (Datamonitor, 2005).

A multi-methodological research design

The investigation of pay practice at multiple levels requires the use of multiple methods in order to avoid the risk of 'methodological myopia' (Kessler, 2001). Complementing theory reviewed in Chapter 2, a mix of quantitative and qualitative methods is used at multiple levels of the exploratory research where deemed appropriate. Quantitative analysis of proprietary industry-level pay trend data provides a portrait of developments in pay within the UK FMCG sector for the period 1996–2000.

The level of analysis is shifted down to the level of the company and strategic pay practice within a sample of FMCG case studies is explored using the multi-level framework of pay approach, design and operation to understand more clearly pay strategy, policy and practice. Primary and secondary data are gathered on case study company pay practice, using multiple methods, including semi-structured interviews and a desk-top review of company documentation. The 'triangulation' of data using multiple methods is deemed an appropriate strategy for the exploration of strategic pay practice because '[n]o single methodological approach is self-sufficient and capable of producing well-rounded theory that simultaneously maximizes the research quality criteria of construct validity, internal validity, external validity and reliability' (Parkhe, 1993).

FMCG pay trend analysis

The availability of detailed pay data in the public domain is extremely limited (Nash, 2003). Researchers intent on using public domain pay data are constrained, principally, by the unwillingness of organizations to disclose information that is highly sensitive personally and commercially. Those seeking to gather data directly from organizations face a further challenge. In addition to commercial sensitivity, the resources (financial and technical) required to collect and collate pay data from individual firms to form an aggregate picture of industry-level pay practice are considerable. Very few academic studies have used detailed pay data as a result (Kessler, 2001).

Within the commercial sphere of competitive intelligence, market research and professional services, a great deal of pay data is collected each year, however, for the purpose of providing competing organizations with detailed analysis of aggregate pay levels within their given labour market. This data is typically gathered, analysed and disseminated by an impartial third-party organization, such as specialist consultancy firms or commercial research bodies. The data used in this study was collected by a specialist pay benefits consultancy firm during the period 1996–2001 on behalf of a 'club' of 30 FMCG organizations operating in the UK and internationally.

The dataset contains information from between 25 and 30 organizations (varying year by year), including detailed pay data broken down by level and occupation for a range of 25 managerial positions. Data was collected from each company, for all 25 positions for each year of the survey (1996–2000 inclusive), on (a) base pay; (b) bonus; (c) long-term incentives (including share options); (d) discretionary cash allowances; and (e) benefits. In sum, the data permits the development of a *total remuneration* portrait of managerial pay in the UK FMCG sector for the period 1996–2000.

Consistency of role matching between like roles in each of the participating sample companies was achieved through a process known as job matching.[2]

All participating firms provide detailed data on all aspects of the matched roles' pay profile.[3]

Quantitative pay trend data were analysed using standard statistical conventions and processed using Microsoft Excel. The quantitative analysis of FMCG industry pay trends for the period 1996–2000 illustrates clearly the collective movement of pay determination within a specific sample of firms. Within the multi-level framework used, the quantitative industry pay trend analysis applies primarily at the first level – the level of industry. It provides useful background to pay developments within individual companies, with the industry and FMCG labour market being an important aspect of the context in which individual case study company pay practice is determined.

Case study research

A key objective of the study is to delve more deeply into the workings of strategic pay practice to understand better the 'dynamic interplay' of complex processes of pay determination and the resultant outcomes, and also the impact in performance terms (Gerhart and Rynes, 2003).

Given the exploratory nature of the research, a series of in-depth case studies was deemed to be most appropriate methodologically (Miles and Huberman, 1994). Case studies permit a greater degree of investigative flexibility and depth when dealing with complex phenomena that are poorly understood and embedded within a particular context (Bonoma, 1985; Dyer and Wilkins, 1991; Feagin and Orum, 1991). An additional strength of the case study method is its ability to integrate information from multiple sources (Eisenhardt, 1989; Yin, 1994).

Adopting the case study approach permits the capture of not only the complexity but also the situation-specificity and changing nature of the firm and its environment, which would otherwise be neglected by the more positivist, quantitative approaches (Porter, 1991). Detailed comparative case studies provide an opportunity to understand processes in context, such as pay determination, drawing on the significance of the interconnected levels of analysis (Pettigrew, 1990). Any organizational process needs to be understood within both the external and internal context in which it takes place. This necessarily requires multi-level analysis of the sort attempted here (Hendry and Pettigrew, 1990).

The chosen methods do have limitations, however, such as the assertion that theory building from case studies may result in 'a narrow and idiosyncratic theory. The risks are that the theory describes a very idiosyncratic phenomenon, or that the theorist is unable to raise the level of the generality of the theory' (Eisenhardt, 1989). Case study research is characterized by high validity but low reliability (Hussey and Hussey, 1997). The lack of reliability in case study research is compounded further by the inability to replicate the data (Kirk and Miller, 1986). Nevertheless, given the scope of the study and the research aims and questions, case study-based research remains the most appropriate method.

Selecting the case sample

A great deal of care was exercised when selecting potential case study participants considered best suited to an exploration of strategic pay in practice. Potential participants were approached solely according to criteria consistent with the research question(s) and the research approach. All case study companies were required to have exhibited market-leading performance over an extended period in terms of annual sales revenue, profit and market capitalization. Secondly, they were required to be deriving the majority if not all of their revenue from the commercial FMCG sector. As the research developed, it was also considered desirable that, as much as possible, the case studies should be comparable across a number of important dimensions. These dimensions included size, organizational life cycle and age, among others.

The net result of careful case study selection and persistent efforts to solicit interest was to secure excellent access to seven leading multinational FMCG companies operating globally and in the UK. All seven participating case study companies are multinational in their scope of operations, each with a significant manufacturing, marketing, sales, research and development (R&D) presence in the UK. All seven firms are large, the smallest employing over 35,000 employees in multiple locations throughout the world. The FMCG industry spans a number of sub-industries. The sub-industries represented within the sample include food and beverage, tobacco, and non-durable household consumables.

Access was secured through a variety of means. Having previously worked in consultancy specializing in the FMCG sector, the author was familiar with two of the sample firms. Using prior experience and involvement as a basis for approaching these two firms, a detailed research proposal was sent to the Reward Directors of each. Having selected appropriate firms according to the case sample criteria, a number of additional companies were cold-called using letters and telephone calls. Existing networks were also taken advantage of, including referrals to long-term clients by my former employer.

The market-leading FMCG case studies

All seven case study companies represent market-leading, multinational firms within the global FMCG sector (see Table 3.1). They compete in some, or all, of the major FMCG markets, primarily on the basis of brand leadership. Their products are marketed and sold in over one hundred countries, in all cases, with manufacturing and distribution facilities in multiple locations throughout the world. Combined, the companies employ almost 560,000 staff in a variety of occupations worldwide, with the smallest employing just under 40,000 and the largest just under 200,000 employees. Their combined annual sales are $160 billion, and pay spend is the single largest operating cost in nearly all of the companies.

In accordance with the intent to research those firms classified as 'leading', and in doing so, selecting the case study sample on what is the *dependent* variable in standard approaches to the assessment of practice effectiveness, namely company performance, all of the firms are long-term high-performers in the global FMCG market. Indeed, the firms are all market leaders in the global FMCG sector overall, and regional and domestic sub-markets, and within their

Table 3.1 Summary of key case study company attributes

	company1	company2	company3	company4	company5	company6	company7
Industry	FMCG	FMCG	FMCG	FMCG	FMCG	FMCG	FMCG
Sub-industries	Tobacco	Confectionery & beverages	Alcoholic beverages	Home, health & hygiene	Confectionery, food & beverages	Confectionery, food & pet care	Home, personal care, food & beverages
Size (no. of employees)	> 50,000	> 50,000	< 50,000	> 50,000	> 50,000	< 50,000	> 50,000
Founded	> 50 yrs	> 50 yrs	< 50 yrs	> 50 yrs	> 50 yrs	> 50 yrs	> 50 yrs
Life cycle	Mature	Mature	Mature	Mature	Mature	Mature	Mature
Ownership	Public	Public	Public	Public	Listed subsidiary	Private	Public
Organization structure	Holding co / country structure	Business unit	Regional structure	Regional structure	Regional structure	Regional structure	Matrix
Market Strategy	Brand-led	Brand-led	Brand-led	Brand-led and supplier	Brand-led	Brand-led	Brand-led and supplier
Scope	Multinational	Multinational	Multinational	Multinational	Multinational	Multinational	Multinational
Performance	Market-leading	Market-leading	Market-leading	Market-leading	Market-leading	Market-leading	Market-leading

Source: Datamonitor (2005, 2006).

specific sub-sectors of the FMCG market. In addition to their sustained high performance, the firms are all seen as highly reputable, and are referenced frequently as examples of best practice, 'excellent', brand-leading firms within the FMCG sector and more broadly. In each of the case study companies, a research 'sponsor', typically working at a senior level within the pay function, was appointed to champion the research internally.

In terms of organizational structure, five of the seven organizations use matrix-style organizational structures, with dual reporting lines on a country and business unit/functional basis. Only one of these uses a global matrix structure, with the other four based around regional matrix structures and geographical territories, for example Western Europe. Of the remaining two firms, one is a formal holding company, with multiple subsidiaries operating under its umbrella ownership and the other is organized along the lines of business units, and not country-based operations. Importantly, the case study firms represent an atypical sample of companies. They were purposefully selected on the basis of the market sector in which they compete, their size and their stage in the organizational life cycle. But, above all, they were chosen on the basis of their long-term financial performance.

Selecting the case firms on the basis of common criteria poses a methodological challenge. If contingency theory predictions hold true, collectively, the effects of the industry (as an element of the environment) might be viewed as a contextual independent variable upon which firms' pay practices as dependent variables are contingent. If conformity of pay practice is observed within the sample of firms – both at the industry level and at the firm level – the standard explanation of the norming influence of the 'industry effect' is both established and powerful (Donaldson, 2001). However, selecting one industry for analysis, FMCG in this case, also allows the researcher to potentially isolate and control for the industry effect as one factor influencing a firm's choice of pay systems. In doing so, it is then possible to differentiate between firms on the basis of the saliency of their pay choices, the effectiveness of their managerial processes and outcomes and so on, because, in terms of their employee demographic and product market, all things are largely equal. Moreover, if conformity of pay practice within the sample is encountered, it is not necessarily reflective of contingency at work. In keeping with the exploratory nature of the study, other explanations may be equally relevant and valid, perhaps even more so, and therefore merit research and analysis.

Semi-structured interviews

Semi-structured interviews were selected as the most appropriate means of gathering qualitative data on the case study companies' pay practices. Over 140 semi-structured interviews were conducted with a representative sample of staff, all of whom were involved in the various stages of the pay determination process within the seven case study firms. All interviewees were nominated by the case study sponsor, following a submission of research requirements by the author (contained within the appendices).

A semi-structured interview[4] convention was used in each case. The same structure was used in each, only deviating substantially to accommodate the relative experience or role of the interviewee and the limits of their contribution. In all seven case studies, stakeholders representing generalist senior management (commercial focus); senior functional specialists (commercial and functional focus); pay specialists (functional focus); HR line managers (function and line commercial focus); operational line managers (local commercial focus); and employees (the experience of pay) were interviewed individually.[5] Wherever possible, interviews were conducted face to face.[6]

Additional interviews

A number of additional interviews were conducted with senior specialist pay advisers and consultants from human resource and management consultancy firms involved in the pay determination process of the case study FMCG firms. Views were also sought from representatives and reward subject specialists of professional associations representing personnel and human resources professionals in the UK.

Secondary research methods

A range of privileged company-supplied information was gathered in the form of formal documentation about pay determination and pay management. Secondary data included company memoranda, presentation materials, formal strategy and policy documentation, pay scheme rules, functional marketing material, internal briefings, brochures and, where available, quantitative data on pay distribution, employee turnover and so on.

In addition to the privileged company-supplied data, a large amount of public domain information on each of the case study companies was collected, including published case studies, company reports and accounts and business statistics regarding longitudinal financial performance. Archival data was also collected in order to understand better the history of the case study firms, and the context in which pay was being determined. All privileged and publicly available secondary data was gathered to support the major research undertaking, that of case study interviews.

Non-disclosure, confidentiality and coding

Researching the management of pay is an especially sensitive activity on a number of levels. Commercially, pay data is closely guarded corporate information, not typically shared outside the organization in the interests of maintaining competitiveness. In three of the seven case studies, non-disclosure agreements (NDA) were signed and completed in order to proceed with the research.

In the interests of confidentiality each case study was coded at random and each interviewee was assigned a code to ensure anonymity. Specific references to unique characteristics of any of the case study firms, such as branded products or product market references, were also removed.

Analysis and presentation of the findings

The study uses a multi-level framework to differentiate between the nature of pay practice, in each of the case study companies, as it is *perceived* at the levels of approach, design and operation. The findings are presented, therefore, according to level. Using this method to frame the findings allows effective comparisons to be made between the prima facie similarities and differences of the case study companies and enables the richness of the data to be portrayed as fully as possible.

There are five findings chapters in total, with a supporting discussion chapter, which, perhaps unconventionally, draws further upon primary data. One of the findings chapters, Chapter 8, brings together the multi-level findings overall to present a portrait of the grounded reality of strategic pay in practice. The remaining four chapters cover pay practice at the levels of (a) the FMCG industry; (b) pay approach; (c) pay design; and (d) the pay operation. The industry-level findings are structured according to the standard convention of pay trend analysis. The three company-level findings chapters, though, require an additional framework in order to make the findings most meaningful.

The three findings chapters are structured according to a framework developed by Zbaracki (1998), but adapted specifically for the presentation of the case study companies' findings in this study. The framework allows for the capture and order of the multitudinous and complex array of phenomena that comprise pay determination in the seven case studies. Applying the same framework consistently also permits comparisons to be drawn across the seven case studies. The framework comprises four elements: *context* (in which pay practice at that level is determined); *variation* (of pay practice at that level); *selection* (of pay practice at that level); and *retention* (of pay practice at that level). These four stages are sequential, reflecting the fact that organizational planning and practice determination are thought of in linear terms by decision makers, so that policy informs practice.

The first stage, *context*, reflects the exogenous influence of technical and institutional properties that influence the determination process. The second stage, *variation*, reflects the stage in the determination process where the stakeholders involved perceive the need for intervention in the form of either change or preservation of the status quo and the decision to do either. The third stage, *selection*, refers to the conscious choice of 'what' the new or existing practice *should* reflect. The fourth and final stage, *retention*, refers to what is retained organizationally as pay practice. Data presented at each level and stage of the pay determination process reflects perceptions of the nature and value of the pay system. Classifying the various aspects of strategic pay in practice at the three levels and various stages allows perceptions of pay practice (nature and value) to be compared *within* and *between* each of the case study companies.

Summary

Within the context of standard approaches to the investigation of strategic pay, and its perceived limitations, this study proposes an alternative approach that aims to explore the phenomenon of strategic pay practice at multiple levels, using multiple methods, both quantitative and qualitative. A quantitative analysis of FMCG industry-specific trends is proposed to address the key question of what firms are doing in relation to pay, and to provide the backdrop for the company-level investigation of individual case study company pay practice. The chosen research design and methods represent the most advantageous approach to achieving the ambitious and important aims of the study outlined in the Introduction.

4
Pay Practice at the Level of Industry

This chapter on industry-level findings reviews trends in managerial pay in the UK FMCG sector for the period 1996–2000. Data were collected by a specialist pay benefits consultancy firm on behalf of a consortium of international FMCG firms operating in the UK domestic market. The industry-level findings allow us to address one of the major research questions highlighted in the introduction: What have FMCG companies been doing in relation to pay? How does this contrast with economy-wide trends, and what are the implications for individual company practice within the FMCG sector?

A portrait of managerial pay in the UK FMCG sector

Economy-wide studies of pay practice such as the WERS series of workplace-level studies (reviewed in Chapter 2) indicate that employers in recent years have moved towards the greater use of performance-based rewards for managerial, technical and professional staff (Cully et al., 1999; Nash, 2003). Most data reviewed in this industry-level analysis of pay practice indicates that the level of managerial employee pay at risk is far higher in the FMCG sector on average, when compared to economy-wide trends. If degree of pay at risk is an indication, FMCG firms in particular are attempting to use pay strategically in comparison to their peers in other industries. When viewed longitudinally, however, we are able to see that the move towards the use of strategic pay in the FMCG sector has been a relatively recent and rapid development.

The 1996 FMCG pay portrait is predominantly one of base pay, with limited short-term incentive opportunity, and no element of long-term variable pay. Moreover, there is little variation between organizations in terms of base pay provision, with the range between lower quartile, median and upper quartile narrower relative to other industries (consult1). There is limited variance between organizations paying short-term incentives. For those organizations competing on wage levels, it is fixed base pay and not bonus opportunity that is the primary means of competitive advantage. The 1997 pay portrait differs significantly from that of 1996 in terms of the emphasis placed upon variable pay. Virtually all organizations have increased the level of available short-term bonus opportunity. Most significantly, a number of organizations have introduced the purchase of share options as an element of pay, representing a long-term variable element of compensation, geared predominantly around base pay, and base pay progression, linked to inflation and labour market increases.

The 1998 portrait represents further progression in the trend towards greater variability in employee pay. In particular, the emphasis placed upon long-term incentives (LTI) and share options, in addition to near-universal coverage of short-term incentives (STI) (bonus), is greater than that placed upon base pay. The FMCG portrait in 1999 is a consolidation of the 1998 position. It has become, in effect, standard practice to base a significant portion of employees' pay on short- and long-term variable performance. However, the form of long-term variable pay has changed to encompass LTI most widely, with share option provision having declined sharply. STI remains at a consistent level with 1998, and base pay increases are in line with the incremental market movement observed in previous years. The pay portrait in 2000 is a further consolidation of variable pay as a significant percentage of employee pay. However, unlike 1998 and 1999, STI in 2000 rises significantly, increasing the emphasis placed upon short-term performance. The emphasis on long-term performance is consistent with the previous two years, if not reduced slightly (see Figure 4.1).

The longitudinal portrait is one of little or no change to the basic composition of junior management pay. Similarly, pay progression for junior management roles is modest over the same period. For middle management roles, the initial focus is on STI (bonus), with a move towards the inclusion of LTI and share options as elements of the variable pay element of the package. Overall, the amount of variability in middle management pay increases, with a broadly even split between STI and LTI and between, we presume, pay based upon individual performance and pay based upon company performance (for example, measures of shareholder value, such as earnings per share, EPS, and total shareholder return, TSR).

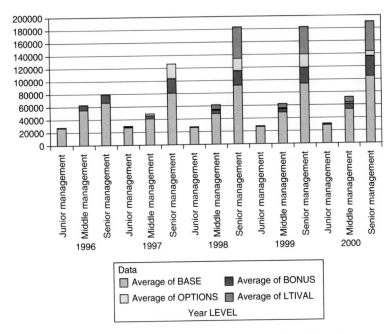

Figure 4.1   Year-on-year increase in total compensation by role level

The portrait of senior management pay (below executive level) is in stark contrast to middle and junior management pay. In the first instance, a greater element of pay is at risk through STI provision, constituting more than 15 per cent of overall pay. The period from 1997 onwards sees the introduction of share options and long-term incentives, which, when combined, result in a marked increase in performance-contingent pay as part of the overall senior management pay package. The inclusion of share options, especially during 1997 and 1998, and LTI, latterly in 1999 and 2000, dramatically increases the overall level of senior management total remuneration. The increase in senior management pay is in stark contrast to the levels of pay progression for junior and middle management. As a result, there is a high degree of relative wage disparity between the three levels of the management population (Table 4.1).

The rapid convergence around the observed pay norms is most vivid in graphical format (see Figure 4.2).

Analysis of the data reveals further high levels of conformity between the sample companies, resulting in readily observable industry pay norms. In terms of the use of short- and long-term variable pay, and the

Table 4.1 Prevalence of pay systems' usage

	Year	n	Number of organizations	Percentage of organizations
Short-term	1996	31	29	94
variable pay	1997	26	26	100
	1998	29	29	100
	1999	23	22	100
	2000	25	25	100
Long-term	1996	31	0	0
variable pay	1997	26	10	38
	1998	29	22	76
	1999	23	19	83
	2000	25	21	84
More than	1996	31	0	0
three pay	1997	26	0	0
interventions	1998	29	8	28
	1999	23	9	39
	2000	25	16	84

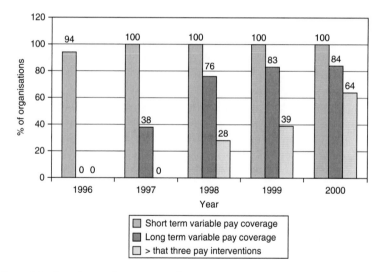

Figure 4.2 Prevalence of pay systems' usage

use of three or more pay interventions as elements of one total compensation package, there is evidence of increasing conformity over the course of the dataset. Virtually all of the sample organizations pay some form of STI, with one conspicuous exception. By 2000, 84 per cent of organizations within the sample include long-term variable pay as an element of employees' total remuneration, when compared to just the previous two years. The data reveals that relatively few organizations (38%) paid any form of long-term variable pay in 1997, but variable pay practices are adopted widely and rapidly thereafter. The most dramatic development is the doubling of the use of long-term variable pay within the sample between 1997 and 1998.

Similarly, in 1996 none of the sample FMCG organizations used three or more pay interventions as constituent elements of one total remuneration package. However, 1998 saw a rapid increase, as organizations increasingly supplemented base pay and bonus (STI) with one or more form of long-term variable pay. The provision of benefits is excluded from the analysis. However, consistent with conformity observed in cash-based pay practices, high levels of conformity also occurs in benefit provision, most notably the transition from traditional benefits' provision to new models of flexible benefits, emphasising employee choice and value for money, self-purchase schemes in the form of additional insurances, medical cover and such like (consult1). A key highlight is the greater use of performance-based pay across the sample of FMCG firms. The widespread inclusion of variable pay, as a significant portion of employee pay, becomes very much the norm in the UK, particularly for middle and senior management roles. There is, therefore, a great deal of conformity of pay practice within the market, and where patterns of practice have emerged on a limited basis in the first instance, such as the use of LTI, widespread adoption of such practices by other case study companies has occurred very rapidly.

What is startling is the speed with which LTI, as new practice, have become the pervasive market norm. Are conventional market forces responsible for such rapid change in the make-up of FMCG pay? Market forces reflect the ebb and flow of labour within the market in this context. Is the importance attached to market forces justified, or are there other dynamics at work?

Choosing to conform?

The observed pay norms within the market are not unexpected. The FMCG data confirms the economy-wide trends observed within the analysis of the WERS data towards the greater use of variable pay (Milward et al., 2000; Cully et al., 1999). Moreover, the increasing use of a number of pay interventions, either performance-based or linked to role inputs such as behaviours, reflects much of the received wisdom and prescribed guidance of the strategic pay school. FMCG firms, data would suggest, are leading the 'headlong rush' towards the use of variable pay interventions, multiple pay interventions and extensive market benchmarking (CIPD, 2007). The degree to which the FMCG sector has embraced variable pay, market movements and a mix of pay interventions is far greater, however, than general industry practice. Is FMCG pay practice more strategic, therefore?

Is it fair to assume that many of the assumptions that underpin these strategic pay interventions in general practice apply equally to the use of these same interventions in FMCG firms? These assumptions are that pay within the FMCG market is underpinned by (a) an emphasis on performance; (b) is achieved through the use of specific interventions that align the financial interests of employees to those of the organization; and (c) there is an articulated reward strategy that emphasizes business goals (CIPD, 2005). Such interventions reflect the assumption that individuals are motivated by economic rationality, and that levels of employee performance and desired behaviours are, therefore, management outcomes.

A best practice is one that is consistently linked with positive performance outcomes, the implication being that 'some HR practices are always better than others, and that all organizations should adopt these best practices' (Delery and Doty, 1996). Similarly, related practices that are linked to superior organizational performance are often bundled together into high-performance work systems (Wood, 1996; Danford et al., 2004); practice configurations (Delery and Doty, 1996; Delery et al., 1997); and 'bundles' (Purcell, 1999). Wood (1996) cites 'new forms of pay and assessment systems' as a core element of high-commitment work systems. In a review of HR and performance studies, the following are consistently rated as pay best practices: multiple pay interventions, performance-related pay, higher than industry rates of pay, incentives and profit-related pay (Boselie et al., 2001). Sixteen 'best practice' HR interventions that Pfeffer (1994) claims yield superior organizational performance were reviewed in Chapter 2. These include above-market pay (above the market median); the use of incentive pay systems (aligned with organizational goals); profit-related pay; and high levels of employee ownership. The industry-level analysis confirms that the FMCG sector pay practice conforms closely to these prescriptions.

Market positioning is seen as central to the practice of compensation (Lawler et al., 1995). In the face of intense competition for key labour, organizations are increasingly starting to benchmark pay levels against the external labour market, where previously pay levels might have been internally referenced or collectively bargained (Armstrong and Brown, 2001). All firms contained within the FMCG sample of firms benchmark year on year against their industry peers in order to understand better relative rates of pay, for roles at all levels, and in most major occupations. Benchmarking is conducted on a total remuneration basis – the combined value of the financial pay measures to the individual – and includes base pay, bonuses, long-term incentives, allowances and benefits. These elements of pay are combined to reflect a 'total remuneration' estimation of the financial value of the package to the employee.

Benchmarking is further broken down to illustrate position against the competitive labour market, be it the 25th percentile, the market median (50th percentile) or the 75th percentile. Such data are used, in combination with other sources, to inform decisions about pay progression typically for roles and not individuals. As such, the market data informs decisions about pay progression that potentially affect many thousands of employees. The gathering of market data and the conscious and deliberate positioning of pay relative to the market is indicative of pay best practice (Lawler et al., 1995). Budgetary constraints such as ability to pay, or other considerations such as internal relativity, serve to moderate the firm's ability to position itself within the market as desired, but no company within either the pay survey or the sample of FMCG case studies pursues a strategy of 'underpaying', and many seek to better the market median for all roles, or a lesser number of key roles.

With the notable exception of one, all firms within the sample have adopted performance-based pay over successive years, and increased it as a proportion of the employee's total pay package. The performance-based pay interventions typically include bonuses, long-term incentives and discretionary allowance, paid on the basis of exemplary performance in the role. While the data tells us nothing about the definition of *performance* within the FMCG firms – the basis upon which performance-based pay is awarded – we are able to infer that (a) both short- and long-term variable pay is pervasive; (b) nearly all roles, including junior management, have performance-based pay as an element of package, indicating that FMCG organizations are embracing 'broad based' incentives (Marler et al., 2002); (c) it is senior management roles that are most incentivized, through three interventions typically; (d) as a result, senior management pay has increased dramatically over the survey period; and (e) the speed with which firms that comprise the industry have moved to adopt innovations in reward is very fast indeed, implying both a willingness to effect change *and* the ability to do so.

Integrated pay systems are a form of the bundling of employment interventions reviewed in Chapter 2 (Armstrong and Brown, 2001). All of the sample companies have chosen to benchmark themselves on the combined value of all financial pay interventions including benefits – total remuneration. Thought is clearly given to the overall value of pay to the individual, when managed as a system. Moreover, the elements of the total remuneration system of pay appeal to different aspects of employee performance (Armstrong and Brown, 2001). Base pay typically reflects the market value of employee proficiency in the role. Bonus reflects performance against STIs, providing an incentive typically geared around performance outcomes. LTIs emphasize the long-term return on shareholder value by aligning employees' long-term interests to those of shareholders through employee ownership. Benefits, while not performance-based, confer security and protection, permitting the employee to participate in a range of core and ancillary benefits that are typically wholly subsidized, much reduced in price or not available elsewhere (Zingheim and Schuster, 2000).

Summary

What, then, do the observed pay norms represent? Do they corroborate existing empirical research regarding the existence of best practice in pay, and indicate that such best practices are pervasive within the FMCG market? Does the startling convergence around the observed pay norms provide evidence of best practice in pay? By selecting these best practices, are decision makers acting rationally? Why are companies converging on strategic pay? As indicated by the industry-level data, FMCG firms are using pay strategically. To answer these questions we must go inside the organizations.

5
Pay Practice at the Level of Approach

The previous chapter reviewed developments related to pay within the UK FMCG sector during the period 1996–2000. Many of these developments conform closely to broader economy-wide trends and the prescriptions of the strategic pay movement. FMCG companies are engaging widely in pay benchmarking to ensure competitiveness against comparator firms. All bar one of the FMCG case study companies makes extensive use of multiple performance-based pay systems in addition to traditional forms of pay – base pay, allowances and benefits. Data suggest that, as an industry, FMCG companies have embraced strategic pay far more widely than in other sectors and the economy overall. The data indicate that FMCG firms in the UK are using pay strategically.

The context for pay determination in individual FMCG companies is, therefore, one of strategic pay as the industry norm. What is driving these developments in pay at the industry level? Does company-level analysis of pay practice confirm that individual FMCG companies are attempting to use pay strategically? If so, *why* are they and, more specifically, for what *purpose*? The next three chapters address these issues, and others, and draw upon in-depth case study data. This chapter deals with the *approach*-level findings, and brings the lens of analysis of pay practice down to the level of the pay approach, as described in the methodology. In the context of the observed industry-wide developments to pay, it asks: how do the seven leading FMCG case study companies approach the use of pay, and what are the implications for pay practice?

The context of pay determination at the level of the pay approach

The context in which pay practice is determined at the level of approach for all the case study firms is characterized by competitive pressures emanating from the external product market and the institutional operating environment, and, given the size and scope of the sample companies, is global in nature. The seven case study companies are all major household names operating within the global FMCG market, and product and country based sub-markets, and are prone to many of the same contextual conditions and pressures.

The operating environment for all of the case study companies is characterized by limited growth opportunity in traditional markets, uncertainty of demand, intense and tightening competition in emerging markets and, increasingly, the impositions of corporate governance codes of regulation and legislation – the Sarbanes-Oxley Act of 2002, for example. The global FMCG market is particularly challenging in respect of the speed with which consumer demand fluctuates, seasonality and product/brand life cycle. A key change to the FMCG market has been the aggressive and ongoing process of consolidation through acquisition. Throughout the course of the past two decades, dominant companies within the global market have merged with other large firms, or acquired smaller regionally or locally based firms. The result is a market now dominated by large multinational companies, operating across a range of consumer goods sub-markets internationally.

> We're locked in battle with Procter & Gamble, who make [product]. And, you know, it *is* a case of two prize fighters, really, slugging it out in the marketplace and that's never good for profit.
>
> (senior HR generalist, company4)

The nature of the consumer opportunities available to FMCG companies is also undergoing far-reaching change and impacting upon the structure and behaviours of FMCG firms. Globalization has not only removed market barriers and created opportunities in new markets but it has also encouraged FMCG companies to seek expansion in developing economies, given the maturation and intense cost competition of traditional markets.

> It's very tough. FMCG is being squeezed ... we've enjoyed good historical growth, good market share, but we're operating very mature markets that don't have a lot of inherent growth potential, like the technology-based industry that has seen exponential growth in the last five years. Upside of our growth would be four or five per cent. At our highest level, we would see it coming in slightly higher. More realistically, we would experience one to two per cent growth.
>
> (business unit leader, company5)

An additional challenge to the established approach to market adopted by FMCG companies is the increasing power of mass retailers, such as Tesco, Asda/Walmart and Sainsbury's. These companies make large demands on their suppliers, commanding discounts on the cost of their products by virtue of their purchasing power. They also greatly influence consumer demand at the point of sale where competing product is placed side by side, but over which FMCG companies, as producers, have little control. Unlike mass retailers, FMCG companies also have little or no direct route to the consumer and are therefore reliant upon retailers and retailer behaviour. While the fortunes of both are closely aligned, the current perception is that there exists an imbalance of power, skewed towards the interests of large retailers wielding considerable purchasing power and consumer influence.

> The phenomenon of the power of the supermarkets is one of the things that's changed in the last ten years. And that *does* influence what we can do. Yeah? There's no doubt about that. We like to come up with strategies that we hope minimize those effects, but, you know, they *do* have an effect. We've seen supermarket chains taking over other supermarket chains. And every time you take one of the players out, it becomes more and more difficult for us as a supplier.
>
> (senior HR generalist, company4)

The ongoing consolidation of the retail sector has served to reduce FMCG routes to market even further, permitting the remaining large retailers to consolidate their considerable purchasing power. In addition, the larger retailers are no longer confined geographically, operating at a national and international level. Consequently, central price-setting and agreements are becoming the norm which, although it guarantees revenue, is recognized as poor for profit. Moreover, discounted purchasing applies to all transactions, and the result of a single negotiation with a mass retailer, if unfavourable, may result in the loss of many millions of pounds of potential profit. Central decisions by large retailers increasingly influence national and international product trends to which FMCG firms must be responsive if they are to continue to be successfully aligned with consumer preference and demand.

> We're trying to be proactive and get ahead of it [the competition], we always have done, so there is a little bit of us driving, a little bit sooner than is absolutely necessary. But I do genuinely believe that we're not the only organization going for globalization, our customers

are too. So if we can just stay a few steps ahead of them and be ready when they require a global service, then we believe that's the right thing to do. So that's more market-driven, we would say.

(senior operational manager, company4)

FMCG branded products are increasingly facing competition from 'own label' retailer products, which are often viewed as competitive in terms of choice and quality but significantly less expensive. Compliance with legislation and institutional regulation emanating from the external environment also presents additional challenges imposed on the company. Largely as a result of concerns over corporate governance, a raft of sweeping regulation designed to protect shareholder interest has recently come into effect, with which the case study companies are obliged to comply. The Sarbanes-Oxley Act of 2002, the most high-profile piece of recent legislation, has had a profound effect upon companies operating in, or under, US ownership. Regulations aimed specifically at executive compensation are becoming increasingly prescriptive as successive governmental and institutional investor regulation requirements are issued. Within the UK, the Association of British Insurers' (ABI) executive compensation guidelines (2006) represent the most recent in a series of guidelines that prescribe limits to the choices available to companies on the design of executive compensation. Combined with existing legislation, and the pressure of other institutional investor bodies such as the National Association of Pension Funds (NAPF), the freedom of companies to determine executive compensation is becoming increasingly constrained. The effects of such constraints are to encourage conformity of practice as the choices available to companies become increasingly restricted.

Leaving aside concerns with investor protection, FMCG multinational firms are also bound by host country business conduct and employment legislation. In addition to compliance with regulation and legislation, FMCG companies in food, beverage and tobacco face further challenges in the form of increasing consumer awareness and regulatory intervention over issues such as health and well-being. Obesity, like smoking, is now regarded as a serious public health issue in Europe and North America and something that might, through either consumer or regulatory intervention, damage the long-term growth of the industry. The issue of obesity was cited as a significant business challenge by a number of case study interviewees.

Alcoholic beverage producers have come under increasing scrutiny over concerns about alcohol-related illness and public order interests.

Producers have responded by marketing a variety of modified products such as 'lite' beers and low alcohol alternatives to traditional products. Many alcoholic beverage firms have also sought to raise public awareness of alcohol-related illness and injury through sponsored campaigns and research. Indeed, in the interests of corporate social responsibility and good governance, alcohol firms have increasingly partnered with government and non-governmental bodies to promote responsible drinking.

More than any other FMCG sector, tobacco producers have come under the greatest scrutiny. In 2004, the World Health Organization introduced a treaty designed to reduce smoking-related diseases, and this was signed up to by most of the major developed countries. The treaty requires that manufacturers place visible health warnings covering at least 30 per cent of each pack and, most significantly, that government enforce the protection of non-smokers from smoke in work and public places.

> By the time you're established in a market and ready to move on to another, somebody else is in there, you know, notwithstanding patent laws, and you've probably lost the momentum. Equally, you know, you're not making efficient use of your promotion or other marketing money as you launch the new product. So really what you want to do is invent something for, in this instance North Atlantic, and then push it out using one big launch very quickly. And that's a lot of the thinking behind us going into the North Atlantic. And then eventually we'll move on to global.
>
> (senior operational manager, company4)

Firms are not simply responding to commercial challenges and the need to comply with institutional regulation, aimed at promoting corporate governance and shareholder value protection. Firms are also responding to practice trends within the industry and the global economy more broadly. These pressures are institutional in nature and are manifest in the form of industry norms and notions of best practice, associated with superior company performance and stories of success.

> Sometimes it's like a lemming effect? You know, it's just like all these articles get written about it, it's the sexy thing to do and everybody moves in that direction, right?
>
> (management consultant, consult2)

Thus, the case study firms, corporately, are prone to both commercial and institutional pressures. Commercial pressures relate to the changing nature of consumer demand, increasingly mature product markets resisting expansionist corporate aspirations, and overall consolidation of the industry resulting in intense competition between a handful of 'mega-firms'.

> But I think I can understand how companies get into bonuses, but I think the other piece about bonuses is that it's a little bit like following the herd of sheep really. So it's bloody difficult, because the *norm* in the marketplace appears to be that people give bonuses.
>
> (senior general manager, company4)

All of the firms are subject to regulatory compliance in the interests of protecting shareholder value, and also the myriad elements of host legislation in the countries in which they operate. Normative pressures in the form of corporate success stories pervade the industry on a global scale, encouraging adoption in the expectation of similar outcomes.

Variation at the approach level of the pay determination process

As a result of various external environmental pressures illustrated above, both commercial and institutional, all of the sample firms have developed coping mechanisms in the form of successive strategic reviews, and the formulation of new corporate targets and new models of organization. Strategically, all firms have had to negotiate the ongoing tension between cost competition and product differentiation.

> We're in a particularly profitable sector of the fast moving consumer goods business, one that is very controversial, and we are trying to demonstrate long-term value to shareholders, ultimately by showing year-on-year growth in profit. And we have strategies that help us go on delivering that growth, which I would currently sum up as the movement from 'good' to 'great', which probably brings about attaining a leadership position in our business.
>
> (rewards practitioner, company1)

All of the food and beverage FMCG firms in the research sample have sought to align their product portfolios more closely to increasingly cost-conscious consumers, while also still retaining a diverse brand portfolio offering choice. The dual strategy of encouraging a market focus for the business, from product conception, supply chain and finally retail distribution, and asset stripping, represents a significant departure from past practice, for what are in nearly all cases very mature firms, associated with paternalistic structures and legacies of past practice. This presents significant organizational challenges for management. Not least, the market focus requires that the organization seamlessly tailor its offering to consumer demand, necessitating a responsive and adaptable organization. Barriers to such flexibility often stem from the employee base which, while it may be viewed by some as the company's one true source of sustainable competitive advantage, may also inhibit the degree of change possible owing to people's innate aversion to change. This is especially the case during times of high uncertainty, typically associated with the disposal of corporate assets, restructuring and downsizing.

Unlike the majority of the competition, the vision of company1 is to achieve global leadership within the market, principally through organic growth of key market segments and brands, increasing productivity and efficiencies of operation, and, finally, achieving good governance through shared responsibility by all. Enabling the achievement of the strategic goals and the corporate vision is 'excellent organization', consisting of 'winning' leadership, culture, talent and learning.

> So when we started this journey of creating our own reward philosophy, the survey that we did around the world included other employers, and we had banks and technology companies. Walt Disney was in there. It was a fairly eclectic mix. Now we were looking for bright ideas, but we were looking for things that worked with them, but we resisted the temptation of assuming that if it worked for Walt Disney it would work for us. When we saw something that we thought looked good, we then needed to 'sense check it' against the way *we* do things and decide if it was right. So we developed a 'right for us' approach rather than best practice.
>
> (reward practitioner, company1)

Company2 has over the past decade been highly acquisitive, having almost doubled in size as a result. Key corporate objectives going forward include improving profitability and continuing expansion of the operations in emerging markets, which are viewed as the future of the business, given the maturation of traditional markets in Europe and the Americas. In their mission statement, company2's senior management consider the following as critical success factors: (a) investment beating the cost of capital; (b) the consolidation of annual supplier contracts; (c) measuring investment opportunity cost; (d) freeing cash flow; and (e) capitalizing upon the economies of scale afforded by the extensive scale of the group's global business.

In company6, the business strategy is one of transitioning the product offering in both confectionery and food, its two main sources of revenue, from discount high-volume consumer purchasing to 'premiumization'. Premiumization is considered desirable because it is a means of differentiating company6 product within a saturated confectionery product market, and premium products generate higher margins per unit sold. Cost competition is no longer seen as a sustainable business model. In the past, company6 had attempted to shift away from competition based upon cost, by diversifying the product offering to include pet food, ready-made meals and beverages, as well as introducing new brands into its core snack food market. Diversification, however, had not paid off and the company had just emerged from five years of below-target performance. In addition to premiumization, the product strategy also calls for a refocus on core brands of snack food. Organizationally, company6 has, as a stated corporate aim, the ambition to 'make our money work harder'. To that end, it has recently introduced, as a key business measure (and a measure for company-based incentive payments), the *return on total assets* (ROTA).

Company4, facing an increasingly tight product market in the core Western European consumer market, a downturn in the global economy and increasing public awareness and concern over issues such as obesity, health and nutrition, was prompted to embark upon a new strategy emphasizing innovation and efficiency. This new strategic direction included a review of approaches to pay, resulting in the formulation of a new pay strategy, focused on promoting efficiency over expansion.

> I'd say on the growth imperative – which is defined as the new products or extensions in services – that is coming out, that is us driving that, because of our own and our shareholders' growth expectations.
>
> (senior operational manager, company4)

In 2003, company7 implemented a global strategic plan aimed at improving performance and reducing costs and creating a 'delivery mindset' within the company. The strategy had three main targets of (a) top line 5–6 per cent growth by the end of the plan; (b) an operating margin of 16 per cent (profit/turnover); and (c) earnings per share at the low double-digit level. The last two strategic goals have been achieved: production has been streamlined; an enterprise culture has been developed; simplification has been achieved; and efficiency has been hugely increased. The first target, however, was not achieved despite considerable progress at the start of the plan up to 2003. As this was the most important target, there is currently a strategic review under way and a new strategic plan is being put in place.

The new strategic plan emphasizes top-line growth, and both organizational targets and financial targets are more realistic given the current economic situation. It is also viewed as creating greater flexibility to build a sustainable, sound operation, focusing on long-term profitability. The focus is to shift from 'price' to 'innovation' as the primary mode of competitive differentiation.

The plan is, however, still only in its infancy. One of its aims is to simplify the structure of the group and speed up operations by working towards 'One [firm]', with only one company based in each country, and more operations merged at regional level. The starting point is, therefore, to consider what can be done together, and then to deal with the exceptions that arise, where things need to be done differently, in the various local contexts. The number of management positions within the new structure is also being reduced, hence increasing the span of control for remaining managers by three to four fold. While this is creating space for subordinates, it leaves less time available for managers for innovation of new policies and practices, and thus forces more focus on simplicity. The key challenge currently facing company7 is to turn around company performance once again, particularly within Europe.

The company markets itself as 'a truly multi-local, multinational'. In the past, company7 was known for being 'great marketeers', although this is no longer the focus. The new 2010 plan has more of an outward-looking, modest attitude, and is open and sensitive to what is happening in the outside world, trying to identify emerging needs. Company7's aim is to add value by fulfilling its promises to people, giving brand assurance and proactively understanding the needs of the consumer very well, almost before the consumer is aware of his or her needs. The new focus on adding vitality to life applies both to the food, and to home and personal care goods. Company7 also has good relationships with its customers (retailers, wholesalers, out of home channel), using the slogan 'to win with customers'.

And you're going to the most senior people in the organization for this information, and they'll provide you with 'we need to grow our top line, we need to grow our bottom line and, two times our top line, we need to improve our cash flow, we need to ... in our highest margin businesses we want to be market leaders, in terms of market share'. So you could go through a number of these things and kind of say, well how does this support the strategy, the overall strategy of the company?

(global rewards director, company5)

In response to environmental pressure, decision makers within the case study companies have undertaken to initiate change, in the recent past, and vary new practice from the existing status quo. The perceptions of the success of others, competitors in most instances, and the demands placed upon the decision makers by those to whom they are accountable, prompted them to review current practice and opt to initiate change.

Selection at the approach level of the pay determination process

In response to the perceived need for change, the selection stage involves choices regarding the form of change. At the level of approach, selection extends to choices about the philosophy of pay practice, and the principles of the pay design that should best reflect not only managerial aspirations, and the limitations imposed upon those aspirations by environmental pressures, but also the beliefs and values that decision makers consciously subscribe to, and those they take for granted. Senior management indicate the necessity for change in order to achieve strategic objectives, and provide broad direction and guidance in the form of desired outcomes. Additionally, senior management seek to review a range of options for action, formulated by internal functional specialists and supported by external expert advisers. This is with a view to endorsing a particular course of action that they feel best fits the achievement of the stated desired outcomes. While the selection of the form of the pay approach does not reflect formal policy or technical content, the pay approach does take the form of informal and symbolic expressions of aspirational practice, typically articulated in mission statements and corporate communications about vision and values.

And so that all needs to be thought out very clearly because that really creates almost your guiding principles, and through the design and implementation process, you can continuously do checks and balances to say 'is this design element going to help us achieve those guiding principles?'

(management consultant, consult1)

Broad-based pay within company1 is used to 'create alignment of purpose throughout the business and build and maintain a winning organization', emphasizing the use of pay to align employee interests to those of the business, and as a lever through which the business might be developed further. Stemming from the functional mission statement above, the strategic objectives that equate to the principles of pay practice are to (a) create focus and alignment; (b) drive performance; and (c) maximize the impact of reward (internal briefing memo, company1). Creating focus and alignment extends to the desire for alignment of purpose, and a clear line of sight between objectives and outcomes, reinforced by financial opportunity in the form of performance-based pay measures. Differentiation of performance between various units of the business, and individuals within those units, is actively promoted as a means of driving performance. Maximizing the impact of reward extends to competitiveness within the labour market, ensuring parity of pay levels with competitors to attract and retain talent, but also ensuring that the company is not paying over the market rate.

Similarly, the provision of pay and benefits stresses individual ownership and flexibility: individuals being responsible for the personal selection of their level of benefits. Pay is also part of a broader employment strategy, being positioned as key to creating 'an open, confident culture that encourages change and innovation, is shaped by the guiding (corporate) principles, and inspires people to perform and enjoy' (HR strategy document, company1).

And we said, well there are three ... as far as company1 is concerned, there are three things that we believe rewards should be doing. They should be helping us align people to the business objectives. They should be helping us drive performance of the business, and they should ensure that the amount of money basically we spend on rewards around the world is optimised, has its maximum impact. So that we saw as the three roles, if you like, of pay, and then you've got the documents somewhere, and then underneath it you will see a lot of the philosophical strands that will help us deliver that.

So those form a common framework, if you like, for managing pay in company1.

(senior rewards practitioner, company1)

Pay within all seven case study firms is used as a tool for the pursuit of business objectives and enhanced organizational performance and competitiveness. All firms use both short- and long-term variable pay programmes for the majority, if not all, of their white collar, technical, professional and managerial grades of employee. Base pay progression is also typically moderated according to individuals' performance, and in all cases is determined by reference to external labour market movements. Benefit provision, in all cases, emphasizes choice, and personal as well as company responsibility for choices made, and costs incurred.

The pay philosophy within company2 is one of rewarding exceptional performance, delivering value for shareholders and building long-term ownership within the business, through being (a) aligned to the business strategy and corporate culture; (b) driving and reinforcing desired behaviour; (c) being competitive and cost effective; (d) being fair, consistent and transparent; and (e) emphasizing performance-based variable pay to encourage accountability for results, and team and individual-based behaviour (HR brochure and senior management presentation, company2).

For us, pay is just part of a wider, more holistic philosophy and approach, which is based on our belief that motivation and commitment, and thereby our ability to attract and retain talent, is driven by our culture and values, and not our pay.

(senior management presentation, company2).

To that end, the company employs a formalized group-wide pay strategy, representative of most:

- to develop and deliver rewards and benefits programmes in support of the needs of the business, which are externally competitive, within local markets;
- to provide a clear linkage between performance – both individual and business – and the design and delivery of pay and reward opportunities;
- to ensure that reward programmes align personal behaviours with business objectives and are motivational to employees;
- to develop policies and systems that promote and encourage the international movement and development of management talent.

The strategic pay objectives within company4 are for pay to be competitive, differentiated, responsive and consistent, in the expectation that pay will, therefore:

- support the achievement of the global business plan
- better enable company4 to support the global business plan
- better enable company4 to attract and retain key talent
- reinforce the importance of performance management
- respond continuously to feedback from team leaders
- respond to market conditions (company4 corporate memoranda).

Pay is also intended to promote and sustain the following broad-based 'leadership behaviours': (a) visionary, (b) inspirational, (c) innovative, (d) decisive, (e) collaborative, and (f) building talent (company4).

The stated objectives of pay at company4 are to:

- promote sustained success of the company
- assist in the attraction and retention of high-performance staff
- support employee development
- reinforce principles of fairness and integrity
- maximize employee contribution and performance
- be in alignment with the business strategy
- assist change programmes.

Unlike company1 and company2, the selected approach at company3 is not widely communicated. Nor is it clear what values underpin the pay design, nor what the desired pay outcomes are. Similarly, the design principles of pay at company5 centre on highly competitive levels of pay, pay for performance, equitable relativity with peers and the ability continuously to improve deployed pay programmes to reflect better the changing needs of the business.

> I mean, there is ... there is a common reward strategy. Both actually rewards and benefits as well, because the two *do* fit together fairly well in terms of how they're trying to target the overall positioning, so to speak, of the organization. So really, I would say our strategy, in terms of rewards, is to be at the upper quartile level and in terms of benefits to be at the median or average level. I would say that strategy is ... or philosophy, is universally shared, even in the regions.
>
> (HR function practitioner, company5)

Like the majority of the case study companies, both company7 and company5 emphasize their philosophy of pay as being one of total rewards. Financial pay measures are packaged (or bundled) together into a total cash proposition (being the sum of all cash elements of pay, including base pay, bonuses and equity). A total remuneration offering for more senior managerial staff (the sum of all financial elements, cash and benefits) is combined with non-financial measures such as career and development opportunities. Philosophically speaking, therefore, both firms have responded to the perceived value placed by employees on the non-financial aspects of the employment proposition and included those elements within the pay proposition. The implication is that the pay function has responsibility for non-financial reward elements, as well as financial, and that these various aspects of the broader HR contribution are integrated.

Company6 differs from the majority of the case study companies because, while performance is clearly valued, the aspiration is not primarily to create a high-performance working culture, but to be perceived as an employer of choice. The philosophy reflects the widely held view within company6 that performance is secured through the recruitment of the best talent available and not through high-performance measures per se.

> [Company6] aims to be the employer of choice for those dedicated individuals with drive, talent, healthy dissatisfaction and a strong desire to win, who really make a difference. 'We want the best; we'll pay for the best and expect the best from our associates.' Pay should not be the reason someone wants to work at company6. We want people to come to company6 because we run lean, we can spend more per associate, and therefore give more responsibility ('big jobs early'). We want people to work for company6 because of what we can offer in terms of a career.
>
> (corporate documentation, company6)

As a key element of the overall HR strategy, recruitment and rewards are viewed as a supporting mechanism at the level of approach. Indeed, until recently, company6 did not provide any form of incentive pay, viewing it as potentially divisive, and not in keeping with the employment ethos of employee inclusion, participation and involvement. As we will see, however, company6 has introduced performance-based pay in recent years with implications for performance.

Retention at the approach level of the pay determination process

All of the case study companies have a pay approach that is the result of deliberate and conscious determination by leadership operating at the highest levels. The pay approach is determined, primarily, by senior management and subject to board-level management approval in all cases. Moreover, as the selection stage illustrated, the selected principles and values of the pay approach are broadly very similar in response to, largely, common commercial and institutional environmental pressures as they are perceived at the upper echelons of the case study firms. There is variation between companies, however, regarding the form of the pay approach, with clear implications for what is communicated to both managers and employees operating at lower levels of the organization.

> The framework that goes around reward, over and above the grade structure, also says something about the company's philosophy. So whether or not you have a bonus scheme, how big a proportion of your base pay that bonus scheme is, whether or not you have share options, or whether you've other share incentives. Some of these are based on philosophy as much as market practice. You may pay attention to market practice, but essentially it's your philosophy.
>
> (country reward manager, company7)

In addition to being used as a means of communicating 'what is important to us', the pay approach also serves the more practical purpose of acting as a 'guiding framework' for the design and operation of pay at lower levels of the organization, such as the business unit, region or country-specific pay determination. Implicit within the deployment of the guiding framework is recognition that given the size, complexity and diversity of operation within complex multinational firms, centralized pay management does not result in 'best fit' pay designs. Communication of the global pay approach, supplemented by the guiding framework, represents both the aspiration for, and the mechanism by which, a balance between global consistency and local 'fit for purpose' might be achieved. Ideally, the outcome is multiple 'best fit' local variations upon a globally consistent theme.

> I describe it as a framework in which we would expect company1 companies to operate. We would expect the line manager in Australia to be able to look at it and say 'yeah, I can see now that my line

manager is making pay decisions and I see that's one of the elements in this ... it's one of the philosophies'. So, you know, it's about alignment, it's about flying in a formation where we think we need to fly in formation without overdoing it.

(senior rewards practitioner, company1)

However, while all of the firms have necessarily adopted a guiding framework approach, they have done so to differing degrees, with some companies promoting consistency over local fit, and vice versa. Thus, the balance between global consistency and local fit represents a continuum, with companies placed, for better or worse, along that continuum.

For those firms adopting a model of 'light touch' corporate control (that is, emphasizing corporate/global consistency, but primarily devolving responsibility for the design of pay to those further down the organization), the guiding framework, in all cases, is supplemented by a set of minimum standards of practice. The minimum standards represent mandatory requirements to which all within the firm, regardless of role or function, are expected to comply. However, the minimum standards constitute a floor or threshold of practice below which local line management discretion cannot go; the minimum standards still permit a great deal of discretion. In addition to the minimum standards, all organizations, to varying degrees of effectiveness, provide guidance and assistance with processes designed to support the management of pay.

We do the same thing in all sorts of employment principles too, and reward is part of that. But if you have too many centralized controls, then people are not able to use this process to support the business of which you *are* holding them accountable for running.

(reward practitioner, company1)

In terms of what is retained within the organization, the pay approach at company1 is viewed both as a guiding framework for the determination of pay at subsequent stages and levels of the pay determination process. It is not a corporate attempt at control, nor does it limit the scope of managerial discretion to manage pay as deemed best at the point of the interface between the employee and the employer – the immediate line management. Rather, the pay approach is viewed as a set of core principles, which set out in clear terms the basis of pay within company1 – in this case an aspiration and belief in driving performance through establishing a high-performance culture.

I mean in doing it we were very clear that this is not a straitjacket. It's a set of principles, philosophies, tenets – call it what you want – where we want consistency. So how have we gone about it? Let's take one element, and let's just examine how we've gone about driving that. We want to drive base pay through individual performance. So our consistent high performers will get significantly bigger pay increases than our consistent on-target performers, who will get consistently higher pay increases than our under-performers. That's the principle. Now, how do we make that work?

(senior rewards practitioner, company1)

The pay approach also serves the purpose of communicating symbolically what is important to the organization's leadership to employees. In the case of company1, then, in broad terms, pay is positioned as a means of promoting alignment of effort and employee interest to the core values, vision and mission of the firm yet, significantly, not directly but as one element of a broader range of measures – financial and non-financial. The pay approach within company2 is similar to that of company1. Company2 espouses much the same values and aspirations, and articulates them in the form of a formal strategy that is communicated widely and, again, serves as a guiding framework for the determination of pay, at subsequent stages of the process.

The chosen pay approach at company4, company6 and company7, expressed in the form of a formal pay strategy, fulfils the additional role of communicating symbolically what is valued corporately by senior management to employees. Company4 emphasizes performance expectations within the pay strategy, with the implication being 'this is the deal we offer you and this is what we expect in return'. The pay strategy is disseminated to the global organization, in parallel with other important pieces of corporate communication. The effect is to raise the profile of corporate performance above the role of subsidiary businesses and their contribution to corporate performance. The aspiration is clearly to align employee interests, behaviours and productivity to those of the organization at the many operating levels – corporately, regionally and their business unit. In this respect, the pay strategy, in all cases, successfully raises employee awareness of the strategic direction of the company through the linkage between corporate goals and pay.

The pay strategy, as a manifestation of the approach, does not, however, provide a framework for the determination of pay at lower levels of the organization within these three case study companies. As will be demonstrated in Chapter 6 – pay practice at the level of design – the design of pay systems is centralized and not the responsibility primarily of line management. The articulated and symbolically valuable pay strategy does serve to provide a basis for those that manage people – line management – to understand the rationale and principles underpinning the pay systems they are expected to implement.

As noted earlier, the pay approach at company3 is not formalized, nor is it communicated widely. As such, despite sharing much the same content in terms of aspirational outcomes and value as the other case study companies, the approach to pay at company3 remains obscure and is perceived, therefore, by those tasked with the design and the management of pay, and the employees themselves, as ambiguous. The ambiguity and lack of clarity surrounding the pay approach is problematic because, without it, the rationale of pay (for the managed and the managers) is equally unclear. Lack of certainty regarding pay system purpose and pay system outcomes can result in unintended consequences in the form of emergent pay practice being misaligned with the desired approach (as will be illustrated in the pay operation-level findings). The pay approach in company5, in the form of a strategy, like company3, is also not communicated widely, with the result that what is desired in terms of pay practice, and also what is valued by senior management, remains ambiguous. Consequently, there is potentially little understanding of the rationale for pay at company5 both by those that manage and by those that are managed.

> But we made progress, but we were at least allowed to write this year and it just didn't get communicated. But that's better than where we've been in the past, we've never written anything and been told we can't share, we don't want to share anything.
>
> (global rewards director, company5)

Five out of the seven case study firms promote the pay approach, throughout, in the form of an articulated pay strategy. Articulating the pay approach is viewed, not only as a means of defining the corporate position on pay but also as a means of communicating what is considered important to the leadership of the organization. In this form, the pay approach, therefore, is a communication tool and complements additional communication interventions undertaken at a corporate level. Moreover, unlike other communication interventions, the pay approach also allows management the opportunity to formalize those expectations. Furthermore, the pay approach formalizes managerial performance expectations and desired behaviours by incorporating them into the pay determination process. However, despite having formulated a pay approach, two of the seven case study firms do not actively articulate, or promote internally, their pay approaches. Consequently, the pay approach is not used as a communication tool, nor does it elaborate on the rationale for those pay practices ultimately expressed as intended policy.

> We've started to talk about the framework with the international community just last year. So to them that's something that is new and I'm sure it's probably perceived as if it came a bit out of the blue.
>
> (corporate rewards manager, company5)

While these two firms would stress the value of aligning employee expectations and interests to those of the firm, and would further emphasize the role of pay as a means of achieving this, pay does not fulfil this objective. As a result, from an employee perspective, there is an element of ambiguity regarding the rationale for pay, potentially resulting in uncertainty and disenfranchisement, and a lack of understanding on the part of operational line managers regarding their role in the management of pay.

All of the case study companies share very similar approaches to pay, but they do not all articulate their approaches in the form of a clear and constructive pay strategy, and do not enjoy the associated benefits of doing so. However, when asked, no single company would say that it does not purposefully articulate and disseminate its pay strategies. It would be counter-intuitive not to do so – but some of the case study companies clearly do it better than others. It is, therefore, the management of the pay strategy, both in terms of the selection of an appropriate strategy, *and how* it is used, that impacts most on the value retained from pay practice at the level of approach.

Summary

All of the seven case study firms, leaders within the FMCG market, are attempting to use pay strategically. They share a common desire to achieve outcomes of strategic value, and view pay as a means of achieving those outcomes. Pay is universally valued as a powerful 'tool', through which both productivity and positive behaviours might be leveraged in the interests of enhanced performance – individual and organizational. Consistent with the industry-level findings of Chapter 4, the overall picture of case study company pay practice, at the level of approach, is one of convergence around pay practice norms, consistent with prescriptions of strategic pay.

All of the research sample companies face broadly similar environmental, commercial and institutional pressures, and have all responded by developing two-pronged corporate strategies of market leadership on the one hand, and profitability through efficiency savings and financial flexibility on the other. Pay is viewed, by all firms, as an important element of achieving both strategies. Key to market leadership is employee performance and the development of leadership capabilities throughout the organization, for which pay is viewed as an important driver. Pay systems are a means of driving performance but are also a means of encouraging certain behaviours, such as leadership qualities, innovation and a sense of personal ownership for success or failure. In all cases, the elements that comprise the pay approach are bundled with a broader range of employee-related interventions, such as communication, involvement and engagement initiatives, designed to 'foster' a culture of 'high performance' (Table 5.1).

To those ends, pay is viewed as a value-adding activity and is in all cases positioned and marketed as a total rewards proposition, emphasizing a comprehensive and integrated array of financial and non-financial rewards, such as incentives, benefits, work environment, career and succession opportunities. On a practical level, the pay approach is a communication tool that can convey what's important to the organization in how it is executed. In addition it can also inform others of stated aspirations in regard to less tangible aspects of the organization, such as culture, in lieu of precise managerial controls. As such, the pay approach is typically not detailed or technical, nor is it a precise statement of managerial intent, but rather the founding principles upon which the pay design is based, and the rationale for the deployment of pay practices.

All of the case study companies have converged around broadly similar, performance-based approaches to pay, which themselves conform to the prescriptions of the strategic pay school and broader developments within the industry. Indeed, there seems to be one model universally pervasive within the FMCG industry – the strategic model of pay. Emphasizing common design principles, such as alignment, performance, competitiveness and value for money, pay within the case study companies is geared around the achievement of stated economic ends and is determined by management, for whom the deployment of pay, as a managerial tool, is a managerial responsibility. In exhibiting similar models of pay in the form of articulated design principles (such as alignment, competitiveness and so on) the quantitative data indicated (and the case study-based company data would support the assumption),

Table 5.1 Case study company pay practice at the level of approach

Stage Description	Context to Aligned	Variation Aspiration	Selection Content	Form	Retention Perceived impact
Company1	Mission and values	High-performance work culture	Total rewards model	Guiding frame work	Symbolic
Company2	Mission and values	High-performance work culture	Total rewards model	Guiding frame work	Symbolic
Company3	Mission and values	High-performance work culture	Total rewards model	Implicit	Ambiguous
Company4	Mission and values	High-performance work culture	Total rewards model	Code of practice	Symbolic
Company5	Mission and values	High-performance work culture	Total rewards model	Implicit	Ambiguous
Company6	Mission and values	Employer of choice	Talent model	Code of practice	Symbolic
Company7	Mission and values	High-performance work culture	Total rewards model	Guiding frame work	Symbolic

that the sample firms are *choosing* to deploy a range of pay interventions in the form of formal pay policies.

What do the striking similarities of approach to pay practice between these competing firms represent? Is the near total conformity of case study company approaches to pay an indication that the utility and value of strategic pay is such that all leading firms independently subscribe to it? Is it a further indication that strategic pay represents 'best practice' and is therefore universal in its application and appeal, as the level of conformity might suggest? If strategic pay is best practice, and therefore the optimal strategy, does the choice of strategic pay over other approaches indicate rationality on the part of management? As in Chapter 4, at the very least, the approach-level findings confirm the desire of the seven leading case study companies to use pay strategically and represent the first stage of their attempt to do so.

6
Pay Practice at the Level of Design

The previous chapter illustrated that all seven case study companies aspire to use pay strategically and to that end have each developed pay strategies underpinned by largely the same principles. This findings chapter, the second of three company-level findings chapters, lowers the lens of analysis to the level of pay design within the companies. In light of the approach-level findings, this chapter asks specifically: given the desire to use pay strategically, how are firms attempting to do so? Which pay systems are chosen by the case study firms to fulfil the pay aspirations and principles, and on what basis are they selected? Finally, what are the implications for pay system effectiveness as it is perceived by those to whom the selected pay systems are applied?

The context of pay determination at the level of the pay design

Pay systems are designed against the backdrop of the pay approach – the pay strategy. The pay approach defines the aspirations and principles underpinning the design of pay systems – performance-based pay, for example. The pay design, if aligned, should be consistent with the espoused principles of the pay approach. However, as noted in the previous chapter, the pay approach in two of the seven case study companies is not communicated widely and fails, therefore, to inform fully the determination of the pay design. In one of the case study companies, this has serious implications for relevancy and robustness of the design, where the rationale driving the use of pay is not clearly understood by management or employees. The pay design, however, is not purely informed by the pay approach.

Additional external and internal pressures also influence the outcomes of the pay determination process. Although the external pressures include the competitive concerns of senior management, the more important concerns relate to labour market competitiveness, industry trends and competitor pay practice, and regulation to which pay practice must comply. Internal pressures revolve more around the need to ensure relativity, alignment with existing structures and governance. It is worth noting that the context in which pay systems are designed is quite distinct from the context in which the approach to pay strategies is formulated. Reflecting two states of the same pay practice, each is designed in response to different contextual pressures, to which the nature and form of the practice are contingent. Moreover, a key distinction between the case study companies is that determination of the pay design is decentralized in three of the seven, but centralized in the remainder. As a result, pay is determined at the divisional level in three companies and at the company level in the remaining four. This has implications for the perceived effectiveness of the pay design manifest as pay policy.

Centralized pay design decisions reflect those contextual pressures pervasive at the centre, while decentralized pay design decisions are the opposite. Irrespective of the degree of centralization or decentralization, however, the determination of the pay design is influenced, in all cases, by the established principles set forth in the pay approach. As noted in the previous chapter, the values and aspirations of the pay approach are not fully articulated in a couple of the case study companies, with the result that the design of pay systems in those companies is largely unguided and the rationale unclear. The corporate pay strategies of company5 and company3 are not communicated widely by senior management (for reasons that are unclear) and therefore fail to guide the design of pay centrally (in the case of company5) and decentrally (in the case of company3).

In contrast, the design of pay systems in both company1 and company2 is decentralized and determined within the context of business unit operations at the country and/or divisional level. The context in which pay is determined is characterized by the local, and not the corporate business and employment environment. The major UK operating base of company1 hosts, on a single regional site, a variety of functions and divisions including manufacturing, product storage and distribution, shared services and the global research and development division. Approximately 220 researchers, technicians and managerial staff are employed within the R&D division, comprising the global R&D function, and supported by UK-based shared services, operating under the auspices of the London-based UK global headquarters. Located in the regional site are a number of full-time HR managers, who are tasked with the responsibility for designing and maintaining pay systems for employees based at the site, in addition to other employment-related matters. Managing the diversity of functions, units and roles operating within the one site is a key challenge to local line management, as they grapple with the issue of pay and appropriate employee segmentation.

Like company1, company2 functions at a number of operating sites throughout the UK, with business unit HR staff and line management being responsible for designing pay systems. Again, the context in which pay is designed is characterized by local business and employment conditions. The major manufacturing and distribution site of company2 is also regionally based, but there are extensive operations located elsewhere within the UK, with the headquarters based in London. Company2 employs approximately 25,000 employees in the UK, a significant proportion of whom are managerial, professional and technical employees. While there are global product lines that share similar branding, each product line and/or division within the major markets of the company (the UK being one) is treated as a wholly owned subsidiary operation, and as fully autonomous within the 'umbrella' of the parent organization. The determination of pay design is fully devolved to the local management of each subsidiary business unit, working in collaboration with the central pay function, which is itself based in the London headquarters. For both company1 and company2, pay design is determined *locally* within the context of local business unit objectives and conditions.

Company3 is organized geographically, with three territories covering the scope of global operations and reflecting the rapid growth of the company over the past decade. The three geographical territories are the Americas, Europe and International. These cover all employees and markets in which the company operates. Each geographical business unit has its own reward team located within the UK-based global headquarters, and reporting in to the business unit HR director, with a dotted line report to the global compensation and benefits director, also located in London. Within each geographical business unit there is limited reward function representation located within each country, depending upon the size and value of the country-based operation (referred to internally as markets). Despite being located centrally, there is little crossover, or sharing of practice, between the rewards function staff of all three geographical business units. This is the same at lower levels in the organization, between countries selling the same product and sharing the same human capital challenges, despite being in different markets. Pay policies, as they are developed, apply to each of the three geographical business units and may, as a result, be exclusive. As noted in the previous chapter, all policies are developed within the framework of the pay approach, but the pay approach is not articulated clearly, nor is it viewed as a guide to the formulation of the pay design. The result is that pay policies are typically bespoke for each geographical business unit, and apply to numerous different operations, and many thousands of employees, irrespective of local context, culture and business conditions.

Pay within company4 is designed on a regional basis. A European rewards team of five people is placed at various locations throughout the 13 countries that comprise the European territory of the business. Located in the company headquarters in the US, the central pay function is increasingly, and unilaterally, imposing standardized pay policies on a corporate-wide basis, which thereby conflict with the established regional structure. The central pay function exercises a large degree of control and intervenes frequently in pay design, resulting in tensions at the regional level. Company4 is indicative of a trend towards the greater centralization of the design of pay systems:

> So the company is very 'Ameri-focused'. And they're beginning to understand that they need to have some understanding in the countries, but they still want it managed. Primarily, if anything, it's going more towards America than less, and that's because of the European situation. Economically we're not as strong as we used to be, we're certainly not growing at the same rate, and I'm sure everyone has said this, we're not growing at the rate that everyone predicted, which I have to say was, you know, your usual hockey sticks, you know, a little dip and off we go.
>
> (senior reward director, company4)

Consistent with the experiences of other case study firms, the slowed growth of company4, relative to past performance and, as a consequence of the core markets maturing, together with increasing cost competition, has resulted in efforts to regain greater control of the organization, rationalize the cost base and maximize the opportunities for economies of scale, as they are perceived by senior management:

> Consistency, common approaches, reduced administration, managing it from the center – it's all those things. And you have to come back and say, 'But what does that bring to the company?' And that's the

dialogue I'm involved in on the global team. So you can see that we're half-way between being a European company in an American organization, to being a European branch of an American company, which is quite different, and not what I thought I was joining, but, hey, it's quite interesting.

(senior reward director, company4)

The implication of greater centralization of decision making at the corporate level is that it conflicts with the established patterns of pay determination at the regional level. Centrally imposed performance targets and measures do not necessarily best fit the regional organization. The challenge for company4 is therefore one of regional design, being increasingly constrained by the centralist intervention of the US-based corporate pay function. It is a clash between levels of management within the firm, with the interests of regional and local management losing out to those of management operating globally/corporately.

Like company4, company6 is a regionally structured organization, with independent pay functions located in each of the four regional territories of the firm – the Americas, Europe, Asia-Pacific and Latin America. The European rewards team comprises six dedicated full-time staff located throughout the major European country-based operations of the company. Each member of the 'virtual team' reports directly to the European compensation and benefits manager, and has a dotted line reporting relationship with the global rewards director located in the US. The regionally designed pay policy applies to all European-based operations of the US-headquartered parent company. In compliance with host country legislation and codes of regulation, concessions are made to local labour market conditions, but pay systems are purposefully standardized across the European territory as much as possible.

Company7 is one of two cases where responsibility for the design of pay systems resides corporately. It is a particularly large company, with almost 200,000 employees, and operates a complex matrix structure in order to provide clarity around reporting lines for its business units operating in over 120 countries. The central pay function is relatively small in comparison to the size of the firm and operates out of the corporate headquarters in London. The pay function operates with small teams of HR support within each business unit and/or country operation. These local HR units are responsible for overseeing compliance with host country regulation and legislation and pay benchmarking against the local labour market.

The locus of pay design determination rests at the centre, however, and for the vast majority of managerial staff is not devolved to local management. The challenge is applying globall the centrally determined pay systems to the regional and local organization:

> What I mean by that is reward is one of the few places where we have a history of global systems, yeah, which certainly in the last sort of seven/eight years the trend has been towards having one set of policies for key elements of reward that are set globally. And then at regional level, the world is all about making it fit. And in Europe we've been very good citizens and we've basically taken the global model and we've made it work, yeah?
>
> (senior reward director, company7)

Company5 is the most centralist of all the case study companies in terms of pay design. Like all of the case study companies, the rewards function is represented throughout the various levels of the organization – corporately, regionally and locally – in the form of country reward managers and line unit HR managers, with responsibilities including pay. Pay is designed at the corporate level and applied on a broad-based framework to the entire global management population of some 30,000 staff. A further contextual factor, unique to the case study sample, complicates the determination of pay design at company5. This is the intervention of a parent company in pay decisions and the requirement to ensure that a number of practices conform to parent company practice:

> Actually it is, I mean in some cases, it *is* dictated and driven by [the parent company]. So for example, the [management bonus] plan is a ... is an example of that. [Parent company] are the ones who decide on the target percentages by band for the upper levels. They also ... not only does the [company5] board have to approve the business unit ratings that get used in the plan, it then goes to the [parent company] board for them to approve them, same with the pay-outs. So once we've been through the process and the decision has been made about, you know, how much each individual is going to get, it gets reviewed not only by [company5] and approved by the [company5] board, but gets reviewed by [the parent company] and approved by the [parent company] board.
>
> (HR function practitioner, company5)

There is only limited local discretion to determine the form and method of employee pay, even for relatively junior managerial staff. Even centrally, pay decisions are subject to the approval of management within the parent company. Such decisions by both the parent company and the management of the FMCG subsidiary, itself a very large household name, are binding. There is scope, however, to develop additional pay beyond those prescribed from the centre, but experience from elsewhere in the organization would suggest that this rarely takes place in practice:

> We here in [HQ] will provide them with some guidelines for the programme, but, you know if they'd wanted to, you know, go down the path of designing an incentive programme for the employees in Belgium, for example, that would be something that they would be empowered to take the lead on. Well if you believe that you should align our incentive programmes, also that they have better line of sight, then you could argue that those people are in a much better position to know what's appropriate in Western Europe, than we are here in [the US]. Because we're not going to presume that we know everything in [the US].
>
> (corporate rewards manager, company5)

Overall, therefore, the context in which pay is designed varies between the case study companies, with implications for the content, form and impact of the intended pay practice. This variation is principally between central or devolved design pay systems. If centralized, pay is typically designed by specialist pay function staff located within headquarters, who necessarily hold a corporate perspective of the role and value of pay systems. While not global, regional pay teams still apply standardized pay systems to many thousands of employees. When decentralized, the pay design is informed by local business and employment conditions, often in contrast to regional or corporate conditions. The findings indicate that pay systems are contextually highly sensitive. This is exacerbated at the design stage of the pay determination process, where the context in which, prima facie, the same pay systems are designed varies greatly between the case study firms. Such differences, it will be argued, profoundly influence the nature and effectiveness of what, ultimately, becomes operational pay practice.

Variation at the design level of the pay determination process

Within a global, regional or local context, the choice to reform extant practice is driven by the perceived need for change. The need for strategic change typically drives the approach, and considering varying the approach marks the initiation of the design process. Critically, pay function specialists consult both inside and outside the organization, searching for inputs into the reward design determination process. In attempting to define the purpose, the specialist pay functions of all the firms embarked on a process of information gathering, consultation and communication in order to understand better what might constitute a successful 'fit for purpose' pay system and, therefore, pay system success. However, the means by which the firms approached this process of gauging opinion varied widely, both in terms of methods and extent, which had implications for the realized design.

> At the design phase, it's really, you know, a lot of this is kind of where they start to weld together, it's the interviewing, it's the syndication, it's testing different designs, it's modelling the cost. In some cases, organizations do focus groups, you know, to actually test the design with the line, with HR, in some cases potentially even with employees, to see what the reaction is so that it can be refined. And then obviously in that process you're also designing what the communication and the training is going to be to roll out the programme.
>
> (management consultant, consult1)

As a result of the internal assessment of pay design requirements, the variation stage also marks the point at which functional specialists, operating under a senior management mandate, choose what the intended pay policy is ultimately designed to achieve. As is illustrated, there is significant variation between the case study firms in this respect.

Formulating what is 'intended'

Aspirationally, company1, company2 and company3 purposefully seek to align their pay systems with the goals and objectives of the local organization as this is the best means of ensuring the alignment of pay systems to business goals. The 'fit' of the pay system to the local organization is what is considered most important from a design perspective, and responsibility for the design, as illustrated in the previous section, is devolved to local line management. Corporately, local fit is what matters most, and central pay function staff do not actively get involved in the design of pay systems for the subsidiary business units, save for providing technical, legal and process assistance and advice.

In company4 and company6, the regional reward teams gather information and perform extensive consultation and communication in order to scope further the precise requirements for the introduction of a new pay system. The aspiration is different, however, from that of company1 and company2. Whereas the determination of the pay design in company1 and company2 is managed locally, with the result being alignment to local business unit goals and not those of the regional or corporate organization, local business units in company4 and company6 are expected to conform to the regionally determined pay programme. Company6 and company4 differ from each other, however, in respect of their motivation for wishing to encourage conformity to a largely centralized pay system. The concern at company6 is one of good governance. Their belief is that it is through centralist intervention that employees are not disadvantaged by the pay systems deployed. This is in line with their powerful code of ethics openly stated in their approach to pay. 'Mother knows best' is a phrase much used at company6 and reflects the flip side of what is traditionally a very paternalistic firm. There is a belief that the interests of both the firm and the employee are mutually best served by management acting in the interests of both. In the case of company4, the rationale is quite different. The conformity of local businesses to centralist pay design reflects a lack of confidence by central pay planners/management in the ability of the 'business' to determine and manage pay in the best interests of the business, even at the regional management level. This results in 'creeping centralization' and the imposition of both centrally determined systems and targets.

> It's a profit-driven company. They want to have profit, and the only targets they have are profit, growth targets, sharing targets, and something of this one, ya? And they want the business moved, and we have better results, and they look at ... and they also ... they don't trust the people, they are thinking the targets are not smart enough maybe ... and could be that they're thinking, 'Oh they're not smart enough so we use only corporate targets.'
>
> (reward manager, company4)

Like company4, but perhaps even to a greater degree, company5 commands conformity of the international business to largely centrally determined pay systems emanating from the US-based headquarters.

> You know, in the role I have I don't actually interact with line managers outside of North America. You know, the distance just doesn't do it. Whereas I have that regular interaction more or less, you know, here in the States, where the line managers are sitting in the building and

you're ... you know, you're meeting with the folks and you know where they're coming from and what's on their mind. And you have a better way of, I guess, gauging based on those conversations, the extent to which some of the messages that you're communicating are sinking into the way they think. You know, I tend to get those clues indirectly through the conversations I have with the region compensation people, for example, and, you know, some of the regional human resources people.

(corporate rewards manager, company5)

Again, reflecting a position that corporately determined pay systems fit the business best, pay systems are designed to align employees to predominantly corporate, financial targets irrespective of role, function or location. Company7 also prescribes pay systems designed from the centre, but the emphasis is not only on purely centrally determined financial targets and also includes scope for the inclusion of local non-financial performance measures. The purpose of pay is thus to encourage corporate fit – the sense of one company – as opposed purely to aligning pay to the business priorities of the local organization.

Referencing practice internally

Before the introduction of a new pay system, or the revision of an existing one, the specialist pay function within each firm performs extensive consultation internally, seeking to solicit opinion of what is required in human capital terms by the business, and to understand better what is required of any pay system introduced.

If we're not clear at the top end what we're trying to do with that, I don't think we should be surprised if by the time it gets down to here that people are also a little unclear. And, to be honest, if actually our intent is just we're going to match the market, then fine, that's what we should say and we shouldn't try and dress it up in anything other than that's what we're going to do, yeah? So that's what I'm saying. I think we've got a great opportunity to sort of rethink what it is that we're trying to build. I know it's not as simple as that, but try and draw a picture, this is what we want, or if we did it this way, well what would the levers be that we would pull?

(senior reward director, company7)

The process of consultation was also a feature of the pay determination process at the level of approach, but this involved consultation with senior management and was driven by the desire to use pay as a means of aligning employees first and foremost to the business strategy. At the level of design, consultation is not with senior management, but typically involves soliciting opinion from business unit leaders:

> We've been through that whole reward architecture debate where we'd actually talk to people. This wasn't just me, or me and a couple of others, thinking in a dark and smoke-filled room. This was a process of saying to relatively senior management in the organization, you know, what is the role of annual incentives and what performance should it be based on, you know. So we'd had that debate.
>
> (senior rewards practitioner, company1)

The variation stage of the determination of the pay design is the opportunity for the participation of 'business leaders' in the development of pay systems that they ultimately will be expected to adopt. It is apparent that within each of the case study firms soliciting opinion is regarded as important, not only to inform the design of pay but also to instil a sense of ownership and involvement with those being canvassed. Performing such consultation and data gathering is an essential step in attempting to ensure that the pay systems being designed are aligned well, not only with the business strategy but also with the organization(s) into which they are to be introduced:

> I guess what I would probably do is I would envision convening a group, or a couple of us, to talk through some of these things in terms of the messages that we want to communicate and have a discussion along those lines about what things seem to be the best fit given the direction we have as an organization. You know, how do we want to position the messages? Are these the right messages to position?
>
> (corporate rewards manager, company5)

Each case study company has a different approach, however, to the process of soliciting opinion. Some case study firms perform extensive internal consultation and information gathering, while others do less. Company1 and company2 conduct significant consultation but, as pay design determination is decentralized, this means that it is more in the interests of stewardship and good governance, with the intention of satisfying internal stakeholders, senior management, external stakeholders and regulatory bodies. On the other hand, while a great deal of internal consultation is performed in advance of pay system reform, such consultation in company4 is limited, largely, to issues of compliance, such as observing local employment laws. The experience of business leaders would suggest that this is not fully in tune with the business need:

> The rewards team sits in a HR department and has very, very little contact with the business. It's not out there, it hasn't got a finger on the pulse, it's not, you know, day to day, it's not talking to the business leaders, it's not out there seeing what the problems are. It tends to be, and I hate to use the term, it tends to be a little bit ivory tower-ish, and it sits in a ... in a kind of theoretical bubble within the HR department.
>
> (line unit HR manager, company4)

The focus of the pay function in company4 is largely technical and not business orientated, which is a consistent theme across a number of the case study firms. The scope is defining what is possible and not necessarily what is desired. In company7, the sheer size and complexity of the diversified organization and the relatively small pay function prohibit comprehensive consultation and information gathering, leading to a reliance on numerical forms of information, such as the results of employee attitude surveys. The means by which opinion is solicited also varies widely, with the case study firms using a variety of methods but, in all cases, struggling to develop comprehensive pictures of the business need. Methods of solicitation range from one-to-one 'water cooler' conversations to more formal mechanisms such as interviews, data collection, surveys of line manager opinion and analysis of employee attitude surveys.

> We do have quite a few sort of cultural tools where we ... our culture team actually travel around the world and assess various markets, it's called World Plus ... about various markets, about their culture and at what stage their culture is and ways to improve. And that is all around the guiding principles. And they developed the guiding principles on to identify sort of ... they call it the 'body and soul' of the organization, and it just helps the operating companies to think about where they are and what they need to do in terms of embedding these sorts of principles within the organization.
>
> (corporate reward manager, company1)

There is a natural conflict of interest that requires reconciliation in order to design a robust and well-aligned pay system. The conflict occurs naturally between the specialist pay function and what is perceived to be required by generalist line management and senior management. Very large differences in opinion regarding the definition of effective pay can occur between the disparate managerial groups. The implication of this is that each, as a stakeholder group, values different things in pay terms. Nor do they share the same experience of pay. The management of pay for line managers is one aspect of managing people, itself merely one aspect of a challenging role with broad responsibility. The amount of time and effort line managers are prepared to devote to providing inputs into the pay determination process, through performance management, calibration of ratings and other such activities, is naturally limited. Moreover, as a result of their relative inexperience of pay, especially technical issues associated with pay design, and a lack of familiarity with the law, the expectations of line managers, when viewed from the perspective of the pay function, are often unrealistic and undesirable:

> But one of the things you can do is if you were going to be doing that is actually to have some focus groups, to talk to some of your senior managers or junior managers, and that's a very fraught thing, I believe, on reward. And, um, we'll pick it up in team leaders in a minute. But, quite often the business wants to do something, which is with their perspective. And HR's role is quite often to say, 'I know you would like to do that because we're all good news merchants, we love giving good news, but actually that's not a good thing to do.' I'd take all of that away and give it a good stir and come up with a few suggestions. I would never say, 'Would you like to design it with me?'
>
> (senior reward director, company4)

If the pay function and the personnel within it are perceived negatively, their ability to fulfil the already challenging task of gathering salient information is further impaired. Clearly, the strength of the pay function is a key determinant of the quality of information it is able to glean about the required business need, and what might comprise a good fit – both of which are critical to the quality of the pay design.

> It's very much a stakeholder process and is probably fairly informal rather than formal. So the corporate expertise team, you would hope, would constantly be sounding out the stakeholders around the world

to make sure that they're in touch with what's happening both at [company7] and the different markets it operates in.

(country reward manager, company7)

Observing the process of solicitation within a number of the case study firms would suggest that, while formal mechanisms such as communities of practice and forums are clearly important, internal referencing is best performed when complemented by informal personal relationships, established through shared experience, with networks of interested stakeholders inputting voluntarily into the solicitation process. Social capital is an important aspect of the informal organization upon which the effectiveness of pay systems is contingent, but is not well documented within the literature (Napathiet and Ghoshal, 1998).

Referencing practice externally

The referencing of practice is, however, not solely internally focused. All of the case study firms extensively solicit external company practice at the variation stage in the determination process. Competitive labour pressures encourage conformity of pay levels – a median position by default. This is as illustrated by the industry-level data presented in Chapter 5. However, pay specialists within each firm also benchmark on the basis of what others are doing and, in doing so, render themselves prone to institutional pressures encouraging the adoption of best pay practices.

A key principle of each case study company's pay approach was the attraction and retention of desired talent. The principles translate directly into practice at the level of pay design because realizing the principle requires the establishment of competitive labour market rates within the host operating environment where the labour is required. A minority of the managerial population are recruited on individual terms and are expected to operate regionally, or perhaps even globally. The vast majority of employees are recruited on terms devised in specific reference to a single country (or region within a country), which equate to a labour market rate for the role. A significant portion of the determination of the pay design is the gathering and analysis of labour market data used for this purpose. To facilitate the gathering of such data, all firms within the case study sample participate within an FMCG salary survey 'club'.

Similarly, it is apparent that pay designers actively engage in pay *practice* benchmarking against competitors and other admired firms, albeit on a more informal basis. Using the existing network of the salary survey club described above, pay function specialists meet frequently to share experiences and learning. Such an 'external' perspective is valued universally, as it provides a basis of broader experience upon which to draw when fulfilling the mandate required by the pay approach, to which designers are required to respond by the executive, the stakeholder group most involved with the determination of the pay approach. Despite competing for both product and labour, all of the case study firms engage in the same salary survey club of companies and frequently share experiences – such information forming a significant feature of the externally sourced context influencing the outcomes of the pay design determination process. The pay design is, therefore, determined not only in response to the pay approach but also influenced by a number of competing forces emanating from both the internal and external environment, and from various levels of the organization:

> I want to make sure I'm paying the bonus for the right reasons, okay? So that's sort of ... now, if *no-one* pays a bonus, would *I* pay a bonus? Well, I might be a market leader in this. And I think it's very cool, or very effective, to give people a pile of money once a year, as a result of the business objectives. If we were, let's say, really *only* focused on quarterly objectives, I might want to pay people a bonus on a quarterly basis. The companies, and I think I mentioned this last week, the companies that go for full base salary, or for higher base salaries at the expense of a bonus, under ... I think they *understand* that the bonus is possibly not motivational, but I think they lack the ability to be able to manage their costs as a reflection of the business results.
>
> (global rewards director, company5)

In addition to benchmarking pay practice informally through external networks, all of the case study firms also formally use consultants to varying degrees when designing pay systems. Underpinning their efforts both informally to benchmark external company practice through the use of mutual-interest practitioner networks, and formally through the use of consultants, is a belief on the part of pay function personnel that what works elsewhere is of relevance to them. Moreover, what works *well* elsewhere is something that may work well within their own organization. Clearly, benchmarking is a useful exercise, providing pay designers with the opportunity to learn from the experiences and insights of others. This in turn informs and improves their capacity to choose strategically. However, it is also obvious that some firms benchmark external practice more than others and, in addition, benchmark against specific firms considered exemplary and influential in the hope of emulating their success. Interestingly, these specific firms such as General Electric and Procter and Gamble, as examples of 'influential others', are cited frequently and universally as examples of best practice and are the subject of considerable scrutiny.

The variation stage of the determination of the pay design is character-ized therefore by those who, whether located centrally or locally, solicit and canvass opinion about what operationally the pay system should be designed to achieve. They do so within the context of desired outcomes, which have already been defined by senior management within the pay approach. All firms consult stakeholders both internally, such as line managers, and externally and make extensive use of consultants at the design stage. There are, however, a number of competing interests at work within these large and complex case study companies. When design is devolved, the interests of local line management are represented most. When design is centralized, and the application of the design is universal, the design process becomes prone to multiple competing interests from those for whom the intended pay design will be binding. Moreover, the greater the degree of abstraction (centralization), the greater the degree of technical input required by pay function staff to balance these competing interests. For example, maintaining internal equity will conflict with the management's perceived business need.

Selection at the design level of the pay determination process

When viewed at the level of design, the pay systems selected and deployed by the case study firms are strikingly similar. In terms of *how* they go about configuring both the content and form of the selected pay design, however, they are quite dissimilar, with implications for the perceived impact of the design as policy in terms of role, value and appli-cation. Having consulted about practice, both internally and externally, the case study-based data would suggest that the selection stage is where pay specialists choose the content and form of the intended pay design. It is perhaps no surprise that, once again, we encounter a good deal of conformity of pay policies between the case study firms. However, despite the similarities of the intended policies, the way in which firms have formulated those policies varies, with a resulting impact upon the nature, form and outcomes derived from the pay policies. The selection stage typically involves functional specialists attempting to design the precise form and content of the pay system to be applied.

This will correspond with the principles of the espoused approach and the designation of technical elements of a formalized policy considered an appropriate best 'fit' with the organization as it is understood by the functional specialists. Formulation may take the form of either (a) organic development of a firm's specific reward scheme; (b) the adaptation of an existing practice to reflect better the principles and properties of the espoused approach; or, most radically, (c) the wholesale importation of practice from outside the organization; or, most likely, (d) a combination of the three.

All case study firms underpin internal pay relativity (the variance of earnings between roles and occupations at all levels of the organization) using job-evaluated pay structures. Extensive use of broad bands, which compress the job-evaluated pay 'spine' points into groupings of typically less than ten bands, is commonplace. Similarly, the evaluated roles are placed within broad 'job families' permitting cross-comparison on a national, regional and global basis. The use of job evaluation frameworks ensures that employment costs are managed and controlled; equity and fairness between roles, functions, levels and locations is maintained; and there are consistent, clear and defensible links to external labour market rates of pay. All firms use references to the external labour market as the means of defining pay levels and yearly annual pay increases in line with inflation and labour market movements. All of the firms operate median rates of pay for the majority of roles, but pay a premium for 'key talent', typically offering an upper quartile rate of pay. As discussed already, firms gain access to market data through specially created pay survey clubs administered, typically, by consultants, and through consultants' existing databases of market pay rates. Base pay progression (pay increases) is in all cases linked to individual performance within the role. Performance is defined as performance against key personal objectives and assessed in all cases in terms of a Likert scale (such as 'meets expectations', 'above average', 'exceeds expectations'), against which a salary increase value is placed, and is typically limited only by budget.

> We can't realistically go forward year on year giving inflation or inflation plus the increases to base pay when we're ahead of the market ... so depress base pay increases sensibly and start to put more pay at risk. Putting pay at risk, it addresses a very long-standing equity issue that we have on site, because in the last couple of years [managerial, professional and technical] employees have said these guys are getting bonus when we don't, you know, we're all contributing to the same goals

and it doesn't seem clear. So it addresses that and also we believe, you know, it gives a message to our employees who are at that level that, you know, we want ... about working towards the same goals and on that basis we should all share in the success. Will it drive different behaviours in the business? I would suggest not.

(line unit HR, company1)

But where base pay was once the cornerstone of the pay offering, being linked to tenure and emphasizing equality of pay and job security, performance-based elements are now the focus of the pay offering within the case study firms. All firms include, as an element of *total cash compensation*, a significant proportion of pay at risk. The level of pay at risk is defined as a percentage of base pay, and for junior to middle management staff, on-target bonus awards typically range from 10 per cent to 25 per cent of base pay. Long-term incentives also comprise 'pay at risk' and each case provides options for employee participation in a variety of all employee share ownership programmes (AESOPs), most of which offer significant discounts to the listed value of company stocks and provide employees with the opportunity of equity ownership in their employer. All firms also provide a comprehensive range of benefits over which individuals are able to exercise considerable discretion, selecting what suits their personal circumstances best from a 'cafeteria style' menu of options.

The move towards the greater use of incentives as a proportion of an employee's total cash compensation removes the purely fixed cost of base pay and confers upon the employee financial risks (potentially diminished earnings) that would otherwise be the sole concern of the employer. Variable pay, contingent on company performance, permits firms to 'flex' labour costs to some degree in line with the performance of the firm. All firms have adopted a *performance-based* approach to pay and either (a) promote the use of performance-based pay systems by providing a guiding framework for their design and adoption within the constituent elements of the organization; or (b) centrally plan and adopt standardized performance-based pay interventions. These are, typically, company performance-based incentive systems for the broad based professional, technical and managerial employee population. The use of centrally determined standardized incentive programmes is problematic in some cases, and arguably does not fit well with the value-adding aspects of the pay approach, but does serve to limit the risks facing the business by reducing fixed labour costs.

In terms of both the pay approach, expressed in the form of strategy, and the pay design, expressed in the form of policy, there is remarkable consistency of practice between the case study firms. However, it is in relation to how these *same* practices are configured in practice that we experience variation between the case study firms and, therefore, in the effectiveness of not only the pay design but the pay outcomes experienced as a result.

How the selected pay systems are managed

Pay function specialists engage in the process of policy formulation and implementation planning based upon a number of inputs, including (a) prior personal experience gained inside and outside the organization; (b) the desired approach as espoused by senior management; (c) the outputs of the consultation process conducted at the variation stage of the design determination process; and (d) expert opinion, technical advice and facilitation from external bodies. Examples of this include benchmarking data and consultancy advice. Additional organizational information, such as financial data and analysis, employee feedback and so on, is also considered within the deliberation process. Initially, a position paper is produced that combines analysis of the 'current state' of practice and the 'desired state', expressed in terms of the approach the leadership wish to adopt to rewards. The position paper is further supplemented by the identification of the degree of the gap, that is, the degree of difference between the current state and the desired state and, as much as can be discerned, any barriers to the successful closing of that gap. What follows next is a detailed breakdown of the principles translated into practice. This includes the specific practices to be used, for example what form of incentive-based pay should be used, the population to which it will be applied, forecasts containing the projected cost impact of the introduction of the new scheme and a qualitative cost benefit analysis of the scheme impact. The technical detail of the selected design is then packaged within a position paper, which is communicated to senior management to review, for the purposes of approval, amendment or rejection.

> I mean, a year ago when this came up, you know, I sort of wrote back to them and said how can we do an international mobility reward strategy if I don't know what our strategy on international mobility is? Now that piece is in talent management and that's fine, yeah? Then you guys have got to work with us to come up with what this is to start with and then we'll help you by putting together the reward package which supports what it is that you guys are trying to do in talent development. But it has to go at the same time, and I think a

lot of the time we still do our projects in isolation and they're done in quite a technical way.

(senior reward director, company7)

All these sources may be used as a means of promoting the relevance and *legitimacy* of the selected design. They may also be used as evidence of the appropriateness of the selected design when communicating the intended policy to the organization in advance of implementation and also to those interested parties external to the organization, for example shareholders, business academics, government and the media.

Retention at the design level of the pay determination process

What is retained as the pay design is quite different between the case study companies as a result of the pay policy approach adopted. In the case of company1 and company2, determination of the pay design is largely decentralized, save for specific measures such as pensions and the share scheme that require central administration and governance. The pay policies, therefore, merely guide local management discretion about the use of pay and the management of employees. Complementing the articulated pay approach, which sets out the corporate position on the desired principles and outcomes of pay and the minimum standards to which all should comply, local pay design determination results in pay being aligned primarily to the goals and unique characteristics of the local organization. Put simply, the approach defines what pay is and what it should achieve, but discretion is left to local management to determine *how* pay should achieve those ends.

In company1, company2 and company3, three of the seven case study firms, the pay design, having been devolved to the local organization, division or business unit, is supported organizationally by the rewards function in the form of guidance on good practice and minimum standards to which all must conform. However, these are deliberately limited, permitting high degrees of local discretion, with the result that both are viewed as a valuable *guide* to the local determination and execution of pay system programmes:

I think we're schizophrenic as an organization. When it suits yes, because we don't really want to do this. Centre, just tell us what we need to do. And if you don't get the balance right, the centre are interfering. So there's a fine line to be trod between the two and we're a little bit schizophrenic. We're getting a little more centralist but from a very decentralized starting point I would guess.

(senior rewards practitioner, company1)

Intervention at company2 by the centrally operating pay function is perceived by line management as guiding the determination of pay at their level of the company. The central pay function is organized on a geographical basis, with specialists assigned a territory that they have the responsibility to support. The role is not one of a 'policing function', however, nor are central pay function representatives able to veto practice (unless it contravenes a minimum standard, such as compliance with local labour laws), but rather they facilitate devolved pay determination in an advisory capacity.

Pay design determination is similarly devolved in the case of company3. However, there is a notable lack of centralist intervention in the form of either an articulated approach to pay by which devolved pay determination is guided, or of any coordinated support from the centre. From interviews based in the line, it is apparent that there is little understanding of what constitutes the overall group-wide reward strategy, nor the aspirations for pay, nor the means by which pay systems should be used to achieve those aspirations. However, senior management have communicated a clear mandate that pay should be used strategically – that is, to support the achievement of business objectives at all levels of the firm and its operations. As a result, line units have attempted to devise pay systems in response to the executive mandate, but arguably lack the experience, skills and the corporate direction to formulate meaningful practice. As will be illustrated in the next chapter (a review of pay practice operationally), the three business units reviewed all exhibit distinct and widely varying pay practice in response to the same mandate, and as a consequence, experience varying outcomes – positive, neutral and negative.

As a result of the high degree of central intervention in pay target setting in company4, the basis of the variable pay systems is unclear and the desired line of sight effect is lost:

When people look at their variable pay, one of the big problems we've had with all the bonuses is how much can you predict, or influence, your bonus? And, you know, if there's a corporate element I can't predict it. One year it's very good, and I haven't a clue why, and the next year it's terrible and yet I thought we were doing all right. Very unpredictable.

(senior reward director, company4)

Well, the other piece of that same problem, or that same puzzle, is the whole issue around ... and I'm coming back to what I said earlier on now, is degree of difficulty, is what I call it. Yeah, if you take *my* business, I mean this year we've been charged with a $40 million turnaround versus last year, that's because the corporation's got a lot of pressure on this particular business and it wants to see the numbers improve. But at the same time, it wants to see significant marketplace improvement. Now I happen to believe, and this is irrelevant for the purpose of my own performance assessment or my own pay package, but I happen to believe that the objectives we've been set are plain bloody stupid and unreasonable. Now how the hell do you mitigate against that?

(senior general manager, company4)

In company6, those same plans, rules and checks, determined at a regional level but informed directly by a remuneration committee operating corporately, are viewed as *limiting* but not constraining because a greater concession is made for local discretion within formal policy. Nevertheless the implication is the same – the perceived impact of centrally determined pay systems is one of a constraint on operational business units, reflecting as they do a poor fit for local conditions, be they business, labour or cultural.

What is retained as pay design in company6 is the attempt to use company-linked, broad-based incentives in order to fulfil the desire, stated in the approach, of promoting mutuality as a principle. In other words, if we succeed as a firm, you succeed as an individual, but this also includes team working and the collective responsibility for company performance. Arguably, as a result of the legacy of past practice, which emphasizes the principle of mutuality on the basis of job security and equality of pay irrespective of performance, the move towards incentivization represents a significant reform to the status quo, and has been met with both passive and overt objection from employees and business unit leaders alike.

Having resisted industry trends towards the use of incentives, and placing significant amounts of employee pay at risk, company6 does so now as a result of poor company performance. Moreover, pay systems are designed regionally by the regional pay team liaising with a central HR/rewards committee in the US headquarters. The pay design, if not global as a result of central HQ intervention, is at least regional and therefore applied throughout the numerous operations of the European business. Thus the move to include pay at risk is a centralized, regional decision and not a local business one, and therefore not sensitive to the unique needs and circumstances of the local business units. Pay policies in company6, therefore, are viewed as limiting what local management might do otherwise, and what might conceivably represent a better fit for the local business.

Company7 is farther along the continuum again towards centralized pay design determination. While the pay design is aligned principally around the corporation, and corporate-level business performance targets, there is a significant degree of local discretion to determine performance and also to select the appropriate markets for base pay benchmarking:

> One of the fundamental issues with the idea of a global standard is the one we talked about at the beginning, which is we may be one business but are we actually all trying to do the same thing? And the answer is no, we're not.
>
> (senior reward director, company7)

Company7 also runs a global managerial incentive scheme designed to elicit the same outcomes as company5, namely promoting alignment to corporate objectives and corporate ownership. Like company5, there is evidence of tensions as a result of the use of mandated universal practice:

> I think when it was done it was something which was sold on the basis of this is something which we believe should apply universally and hurrah, this is something we believe will drive the right things within our business. And therefore whilst I think there was ... I think there was enormous push back at the time, I have to be honest, I wasn't deeply involved in it, but I think there was quite a lot of push back. I think now what's interesting is that there's more of an opportunity to have that dialogue and say to people what do we think is the best thing for us to do?
>
> (senior reward director, company7)

In the case of company5, moreover, the pay approach is not communicated widely, with the result that the rationale for centralist pay determination, indeed the basis for pay itself, is often not well understood within the organization and levels throughout:

> That's sort of where we were a couple of years ago, and this year like I said, we've put together a sort of summary and said, 'Well, look,

you've gone out to the analyst community, you've said this, why don't we at least communicate it out?' And the answer is, 'Well, we already have communicated it out.' And then I said, 'Yeah to analysts', and if you're savvy enough to read the reports you kind of know where we're heading. And someone in my role, yeah, I'm *very* up on where we're going. But someone, you know, in a business unit or in a different role, in legal or in operations may not. So, it's the age-old sort of what can you say, what do you want to say, how do you want to say it? And we're struggling with that I think. I would say that would be not ... clearly not optimum today.

(global rewards director, company5)

Nor can local line units not comply with the mandate determined at the centre by the corporate rewards function:

No, you can't opt out! (laughs). It might [cause tension], but I think the culture is such that, um ... I don't know if that's an option. No one, no one can secede from the Union, as we say here in the States.

(corporate rewards manager, company5)

The area of greatest variance between case study companies, in terms of the gap between intended policy and what is achieved, is that of mandated corporate pay policies. In all of the case study companies, senior management and executive pay is managed centrally by the head-quarters pay function. Executive pay, irrespective of the incumbents' location, role or function, is managed from the centre and is not within the remit of local operations. However, four of the seven case study firms also extend centralized pay policies to the broad-based managerial population and lower. Referred to under a number of different terms (and often referred to as 'global schemes' in reference to their universal application across the firm), these mandated pay practices are schemes for eligible employees, often numbering in the many thousands, and are a significant element of their total cash remuneration. Irrespective of incumbents' role, level or function, or the conditions of the local environment in which the incumbent operates, the global schemes apply.

Company5 operates a global management incentive plan (MIP) for all technical, professional and managerial employees based upon perform-ance against corporate targets:

In International they wanted to drive incentive plans down to lower grades, because they had only been providing MIP to the director level and above. And so in some ... in many cases, they just took the same plan and looked at it and said, 'Well, this is what the US is doing, let's mirror this' ... there was a big push from the top.

(HR function practitioner, company5)

The purpose of such a scheme is to promote a sense of 'corporate ownership' and 'alignment to the corporate goals'. Being a US-based firm, however, the scheme is founded primarily upon the experiences of the US-based businesses and was developed first by the headquarters' rewards function and rolled out across the world as a mandated programme. Its universal application is a source of frustration for the international operations of the business. As a result, the centralist imposition of such pay systems is viewed as constraining from a business unit perspective, preventing operational line management from adopting alternative and, from their perspective, preferable courses of action with regard to the management of their people.

Summary

The case study companies' corporate pay strategies – the pay approach – were determined in a context characterized predominantly by external, competitive and institutional pressures. These pressures encourage regular corporate revision of the principles underpinning pay so that they better reflect performance concerns. In all cases, pay is valued as a means of leveraging enhanced organizational performance and, corporately, competitive advantage. At the next level of analysis – the pay design – pay specialists respond to these strategic pay aspirations of senior management by attempting to formulate technical policy through which the desired pay outcomes might be achieved. They do so, however, in an environment distinct from that of the pay approach. The context in which the pay design is determined, expressed most often as policy, is quite distinct from the context in which the pay approach, expressed most often as strategy, is determined.

The context in which the pay design is determined is characterized less by external competitive pressures, and more by external concerns over legitimate pay practice and compliance with regulation, and internal concerns over relativity, equity (fairness), governance and performance. Pay systems are designed in response to a variety of inputs, which add to the complexity of what is naturally a highly technical process. There are many obstacles that the pay function must overcome in attempting to formulate robust and relevant pay systems, but they do so with varying degrees of success. Moreover, in each case study company reviewed, the outcomes of pay system introduction were unknown a priori. In the face of such uncertainty, a significant finding is that pay specialists reference external pay practice, typically that of prestigious others. This is used as a basis for pay practice selection in lieu of certainty over the financial returns derived from the introduction of a new or revised pay system.

In the context of externally referencing the practice of 'influential others', all of the case study firms share the same profiles of pay intervention as a means of fulfilling the aspirations stated within the pay approach, and in keeping with the principles of the shared pay approaches – performance-based pay systems, for example. Market-linked base pay is the norm, with all firms benchmarking against the FMCG industry and general industry, according to role and level. All of the case study companies, perhaps reflecting their standing within the FMCG sector as market-leading firms, choose to benchmark against the upper quartile position within the FMCG professional, technical and managerial labour market. Internal relativity of pay is maintained through a combination of job evaluation and broadband pay structures. In the majority of cases, this is on a regional and/or global basis, for example global grading systems (Table 6.1).

Multiple forms of short- and long-term incentives (STIs and LTIs) are used widely on a broad-based basis, with significant amounts of employee pay placed at risk, even for junior staff. In the case of STIs, bonus in other words, a combination of measures of performance is typically used, pay being contingent upon a combination of either (or all) individual, team, division or company performance. LTIs are provided in all cases in the form of all employee share ownership pro-grammes (AESOP) in the first instance, and LTIs targeted at specific groups. Benefits, in all cases, incorporate significant opportunities for individual discretion being provided flexibly through a 'cafeteria style' menu of options. The similarity of pay practice between the case study firms is striking and, again, conforms to both wider industry trends, and the best practice prescriptions of remuneration consultancies and strategic pay commentary. Such conformity of practice supports further the notion that high-performing firms are converging around specific pay norms and patterns of strategic pay practice.

However, *how* the case study firms approach the management of these *same* pay practices is quite different, with implications for their perceived effectiveness. Within three of the seven case study companies, pay design is devolved to local management, thereby responding to

Table 6.1 Case study company pay practice at the level of design

Stage Description	Context to Aligned	Variation Aspiration	Selection Content	Form	Retention Perceived impact
Company1	Local organization	Local fit	Guidance on good practice	Minimum standards	Guiding
Company2	Local organization	Local fit	Guidance on good practice	Minimum standards	Guiding
Company3	Local organization	Local fit	Mandate	Minimum standards	Mandate
Company4	Regional organization	Conformity	Precise planning, rules and checks	Mandate	Limiting
Company5	Corporation	Conformity	Precise planning, rules and checks	Mandate	Constraining
Company6	Regional organization	Good governance	Precise planning, rules and checks	Formal policy	Limiting
Company7	Corporation	Corporate fit	Practice prescription	Formal policy	Limiting

local business conditions, while operating within the bounds of the guiding framework of the pay approach, articulated as the pay strategy. Central pay function intervention is limited in the design process save for providing guidance on good practice. Line management is also required to observe and comply with minimum standards in the interests of good governance. The perceived impact is that of the central pay function *guiding* the local determination of pay.

In contrast, the regionally based pay functions in two of the seven case study firms make a direct intervention in the design of pay systems that are applied universally on a regional basis. One firm does so on the basis that both employee and business interests are best served through precise planning, rules and checks and by being determined centrally. Such intervention, while valued, is increasingly viewed as limiting the capability of subsidiary operations of the regional business to respond flexibly to local employment and business needs. Similarly, the other case study firm requires conformity for reasons that are not entirely clear.

Within the final two case study firms, pay is designed centrally which, in the context of these global firms, means common systems of pay across all of the operations of the firm – global pay systems covering many thousands of employees. Like the regionally determined pay systems, local discretion is limited and the design is expressed in the form of mandated policy. Business unit compliance is expected irrespective of whether the design does or does not reflect a good fit with the local level operations of the firm. The perceived impact of such a scheme is one of constraint on the discretion of line management: how they perceive it best in the context of their business. The next chapter – case study company pay practice at the level of operation – highlights the operational implications for pay practice once it is implemented. Given the inclination of the majority of the case study companies towards the centralization of pay determination, does pay policy result in operational pay practice as it is intended?

7
Pay Practice at the Level of Operation

In light of the design-level findings, this chapter – the third and final findings chapter of the company-level analysis – asks specifically how effective the selected strategic pay systems are operationally. Do they achieve the desired outcomes set out in the pay approach, such as attracting and retaining valued talent, encouraging productivity and eliciting desired employee behaviours, including motivation, commitment and loyalty? Are the case study companies realizing what was desired in terms of the approach and what was intended in terms of the design? In short, is pay *strategic* at the operational level?

The context of pay determination at the level of the pay operation

The environment at the level of operation in which pay is determined is, again, quite different from the previous two levels. In all case study firms, operational responsibility for the management of pay is devolved to generalist line management supported by line human resources officers. Line management, in the vast majority of cases, have little or no specific training in the management of people or pay systems. While they are responsible, in none of the case study companies is effective people management one of the criteria by which line management performance is assessed – responsibility does not equate to accountability. Responsibilities include, primarily, the achievement of defined business objectives set out within the formal yearly planning process. Each division and/or subsidiary business of the case study firms are accountable corporately for their performance against these objectives and are responsible for employing the necessary level and calibre of employees. However, the discretion to manage pay, a key part of the attraction and retention of employees within the labour-intensive FMCG sector, is in four of the seven case study companies centrally determined and not within the gift of local management. In the remaining three cases, responsibility for the determination of pay is devolved to local management operating within the guiding framework of the corporate pay strategy – the pay approach. The following are examples of subsidiary operations reviewed within the research, all of them being quite different. Reflecting the contextual complexity that influences pay determination outcomes – something not sufficiently recognized by standard theory – the environment in which pay is determined operationally varies widely between the case study companies and, critically, between divisions and business units within the *same* case study company.

One such is a subsidiary operation of company1, located regionally, which is predominantly a sales organization, employing approximately 250 dedicated sales staff along with 50 support staff. The sales force staff are typically of manager level, being responsible for national sales and based throughout the country according to sales territory. At the sales-force headquarters, a senior sales team of five is supported by a human resources team comprising a divisional HR manager, an HR officer and an HR assistant. The responsibility of the HR team is to support sales senior management and the salesforce on employment-related matters, including pay. This subsidiary operation manages employees in accordance with the various human resources strategies distributed by the central HR function at the London headquarters and uses many of the core corporate processes. The design and management of pay is, however, entirely based upon local management discretion.

The significant remainder of company1 located at another regional site differs substantially in terms of employee segmentation, size of labour pool and local organizational structures. In the case of both the UK sales function at one site and the various sub-divisions that comprise the other regional site, pay systems are purposefully aligned to local division and team targets. Thus, not only discretion for the design of pay systems used is devolved to local management, but also pay systems are geared around supporting the performance of the local organization with little or no element of pay contingent upon either company-level performance or based upon targets defined at the centre. Control from the centre is exerted through the requirement that pay is managed within devolved budgets. Assistance is available from the corporate rewards function, but discretion is an entirely local affair.

The country operation in the Far East is considered a key growth market within the International business unit of company3, itself a key area of growth opportunity for the firm given tight competition and the maturation of traditional markets in the Americas and Western Europe. The sales branch located west of the capital employs 12 sales staff. Covering a large sales catchment area, the sales team services over 600 venues and 92 retail wholesalers. People management is entirely devolved to the branch manager, operating under the remit of the regional sales manager, himself reporting to the director of sales at the country level. The eastside sales branch employs ten staff including eight sales representatives. Like the westside branch, people management is devolved to local line management, being the district sales manager, operating under the framework determined by the country sales director.

Both the east and west sales branches face considerable challenges to successful business operations, but vary considerably in employment terms in the responses necessary to face these challenges. Not least are the challenging market conditions from intense competition with subsidiary operations of other FMCG multinationals, but also the volatility of the country market. A significant proportion of sales revenue is derived from bulk sales to retail wholesalers acting as the middleman between company3 and retail outlets. A number of these wholesalers have in recent years gone bankrupt, with the result that each sales district has suffered the loss of major customers. In the east branch, one recently bankrupt wholesaler constituted just under 35 per cent of the total sales volume. Such bankruptcies, a market factor beyond the control of company3 sales staff, profoundly influence their performance and related incentive payments.

Company6 UK represents one of the largest operating subsidiaries of the European regional business and is their largest operating site. All of the company6 brands and products are produced at their out of London site, which currently employs 6000 employees, of which a significant number would be classified as managerial, professional and technical. In addition to production, this site also hosts research and design, the finance function, the HR function and shared services. It is also a major distribution centre, and company6 product is shipped throughout Europe from this site. In recent years, company6 has consolidated its regional operations into a few 'mega' sites, of which this is one. While it formerly operated out of 12 sites in the UK, the company now houses the majority of its operations from this location. Within this site, line management from manufacturing, finance, marketing, HR and R&D were interviewed. As noted in the previous chapter, discretion over terms and conditions of professional, technical and managerial employees, including pay, is centrally determined at the regional level. There is, therefore, a great deal of consistency between the level and occupations of managerial staff employed at the site, as a result of the standardized approach to pay, despite the wide diversity of occupations and functions.

As examples, therefore, the business units mentioned all represent subsidiary operations of an umbrella parent company, but vary in terms of size and function and employment requirements as a result. Each represents a unique context exhibiting different attributes – organizational, managerial, cultural and so on. Importantly, irrespective of the nature of the work being undertaken, responsibility for performance is devolved in all cases to local line units through a common system and set of budgetary controls used in all cases. Consequently, the same intended pay systems are introduced into, in many cases, quite radically different contexts. The results, as will be illustrated, can be that the intended pay design reflects a poor fit for the local context into which it is introduced, and becomes, therefore, potentially marginalized, rejected and/or subverted.

Variation at the operation level of the pay determination process

The introduction of a new pay system is, operationally, a highly disruptive event. The findings show that, in a number of cases, if there is a sufficiently poor fit with the employment context into which they are introduced, the intended pay policies may be subject to line management (a) amending the design to reflect better the local environment; or, more extremely, (b) rejecting it altogether and maintaining the prevailing status quo. The choice to either amend or reject the intended design is not necessarily fed upwards to either the pay function or senior management. Functional specialists seem often to exercise very little control over the process of implementation; what information they do receive is mostly financial rather than qualitative data on operational controls or decisions.

In the context of local managerial objectives, the local technical and institutional environment and the need to manage ongoing work without disruption, managers select elements of the intended design for implementation and long-term operationalization. The persistence of prevailing structures naturally forces line management to consider change as either a break in the existing stream of activity (revolution), or an amendment to the existing stream of activity, with change being achieved incrementally through an iterative process of reform (evolution). In the vast majority of cases, even a minor disruption to levels of production or work is often viewed as unacceptable, given highly demanding performance requirements.

Implementing locally determined pay systems

In those cases where pay design decision making is decentralized (as with company1, company2 and company3), line management enjoy much greater discretion to define the purpose, content and form of both the pay design and operation, in the context of their locale, within the guiding framework laid down in the espoused pay approach. The pay approach in company3 is not clearly articulated, with implications for what ultimately emerges as practice from a corporate perspective. In all cases, however, the issue of fit and the contextual sensitivity of pay systems to local context is clearly highly important.

> There's only one group research and development centre in the world in [company1]. It's a unique environment. And in the same way that every good company has a unique social and geographical environment, I suspect that most management teams would probably say, sure I want some direction on certain things but beyond that please let me run my business as I see fit. And as long as I'm delivering the results, why should you care? You know I'm operating legally, I'm operating to our business principles, all the audits are fine and I'm delivering the profits and my people are happy, let's get on with it.
>
> (business unit manager, company1)

The predominant UK pay system within company1 emphasizes alignment with the needs of the local organization. The local organization is defined as subsidiaries of the overall holding company, or specific 'brand' organizations, managed on a country-by-country basis to ensure compliance with host country regulation and legislation. Consequently, within the overall structure of the corporate pay framework, pay is largely determined on a subsidiary basis by local management, in coordination and consultation with both local and corporate HR departments. Local management, therefore, have the autonomy largely to manage pay as they deem fit, while relying upon the central pay function for guidance and technical advice. Increasingly, the central pay function is championing the use of core processes supporting effective pay management, such as performance management techniques. They do so on the basis of attempting to raise line management awareness about the issues and effectively marketing 'good practice'. The emphasis is not, therefore, on prescribing specific pay practice at the business unit/subsidiary level, but promoting awareness and attention to the importance of process to pay system effectiveness:

> I mean, now being at the coalface, having been at the centre, I think the local autonomy is incredibly important. I think, you know, we need ... there are certain things that we need from [corporate HQ] in terms of long-term strategy, more direction, approval for various things, but ultimately we should be left to get on and run our business.
>
> (business unit manager, company1)

Company2 shares the same corporate aspiration that line management should develop pay systems autonomously that suit local business conditions, thus ensuring local fit, but within the overall guiding structure of the corporate pay approach. Much like company1, pay practice is therefore necessarily emergent, with the systems deployed representing multiple variations on a theme – the theme being the pay approach. Minimum standards are imposed, however, ensuring that, irrespective of the autonomy of local management, governance is ensured through compliance.

Company3 also emphasizes the development of pay systems locally and values corporately the autonomy of local line management to do so. Both the design and the operation of pay are devolved to local line management. However, the design of pay is determined on a country basis and applies, as noted in the previous chapter, to all of the end-market operations of company3 operating within that country, irrespective of market and organizational conditions. Nevertheless company1, company2 and company3 remain examples where pay is managed locally in terms of both design and operation. All three are solid examples of the determination of pay being decentralized. However, company3 differs from both company1 and company2 in one important respect.

While company1 and company2 devolve pay management to line management for the vast majority of their technical, professional and managerial employees, they do so on the basis of a set of espoused principles and aspirations – the corporately articulated pay approach – and support the local management of pay by championing a core set of processes and minimum standards to which all must comply. In the case of company3, however, little is provided in terms of either an articulated pay approach or supporting processes championed from the centre. The consequence is that local line management devise pay systems in response to a corporate mandate to do so, but with little guidance or structure on how to do so effectively. There are manifest implications resulting from a lack of either a clearly articulated approach to pay or guidance for pay system effectiveness in company3, which are discussed in greater detail in the remainder of this chapter.

Implementing centrally determined pay systems

The remaining case study companies, company4, company5, company6 and company7, differ quite radically from the first three case study companies because determination is largely centralized, with clear implications for the operational determination of pay locally. The pay design (policies) disseminated in each case are highly instrumental in nature, containing very precise technical content and expressed in the form of formal policy. Pay practice effectiveness is measured in large part in the degree to which realized pay practice reflects intended policy – ensuring corporate-wide consistency of practice. The challenge for both the pay function and line management, as two distinct groups involved in the implementation process, is to integrate the intended pay policy with ongoing work and existing pay structures and practice.

Company4 determines the pay design on a regional basis in response to impetus from the global pay function operating corporately at the US headquarters. The centralization of pay regionally and the dissemination of globally determined targets is not unproblematic. Indeed, as a result of successive reforms to the pay systems used, each of which are imposed on operational business units centrally, local management is wary of the introduction of new pay systems, suffering, in the words of one interviewee, 'battle fatigue':

> What the company's trying to do is make the pay fit its goals. So actually what we do is we try, and every year we reinvent the wheel. ... Every year we reinvent a scheme to try and get rewards that meet the company's goals. And every year we get it wrong for at least 50 per cent of the people because all sorts of reasons. So my view is why, why do we continue to do that?
>
> (senior operational manager, company4)

Ostensibly, the use of pay as a means of aligning employees to the goals of the business and the achievement of corporate goals is a core tenet of strategic pay. However, as the company evolves in terms of both mission (corporate strategy) and composition (organizational design), so too must pay. In the case of company4, the inflexibility of pay systems, owing to the rigidity of the prescribed design, results in pay systems that are often a poor fit regionally and locally, being changed frequently, not in response to change in local contextual conditions, strategic and organizational, but corporate contextual conditions. New or greatly amended pay systems are introduced and reformed rapidly with the result that they are rarely embedded as established and effective pay practice:

> But we've kind of gone into overdrive just lately. We've got HR initiatives coming out of our ears. We've got corporate initiatives going on everywhere and they're all driven out of HR, because there seems to have been a sort of ... there's been a significant realization within [company4] that we have a lack of strong leadership and that we have a dearth of talent in certain areas of the organization. And in order to do that, we've leapt to, 'Ah-ha, we need to strengthen HR.' And I'm not kidding you, twelve months ago we had *one* VP of HR in the entire European ... in the entire global organization, I believe we have seven now.
>
> (senior general manager, company4)

This quotation provides a valuable insight into the use of pay systems, with implications for their effectiveness. Contrary to the objectives of pay detailed in their approach to pay, and the intended policy identified in the previous chapter, the extract suggests that the motivation for use of pay is not strategic in the standard sense, but a tactical response to the failings of corporate leadership. A common theme running throughout line management interviews, in cases where pay determination is centralized, is that the underlying and implicit rationale is not the use of pay to elicit strategic outcomes in the form of productivity and behaviours, but as an additional means of corporate control. It would seem that strategic pay practices are used in lieu of strong leadership.

In company7, pay systems are perceived by line management as limiting their ability to manage their people best locally. Company7 has a history of being notoriously centralist in pay determination, using global standards that bind all operations to a common structure. Such structures are widely perceived by line management to be overly prescriptive. In company5, a major competitor of company7, the experience is similar:

> I think it is [too one size fits all] to a certain extent. We've ... I mean, we have a standard global bonus programme, for example, which is applied. Interestingly enough, in the US they only apply it to the

director level and above and they have different programmes below that. In International, they've used the same programme that we use for the director level and above in the US, but what they've done is used the same target percentages that the US uses for the lower levels in the other programmes.

(HR function practitioner, company5)

Again, the imposition of 'global standards' is universally unpopular with line management who feel they lack relevance and, worse, direct employee efforts to the wrong ends. This is recognized by pay function personnel, but centralist intervention in local pay determination persists reflecting a belief in 'global alignment'. Nevertheless centralist intervention is not entirely prescriptive:

I think the thing you've got to sort through as an organization, philosophically speaking, is whether those things that are so important to you that you believe there is value in having global alignment irrespective of what local market conditions indicate, then what are those things that, you know, well, it's okay and it makes sense to go local and we shouldn't be upset about here centrally. I don't know that we've really grappled with all those questions. It's been a bit of a learning process for everybody.

(corporate rewards manager, company5)

Company6 shares the same challenge, but the underlying rationale and purpose of central policy is different, however. As noted in the description of their pay approach, centralized policy in company6 is not the result of a manifest desire for corporate control (arguably the reason in other case study companies), but reflects instead a 'mother knows best' attitude by senior management and the centrally located (operating at the regional level of the firm) pay function towards the management of pay. Deemed to be of such high importance, organizationally and in terms of employee welfare, pay is not left to the responsibility of line management and is therefore necessarily standardized. The pay function, acting on behalf of the influential 'remuneration committee', prescribes policy to protect the interests of employees. The view is that senior management acting corporately (regionally) know better what is required for the business in pay and employment terms than line management managing the day-to-day employment relationship:

There's a very, very interesting dynamic going on there, which I don't completely understand myself, which is something about … and

I don't know if it's just in our organization where to some extent we haven't given people as much local freedom as they probably needed and therefore people have lost the skills capability and confidence to do it themselves, or whether there's something very much deeper and profound going on, which is actually people think they want to have control over something but actually they don't want to have control over it at all.

(senior HR practitioner, company6)

This long-held approach to pay is changing, however, as the company, in response to the need for product diversification in order to maintain competitiveness, increases in complexity and inclines more emphatically towards prescription. Managing the inherent tensions over the extent to which control over pay determination should be retained at the centre or devolved to line management is a source of tension and pitches the pay function frequently into conflict with line management to the detriment of pay system effectiveness.

The contextualization of centrally determined pay policy

Where pay determination is centralized, line management must necessarily adapt policy to local conditions. This is manifestly not an easy process. The 'contextualization' of global standards requires a great deal of managerial time and effort, with the ever-present risk of failure and the associated consequences. There are numerous examples of line management resistance to the centralist prescription of standardized policy. Line management face the choice of either accepting the mandate for change, or attempting to execute pay policy in line with the expectations of the pay function, acting on behalf of senior management. Alternatively, line management may also react by rejecting part or all of the intended design, despite a corporate mandate requiring its adoption. Furthermore, the intended pay design may be subverted in favour of maintaining the status quo, or alternative practice perceived to be of greater benefit in the local environment.

Well, yeah, there's sometimes people like me kind of working with the line, kind of almost, if I say collude that probably puts it too strongly. We will find ways around to help our business partners, because they will sit there and say things like, 'Well, I really do need to help retain this guy, motivate him, but you know the reward team is saying that, you know, we can't give a salary increase above a certain level, you know, it's nonsense, dah-di-dah-di-dah, can you help me?'

So we will sit there and I will come up with, hopefully, a solution which means that we can reward somebody in a different way, but it's not via a salary increase, so it doesn't come onto the radar screen of the reward team, if that makes sense.

(line unit HR manager, company4)

The contrast in some of the case study companies between what is intended in policy terms and what is achieved as practice relates, in large part, to varying interpretations of the same policy. Inevitably, much of the disconnection between the three dimensions of practice – the approach, design and operation – is a result of varying interpretation of either the espoused principles of the pay approach, especially where decentralized, and the intended design where centralized. As policy is cascaded throughout the organization in the state of prescriptive rhetoric, it is inevitably interpreted differently by those whose involvement is required in the pay determination process. Each stakeholder involved (line management, for example) in the implementation of the policy (translating it into practice) brings to the process unique values, perceptions and capabilities. Line management capability in the area of people management varies widely, it is perceived, for reasons that are not well understood. Managers, as individuals, inevitably interpret the same policy differently, as a result of their own personal values, beliefs and abilities, whether they be known to the individual or taken for granted. The implication is, therefore, that within the pay determination process there exist multiple opportunities for divergence between the intended substance of the policy and the implemented reality of the achieved practice, simply because policy is interpreted differently.

It comes back to the obsession that perhaps HR practitioners have designed. We are always seeking for the perfect reward system, the perfect appraisal system, what have you. Actually it doesn't matter. If it's 80 per cent okay you can make it work, but the mechanism for making it work is delivery, and if you spend a hell of a lot more time in making delivery more effective you may get better results. And the key to your delivery is probably your line manager because if you give him a perfect system then you'll find he'll have no option but to implement it perfectly. We never give him a perfect system.

(country reward manager, company7)

In such cases, the misinterpretation of results is often discreet and not easily understood, despite being a key factor in severing the alignment of pay practice to intended pay policy. This is not necessarily an undesirable consequence of a decentralized structure, but rather a practical reality of large organizations. The variation in realized pay practice highlights that when decentralized, pay determination results in emergent practice. In line with the espoused values and pay outcome aspirations stated in the pay approaches within both company1 and company2, operational line units within each firm have developed locally determined pay systems designed to support the achievement of local business objectives. The result is the *emergence* of a number of related pay systems across the global organization representing variations on a theme – the firms' approach to pay. Where pay determination is centralized, by degree (regionally or globally, for example), the experiences of the case study companies suggest that the introduction of intended policy can be highly challenging. Developed centrally in the context of the corporation overall, and in response to the needs of the local organization as they are perceived by headquarters staff, intended pay policies often reflect a poor fit when implemented. A common implication is the subversion of intended policy in favour of existing or alternative practice more in keeping with the prevailing status quo of the local organization. The introduction of a new pay system, whether centrally or locally determined, is a process fraught with tensions. In particular, the tensions between the pay function and line management are felt acutely as the pay function attempts to promote the adoption of pay systems in line with intended policy, to be met with considerable resistance from line management and employees.

Selection at the operation level of the pay determination process

At the selection stage of the determination of the pay approach, the divide between central and devolved pay determination results in significantly different pay outcomes being experienced in each of the case study companies. In the context of line management determination of pay, the selected role for pay differs substantially from that intended centrally by the pay function. The implication is that firms using the same pay practices, for example incentives, do so for different operational reasons. Notably, variation in intent is divided between centrally imposed use of pay in what is perceived as a means of corporate control, and the commitment styles favoured and adopted by local line management, where they have discretion to do so.

Devolved pay management

Pay within company1, as noted, is devolved to the line organization. In response to local business needs, line management universally use pay as a means of reinforcing additional local people management initiatives not driven from the centre. Where they have the discretion, line management construct bonus systems, as per a corporate mandate to do so – company3, for example – as *rewards* and not incentives. Bonus payments do not respond typically, therefore, to specific individual targets, but a combination of team and/or division performance, and are paid on an annual basis. The precise amount or value of the payment is unknown to employees in advance of payment, which effectively negates any 'line of sight' effect. Bonuses are, therefore, reactive to perceived individual performance, and funded by overall team and/or division performance, and are determined retrospectively and not according to a fixed or predetermined formula. Potentially bonuses may be awarded in spite of below-target performance, if it is felt that non-payment would corrupt the 'deal' that characterizes the employment relationship locally, or would be perceived as unfair and therefore a source of conflict – discreet and manifest. As a result, there is often little or no discernible line of sight between individuals' performance and performance pay outcomes.

Not only are individuals not incentivized on their personal performance, but their contribution is aggregated to that of the whole – team performance, for example – purposefully to foster an ethos of 'shared responsibility'. Strategic pay systems are not used, arguably, to generate the outcomes promised, but support instead additional measures considered more important, such as recognition, freedom to develop, career opportunities and others. Performance management continues to play an important role in fostering and perpetuating expectations of performance, but where line management have the discretion to pay, they rarely seem to do so. The linking of pay to individual performance is universally viewed as operationally problematic, and it is avoided where possible – a finding that challenges the trends towards the use of individual performance-based pay identified in the literature review.

> But what I have sort of witnessed over the past few months certainly is that it's time for appraisals to be done, so there's a panic and oh, I'd better get my objectives sort of filled in and people doing everything retrospectively, and I think certainly that doesn't necessarily help when it comes to … if you've got someone that's underperforming throughout the year with regards to their development planning and

things like that. I think that if it's something that we can get people to buy into and to actually go through and make sure that they are doing the mid-year reviews and things like that, it will certainly help with underperformers.

(line unit HR officer, company1)

Such arrangements are indicative of high trust/high commitment workplace arrangements. The post hoc award of incentive pay is intended not only to comply with the espoused pay approach, which is viewed as important at the grass roots level of the firm, but also to reinforce culturally what is important both corporately (company vision, values and mission) and operationally (business unit performance targets and local management styles). Operationally, therefore, pay within the line units researched in company1 and company2 serves to reinforce, culturally, expectations of performance and values.

Centrally determined pay systems

Despite the devolution of pay determination to local management in company3, financial targets remain imposed from the centre. Local management have discretion over the form of pay, and universally use some form of incentive, but do not have discretion over the targets set and little control, therefore, over pay outcomes. The use of incentives does serve to align employee efforts towards the regionally determined business goals, but whether those goals are appropriate is a matter of contention at the level of the business unit.

It is widely perceived that the centrally imposed targets do not take sufficient account of local business conditions, especially volatility within the market. In the case of company3, line unit sales managers have significant proportions of their pay placed at risk based upon performance against targets that are considered unachievable:

I think one of the things that the individual element has done is force line managers to actually do something about performance management. It was quite easy before, yeah there'd been calibration with HR, but essentially you could still say 'oh you know, I think you've exceeded or you've met', if it would be too difficult a conversation otherwise. Where they have to make a financial decision on the back of it, where they only have so many options to allocate, only so much cash to allocate for a bonus, and they know they're going to have to have a conversation about that and it's, you know, Jack or John that's going to get it, it can help to put behaviour in there that they need to have that conversation, or at least make a call where they could possibly have avoided it before.

(line unit HR manager, company3)

The use of performance-based pay measures within the European operations of company4 serves to encourage line of sight between individuals and performance goals, as per the prescriptions of standard theory. However, it is widely perceived within the line organization that, again, the targets set centrally are misallocated and do not represent realistic targets for local business unit performance. Targets set, both individual and business unit performance-linked, are considered either too hard or too soft. In the case of the former, there is widespread evidence of line management 'testing' the system by asking for exceptions and finding loopholes through which they perceive they can avoid the conflict that would result through compliance. Line management is, in effect, finding ways around centrally determined pay systems and centrally imposed targets:

Well, sporadically, and people are very creative. But actually the process is quite tight, so there's not a lot of leeway, and, as I say, people are creative, so people will always find ways around processes and strictures.

(senior operational manager, company4)

The perceived rationale for the introduction of a centrally imposed pay system is also discordant with the espoused strategic principles and aspirations – the pay rationale as it is expressed at the level of approach. Illustrated in this instance by line management sentiments expressed at company4, but not without resonance within the other case studies, both line management and employees perceive the 'true' intent behind pay systems to be one of attempting to exert corporate control. Centrally determined pay systems, when combined with central objective setting and performance management, are perceived as being used in lieu of effective and inspiring leadership:

There's a *big* issue lurking behind what we've just been saying. Because this whole thing about, you know, weak leadership in the corporate sense allowing or permitting bonus schemes and bonus structures to be a crutch for their failings in leadership.

(senior general manager, company4)

The implication is that if leadership – typically senior management – was sufficiently strong, then the use of centrally determined and managed strategic pay interventions would not be necessary. It is also widely perceived that the imposition of centrally determined pay systems reflects a corporate lack of confidence in line management's ability to manage people and performance. Again, the perception is that strategic pay interventions are being used to address organizational deficiencies for which they should not be intended. This reflects the view that it is not pay that fosters an ethos of performance per se, and not incentives that encourage the 'right' behaviours, but other factors, among which strong leadership is considered most important. However, defining strong leadership, much less exhibiting it, is especially challenging:

> I don't know. Well, sorry, that's not true, I do know. The theory is we're trying to engage senior management across the globe in shared agendas around global initiatives, and making sure that it's, it's ... I think it's a clumsy attempt to do something which by definition you can't do, and that is to impose culture. I think we're trying to impose cultural change and behavioural change by setting the bonus scheme to do it, rather than taking on the leadership challenge of changing it.
>
> (senior general manager, company4)

Company4 provides a good illustration of where past negative experiences of pay systems prejudices current or future systems irrespective of their technical or business merit. By being removed from the business, pay function personnel are not cognizant of the 'bad stories' associated with pay, often because it reflects negatively upon their contribution and they are purposefully sheltered from negative sentiment. Where cognizant, it is also perhaps in their interest that such negative sentiment is not communicated to senior management for fear of the function being perceived as having failed. Senior management remain ignorant of negative experiences of pay being both removed, and protected, from the negative discourse emanating from line management and the employee base. As a result, the rhetoric of success is often pervasive at the upper strata of the case study companies, quite divorced from the grounded negative experience at the operational level. The technical experience of pay is largely discreet and localized and not easily shared. The rhetorical experience is, however, explicit and not bounded by personal experience. This represents a clear potential for a divergence between the rhetoric and reality of practice experience and, necessarily, perceived practice effectiveness.

> I was astounded to find that we typically had fairly good policies, not always mind you, however. I mean sometimes I have found people being administered under a so-called policy that's not documented anywhere!
>
> (HR function practitioner, company5)

In reaction against prescribed policy, there are numerous operational examples of emergent pay practice. Emergent practice arises as a result of line management outright rejecting the intended pay design and putting in its place a locally devised system that, it is felt at that level, better suits local conditions. Similarly, the adaptation of intended policy may result in realized pay practice being quite dissimilar to what was intended centrally. Again, the degree to which the central pay function, having assumed responsibility for the pay design, has recourse over such action is limited, as the findings at company5 indicate:

> No. No, I mean even down to ... I mean so much of our finance stuff and that is controlled. And even structures are dictated at the global level, and you have to sometimes say if we put someone in to run a business, should we not trust that that person. ... I mean if we don't trust that that person can make the right decisions to structure that business in the best way to deliver the best possible result, why have we got them in there doing the job?
>
> (HR function practitioner, company5)

Pay system ineffectiveness at company5, and the negative outcomes experienced as a result, are not necessarily communicated nor well understood, often being discreet and therefore difficult to remedy by either the pay function or senior management. For many reasons, not least the wish to avoid communicating failure or perceived weakness, negative 'stories' associated with pay systems operation are often internalized locally by line management and/or the pay function. Positive stories, however, disseminate much further within the organization and serve to reinforce the positive rhetoric around the use of those systems – a rhetoric of success that does not always reflect the reality of operational experience. Positive stories may, in turn, inform further the experiences of others and so on, generating a perception of pay system effectiveness to which those less involved in the pay determination process are especially prone.

Retention at the operation level of the pay determination process

Given that what is practised operationally is potentially not what was intended as policy or desired strategically, what are the resultant outcomes? The final stage of the final level of the pay determination process – retention – depicts what is retained organizationally as outcomes of the enacted pay systems. In light of the preceding findings sections, what are the organizational outcomes experienced? Are they consistent with the desired outcomes stated within the pay approach? Is pay within the case study companies achieving what it is supposed to?

At the operational level, pay within company1 does largely fulfil the aspirations set out within the pay approach across the business units reviewed. Pay is not, however, the strategic lever through which behaviours and performance are leveraged as prescribed by standard theory, but is viewed as a means of supporting the achievement of local business objectives by 'creating an environment in which performance is valued'. Pay is also viewed as an important means of fostering a shared sense of corporate identity. Company1 is a very large decentralized holding company with a relatively small corporate headquarters that acts as an umbrella organization for the myriad autonomous operating companies that comprise the whole. The contribution of pay to the creation of a shared sense of corporate identity and culture is highly valued by both senior management and line management throughout the global business.

Bonus systems, where they are used, are not constructed to incentivize behaviour in the standard sense. In recognition, perhaps, of the difficulties of both defining and measuring individual performance, incentives in all of the operating units reviewed are linked to the achievement of business unit objectives. Individuals' pay is at risk based upon business unit/division and not individual performance. Line management retain the discretion to alter incentive awards, post hoc, to mitigate the negative effects of non-payment in the case of poor performance. Where individual performance conditions are used, and modifiers on incentive payments are linked to business unit performance, they are typically 'soft' measures, which are not formalized objectives as such. From the perspective of the employee, therefore, they are incentives in the standard sense. Where paid out, incentives reinforce line management performance expectations overall and are not linked to individual performance management outcomes. Rather, they are used to foster a sense of 'shared responsibility' and, again, reinforce a culture of high performance and commitment. The provision of incentives is also viewed as important when recruiting new staff:

> I think with the bonus arrangements that we have in the UK ... they're not really set up or constructed as incentives. I would be really surprised if anyone you meet and interview would say that they look at their bonus and really feel that it's pay at risk, or they really feel that it's something that incentivizes them to do their job differently and to behave differently. I think the response you will more commonly hear is 'if I get this bonus I understand what it's based upon and performance is targeted but typically it's not something that really drives my performance during the year'.
>
> (line unit HR manager, company1)

Other aspects of pay, such as the use of long-term equity-based systems, do not, again, elicit outcomes consistent with prescriptive theory. With regard to employee share ownership, a 'sense of entitlement' is pervasive, with the taken-for-granted expectation of an award being commonplace:

> It's very interesting because my previous company had deliberations for quite a long time about introducing some form of share reward scheme, some form of incentive, to drive share ownership. And we had long debates about the benefits of doing something like that because it would encourage more of a shareholder mentality and build a stakeholder mentality with employees. And then I came here, where there has been a share reward scheme and share participation plan in place for many, many years. It doesn't encourage that. It doesn't encourage that at all, you know. That scheme has been in operation for so long that it's ... it's become part of the fixtures and fittings.
>
> (line unit HR, company1)

Overall, therefore, pay is viewed philosophically by many within the company as 'hygiene' – a perspective that does not sit well with standard prescriptions. Pay is universally viewed as important, but it is not the means by which those outcomes of strategic value are elicited. Rather, if employees' need for hygiene is not satisfied, then pay can be a 'terrible brake' on those aspects of the management of people that do elicit such outcomes – principally strong and inspirational leadership. However, indirectly, pay can have a negative impact upon employee morale and motivation. For example, the individual incentivization of senior management against fixed targets can result in negative outcomes if not properly managed:

> You'd find some ... particularly towards the end of the year, one or other senior manager trying to get something done which you were thinking has nothing much to do with me, why does he want all this work done? And you find out by a bit of digging that it's one of his bonus objectives. Well, I'm not getting anything out of this, it's not contributing to my objectives, why am I being bullied and pushed and so on to get this work done so that somebody else can collect their bonus?
>
> (rewards practitioner, company1)

Company2 experiences very similar pay outcomes to company1. Pay is, again, valued as supporting the achievement of local business objectives, but it is not credited itself with driving performance. Pay also contributes towards the creation of an ethos in which performance is valued and employees adopt a sense of personal ownership, not only for their personal performance, but for that of the company overall. Despite using a similar profile of pay practice to all other firms, pay is managed in a manner consistent with the heritage of employment at company2 – one of paternalism and mutuality.

In company3, the third and final case study company where pay determination is largely decentralized, the pay outcomes experienced differ from those in both company1 and company2. The outcomes experienced in terms of their value are far more variable, with some business units seemingly benefiting a great deal from the attempts to use pay strategically and others much less so. Why is there this level of variability in pay outcomes? Company3, as already discussed, does not clearly articulate the pay approach, which has implications for the impact of pay in practice in two important respects. Firstly, by not disseminating the pay approach in the form of clear strategy, managers tasked with the determination of pay at the local level do not clearly understand the basis for the pay systems they are determining, nor the outcomes they are supposed to elicit. Pay outcomes are therefore emergent and not consistent necessarily with overall corporate objectives. Secondly, employees within the divisionally fragmented global organization do not have a clear appreciation of what the organization values in terms of performance, behaviours, values and cultures. The lack of a clear and meaningful strategy means that expectations of the 'effort–reward bargain' are not managed corporately – only locally, according to local management styles and capabilities.

An additional area of weakness is the lack of governance and process supporting the effective implementation of pay policy. The pay function fails in its contribution to promote the effective execution of pay practice through the use of common processes. At the point of implementation, line management has little or no involvement with the corporate pay function except in cases of dispute where either a central legal, or technical, resolution is required. Similarly, the determination of executive pay, including international assignee pay, commands the personal involvement of the corporate pay function, but broad-based employee pay is not considered part of their remit, being instead the responsibility of line management. Furthermore, little is provided to line management by way of support at the point of implementation, merely a corporate mandate and minimum standards to which line management must comply.

The degree to which these minimum standards are enforceable, however, is questionable. The corporate pay function does not facilitate either knowledge sharing or its transfer between line management in separate divisions, countries and business units. Thus, experience and lessons learnt from the implementation of pay systems is not widely disseminated. As a result, the impact of pay, in terms of its perceived value, often fails owoing to poor *management*:

> So you've sort of got the objectives, how they've performed against them, what you've accomplished throughout the year, you've got line management at the end of it saying 'okay, well, I think you're "exceeds"', they put in their reward proposals on the back of that and then they need to have a conversation with their report at the very end saying 'we agreed you're "exceeds" and that's translated into X bonus, X salary review, X stock options'. If, as I still see, that ends up being an envelope shoved under someone's keyboard with the letter in it, it's just so bad. I don't know why you bothered putting the effort into calibrating and everything like that 'cos the amount that the individual's got is completely lost, it's just … gone.
>
> (line unit HR manager, company3)

Despite attempts to the contrary, pay within company3 does not result in outcomes of strategic value. Employee disengagement and demotivation were observed in a number of line units. As a result of a lack of clear strategy guiding devolved pay determination, and communicating to employees what is valued corporately by senior management, combined with a lack of supporting processes, pay does not do what it is supposed to do in company3.

At company4 the pay outcomes experienced are appreciably more negative, but for entirely different reasons. Here pay determination is centralized at the regional level, and the pay outcomes experienced are mixed and often negative. The centralized pay systems – incentives especially – negatively impact upon employees within the European business for a variety of reasons. Despite being tied to individual performance as well as regional level company performance, the incentives used do not encourage a line of sight between the contribution of the individual and their pay. The basis for performance pay, when awarded, is not well understood, leading to a number of negative behavioural outcomes that are common to many of the case study companies. Where incentive payments are in excess of what was expected, it establishes a precedent for future payments and fosters a sense of 'entitlement' that is not easily overcome. Where incentive payments are negative, employees feel unduly penalized for factors beyond their control. These factors extend to corporate performance overall – 'how much difference can one individual make' – to changes in personal circumstances, to which the incentive systems are not sensitive. In both cases, the payment systems are not sufficiently sensitive to the dynamic and fluid immediate environment of line businesses, with implications for their perceived effectiveness and, by extension, their value.

> So we have got a real mixed bag, and the faster the business changes and this evolves, the harder it is for the reward process to catch up. You know, I'll give you a personal example. My scheme for this year has changed twice, and, because my role has changed twice during the year, just slightly, and now I'm going to be rewarded on something actually I've nothing to do with anymore. So not that I'm any less motivated, by that, but you just feel, well, we've put a lot of effort into aligning me up to what I can influence and we've failed, you know! I'll just get paid what I get paid, at the end.
>
> (senior operational manager, company4)

Company4 is a good example of where a technically sophisticated incentive scheme, which is consistent with the principles of best practice, is perceived as operationally ineffective. By virtue of being *perceived* as ineffective, much of its potential impact is diminished. Irrespective of technical merit, all line management representatives interviewed spoke critically of pay at company4 and viewed pay as an element of corporate interference to be resisted and/or mitigated. For them, the pay systems determined centrally (regionally) induce conflict and malcontent that requires careful management. The implications of linking pay to performance are employee disengagement and demotivation – key challenges for line management to overcome:

> People have worked their arses off against objectives which have been stretched and stretched and stretched by senior management who didn't want to accept the numbers. And, therefore, the workforce has now paid the price of not only being literally short-changed versus the marketplace in terms of their overall net pay, but they actually feel like they're failing. So, actually, you know, bonuses are great when things are going well, or when you're actually paying in line with your policy. What happens when businesses go through tough periods, where either because the periods are tough or because other elements of the business are not going well, the stretch objectives set by senior management are potentially unobtainable, then that has a *massively* detrimental effect on morale.
>
> (senior general manager, company4)

Incentives are contentious and divisive from the point of view of internal relativity. In the case of the largest European division of company4, performance against stretched divisional targets has been modest, although this is still recognized as a considerable achievement, given challenging market conditions and being better than the performance gains (revenue and market capitalization) of competitor firms. And yet, by the predetermined performance standards of the incentive system, incentive pay linked to divisional performance must reflect the 'modest' performance, with the result that the level of incentive is much reduced. Despite strong performance against stretched targets, the message communicated to staff through the use of incentives is one of recognition for mediocre performance. The signal sent by pay to employees thus undermines the best efforts of local management to motivate and engage their employees to maintain performance against stretched targets. Far from being encouraged to perform against stretched targets through the use of incentives, employees are penalized and ultimately demotivated and disengaged as a result:

> Which is absolutely – oh turn your tape recorder off – it's absolutely f***ing ridiculous, absolutely ridiculous. There are people in back

office, admin type roles doing absolutely *nothing* to drive the value for this company who are getting 70 and 80 per cent bonuses, while people in teams slave their arses off and get 20 per cent. It doesn't figure. It doesn't make *any* sense to me at all. I understand the *convenience* of it, and I understand the administrative cost of the alternative, but unless you can factor in some degree of line of sight, how the hell does it ever operate as an incentive scheme of *any* sort?

(senior general manager, company4)

One implication of the managerial incentive system used within European operations at company4 is that over the four-year course of the incentive it has created a great deal of perceived pay disparity between the various divisions that operate under the European umbrella organization. Some divisions are tarnished with perceived poor performance that does not recognize the reality of their value corporately, or the conditions under which such performance is won. It is not an uncommon phenomenon for staff to transfer between divisions within company4 in the expectation of more favourable pay for the same work. These negative outcomes of the use of incentives are recognized by representatives of the pay function:

When people look at their variable pay, one of the big problems we've had with all the bonuses is, how much can you predict, or influence, your bonus? And, you know, if there's a corporate element I can't predict it. One year it's very good and I haven't a clue why, and the next year it's terrible and yet I thought we were doing all right. Very unpredictable.

(senior reward director, company4)

The implication is that pay is unfair and that line management struggle to reconcile the tensions and conflict that arise naturally as a result. The negative outcomes associated with the pay systems used are not, however, solely confined to behavioural outcomes. Linking pay to performance, for both performance-based base pay (merit) and incentives, requires a number of managerial inputs in the form of objective setting and appraisal. The administration required when linking pay to performance is recognized as being especially time-consuming:

In terms of the administration, it takes forever, it's ... what seems to happen. ... The line's perception is, I think, you complete this job description, it goes into a black box, and out comes a grade. So HR is

perceived to be grading these jobs. HR is in a no-win situation, there
is *no* ownership for the grading scheme from the line.

(line unit HR manager, company4)

The story at company6 is similar. The use of centrally determined
variable pay systems linked to regional and country-based business success has resulted in a number of unintended outcomes. The pay systems
used are perceived by employees as a break in the traditional 'deal',
one of paternalism, job security and strong people management. Weak
business performance and market expansion, relative to the heady days
of the late 1990s, has resulted in much being done to streamline business operations, with implications for the pay systems used. One such
efficiency initiative was to include a portion of employee pay at risk
based upon overall business performance regionally. However, continued
poor performance has resulted in few, if any, payments under the new
incentive scheme. As one pay function specialist commented on the use
of incentives: 'Incentives only work when they pay out' (pay function
specialist, company6). However, as a result of corporately imposed targets,
the incentive programme linked to regional/divisional business performance has not 'paid out' since its introduction in 2000. Moreover, to fund
the 'bonus pot', base pay increases were frozen for a successive period of
four years, with the result that employees received neither pay increases
nor bonus payments and pay fell, in real terms, behind that of competitor
companies. At the time of the research, a manifest consequence of this
was the sharp increase in employee rates of turnover, with pay cited
frequently in exit interviews as the reason for departure.

Again, the message sent to employees within the divisions in which
incentives were not paid was one of failure to meet corporate performance expectations. This did not sufficiently take into account the
unavoidable constraints on the ability of the business to perform –
constraints beyond the control of employees. A frequent reference
made in relation to incentives is: 'I get paid what I get paid. It doesn't
matter.' Far from encouraging performance, incentive pay becomes, at
the very least, part of the 'fixtures and fittings' and, at the very worst,
a factor encouraging the disengagement of employees. This is especially
significant for company6, which continues to pride itself on being an
'employer of choice' – the cornerstone philosophy of its pay approach –
and a paternalistic employer. The introduction of company-linked
incentive pay has served to 'break the deal' of mutuality and reciproc-
ity, both of which are core corporate principles. Pay at company6 is
intended to reinforce a sense of mutuality. Arguably, it does quite the

opposite. In attempting to use pay strategically in support of business success, pay has become perceived as a cost-cutting vehicle.

At company5 the experience of pay systems operationally is mixed, but unlike company6, company4, company3 and company7, pay function staff in many cases are unaware of the failings perceived by line management. The sense of entitlement associated with the company performance-based management incentive plan (MIP) is viewed as especially problematic:

> Mm, I think ... interesting. I would say it does, certainly in terms of attracting and keeping people. And in fact, sometimes keeping people too *much*, because I would say generally, you know, we're pretty generous and often end up keeping folks we wouldn't necessarily want to. But does it ... um, has it really been used to drive the strategies? Definitely not, definitely not.
>
> (HR function practitioner, company5)

A corporate requirement, but funded by local management, the MIP has become, by degree, largely expected as a guaranteed element of pay paid in addition to base pay. Individuals have little or no discretion over participation, and the result cannot be credited to any one individual, and so there is little if any line of sight. The MIP, far from what was intended, is an expensive overhead sourced from local business unit budgets and therefore a brake on profitability, with little or no perceived return:

> So then, you know, if they are intolerant, and part of what helps, or part of what we believe at least for the North American employee, I don't know if it's true or not, but part of our prevailing belief is, for those of us that have come out of the US HR schools, is that there is some sort of motivating factor of having this pay at risk, that somehow drives people to do something differently. If you can't have the same kind of level of risk implanted in other parts of the world then why, you may ask, what is the benefit of doing that kind of thing? And it turns into being another benefit from which you get no reward.
>
> (corporate rewards manager, company5)

At company7, pay operationally is considered a key element in attracting and retaining the necessary calibre of employee and is a means through which, on a global basis and to the entire employee population, the leadership is able to communicate what is considered important for company success, such as performance expectations and desired behaviours. However, both within and without the pay function, pay is not viewed as being universally effective, or the means through which value is necessarily driven. Moreover, the use of pay interventions, such as incentives, is seen as highly administratively time-consuming and expensive and, it would seem, with little evidence of a return:

> Do I think we're doing it well now? No I don't. I think we're spending a lot of money, but I don't think we're doing it well, and that's not a criticism of any one individual, not at all. I think it's just a combination of our history, of where we've got to, lack of clarity in a whole number of areas, but fundamentally not now having a coherent story to explain to somebody why they've got what they've got.
>
> (regional reward manager, company7)

Nor are the pay systems deployed achieving what was intended. In the case of equity-based long-term incentives designed to encourage long-termism of outlook and employee retention, their configuration results in an overly individualistic focus, which stifles collaboration and cross-functional relationships (shared marketing opportunities, being an example), both of which are valued operationally. Arguably, such collaborative behaviours cannot be achieved through payment systems alone, but in the case of company7, the pay systems imposed by the central pay function as a global standard act as a brake on such behaviours:

> I think you know most of our reward systems now are completely individual, you know. Individual base pay, you can argue that our variable pay is a profit-sharing, it is but it still has an individual twist. Stock is individual essentially. Whereas actually in vast swathes of the business, it's about cooperation and, as I say, over a much longer time frame, yeah? A year is not relevant.
>
> (senior reward director, company7)

As in all of the firms, meaningful performance differentiation at company7 is especially hard to achieve operationally. Company7, like many of the other case study companies, uses a Likert scale ranging from 1 to 3, with 1 being below expectations, 2 meets expectations and 3 exceeds expectations. Three categories of performance linked to pay, when applied to many thousands of employees, are inherently problematic and perceived by many as being unfair. Moreover, individuals' performance is not within their gift necessarily, especially with regard to unforeseen events beyond the control of the individual and unknown in advance of objective setting:

> You can get an absolute win or fail [rating] because something happened that you hadn't anticipated when you set the target. Likewise you can get an absolute win because something happened. Neither of them is fair, neither of them will motivate individuals to achieve. And what you're looking for is to get the individual to exert the influence he *can* have in an appropriate way. You don't do that by saying you've got to achieve these particular numbers if a circumstance comes up that you hadn't foreseen.
>
> (country reward manager, company7)

The attempt to incentivize behaviour also has additional negative outcomes in the form of constraints on innovation. As the quotation above highlights, a theme running throughout the findings is the challenge associated with the measurement, and incentivization therefore, of individuals' output. In the case of the majority of professional, technical and managerial roles and occupations, output is difficult to define and difficult to measure. All of the case study firms invest considerable resources in developing robust objective-setting and performance management. However, the degree to which the performance management process can incorporate sufficient sensitivity to individuals' output is a consistent challenge. The measurement of innovation (an example of employee *discretionary* behaviour much valued strategically) as performance is especially problematic:

> I think that's right, but you do focus the individual to accept that there is no innovation and that his job is selling [product] whereas there might well be and you will miss that opportunity by having them totally focused in on something else. We are presupposing that there is ... that there can be no creativity in selling [product]. So the individual who thinks now if I make a tie up with an [x] company and sell a [product], that might increase summer sales of [product] where traditionally they've been a winter sale. I don't know. You do not get innovation from putting targets in front of people.
>
> (country reward manager, company7)

Where such measures are used in the case of company7, it is not necessarily through quantitative measures that these are achieved, but through line management appraisal, which is necessarily subjective and therefore open to criticism. The findings at company7 indicate that attempts to promote innovative behaviour through performance-based pay can have quite the opposite effect.

Overall, the operational outcomes of the pay systems used are negative in a significant number of cases. In company1 and company2 the pay systems are perceived to be valuable as supporting local management and reinforcing a culture of performance and a sense of shared purpose, but they are not behavioural levers, nor are they arguably the means through which employee outcomes of the greatest strategic value are achieved. In the remaining case study companies, for reasons associated with *how* and *how well* their pay systems are managed, pay systems are often perceived as ineffective and, in some instances, damaging.

Summary

At the third and final level of analysis – the pay operation – the findings reveal, in a number of the case study companies, a gap between (a) what was desired strategically, (b) intended as policy, and (c) achieved operationally as pay practice. As a result, pay in these cases does not achieve strategic outcomes. Operationally, pay is non-strategic. In a significant number of cases, attempts to use pay strategically resulted in negative outcomes, including employee disengagement and demotivation. Realized pay practice is not, therefore, the logical extension of rational planning, as theory would suggest, and some firms experience better outcomes than others in pay. This can be credited in large part to *how* they approach the management of their pay systems. The findings indicate that there is a strong relationship between pay system effectiveness and the locus of their determination.

Company1 and company2 are two examples of pay determination devolved to line management. Pay within both conforms to what was intended – namely the local determination of pay systems best suited to supporting the achievement of local business objectives. Corporately, emergent practice is both expected and encouraged, and is guided, but not prescribed, by the pay strategy and the espoused principles, values and aspirations of the pay approach. Perceived positive outcomes communicate the value of pay and its role in attracting and retaining valued talent. It is not, however, nor is it intended to be, an instrumental means through which management is able to drive performance or behaviours. Firms that do attempt to use pay in such a way experience the greatest degree of perceived pay system ineffectiveness – the greatest degree of

Table 7.1 Case study company pay practice at the level of operation

Stage Description	Context Aligned to	Variation Aspiration	Selection Content	Form	Retention Perceived impact
Company1	Local targets	Autonomy	Post hoc reward	Reinforcing	Culturally reinforcing
Company2	Local targets	Autonomy	Post hoc reward	Reinforcing	Culturally reinforcing
Company3	Centrally determined targets	Autonomy	Directional	Misleading	Neutral/demotivating
Company4	Centrally determined targets	Enforced scheme	(some) line of sight	Reinforcing	Neutral/demotivating
Company5	Centrally determined targets	Enforced scheme	Directional	Misleading	Risk
Company6	Regional and/or product	Compliance	(some) line of sight	Reinforcing	Neutral/demotivating
Company7	Corporate and local targets	Enforced scheme	(some) line of sight	Reinforcing	Neutral/demotivating

'gap' between what is intended and what is achieved, and relatedly, the number and severity of negative outcomes experienced (Table 7.1). When pay determination is centralized, there is seemingly a greater likelihood of pay systems producing unintended consequences. Often perceived as a poor fit for local business and employment conditions, formal pay policies are subject to (mis)interpretation by line management and employees at the point of execution, with the result that significant variations of the same policy between different operational business units are evident. If sufficiently misaligned to the business and employment conditions of the local organization, it is also apparent that line managers, in protecting their own interests and that of their staff, may potentially subvert the intended pay system. This may take the form of an outright rejection or, more typically, a substantial revision of the pay system implemented, which may or may not be appreciable at the corporate level. As a result, much operational pay practice might be classed as 'emergent' and not the result of formal pay policy per se. Rather, it represents the best efforts of local management to use pay systems to support the achievement of objectives for which they are primarily responsible.

Critically, therefore, it is important to recognize that the pay operation within four of the seven case study companies is characterized by *divergence* between (a) the intended pay design and achieved pay practice operationally; and, as a result, (b) the effectiveness of those practices; and (c) the outcomes – positive, neutral and negative – experienced. Pay operationally reflects neither what was desired strategically nor what was intended in policy terms. Quite simply, pay practice operationally is not what it is supposed to be in these case study companies. Where there is such a gap between the approach, design and operation, pay is mostly *non-strategic* by the terms of standard theory. Moreover, a number of negative outcomes from attempts to use pay strategically are apparent. Such negative outcomes can serve to limit company performance and potentially diminish value. Consistent with the observations of the previous chapter, it is clear that the greater the degree of centralized pay system determination, the greater the likelihood of unintended consequences and negative outcomes that result from attempts to use pay strategically. Such issues are discussed within the overall context of the findings at all levels of the pay determination process in the next chapter, on the reality of strategic pay in practice.

8
The Reality of Strategic Pay in Practice

Responding to a need to improve understanding of strategic pay in practice, this study has presented findings on the pay practices of leading companies that challenge the strategic status of pay. All of the case study companies aspire to use pay strategically in line with prescriptions of standard theory, and all largely select the same configurations of 'best practice' pay systems on that basis. However, the findings also demonstrate that all of the case study firms experience significant managerial difficulties when attempting to 'operationalize' these pay systems.

Operationally, in a number of the cases, pay practice does not reflect what is desired or intended strategically, and does not therefore yield outcomes of strategic value. Pay is non-strategic in these cases. The case study companies' findings also reveal that when attempting to use pay strategically, a variety of unintended and negative outcomes are also experienced, with the result that these so-called strategic pay systems potentially consume and/or diminish more value than they create. This chapter will discuss these issues and other overall themes to emerge from the findings.

A multi-level portrait of pay practice

Using the multi-method approach to understand pay practice at multiple levels, preliminary analysis of industry-level data confirmed that the vast majority of private sector firms operating in the FMCG sector in the UK use pay systems that would be characterized as strategic according to the prescriptions of the literature. All deploy flexible base pay structures linked to market movements on a yearly basis. All, bar one, place significant levels of pay at risk through the deployment of at least one form of short-term incentive bonus system for all white collar employees. All use one or, typically, two forms of long-term incentive pay for all white collar employees. Finally, all use a comprehensive array of financial benefits emphasizing choice and value to the individual.

Drawing upon case study-based research within seven leading multinational firms operating in the global FMCG sector, the findings at the next level of analysis, the pay *approach*, reveal that all firms aspire to use pay strategically to promote alignment between their employees and the mission, vision and values of the firm. All of the case study firms emphasize the value of high-performance working cultures and have developed total reward models of pay to those ends. Thus far, they all correspond to both FMCG industry pay norms and conform to prescriptions of strategic theories of pay. Like the industry-level data, the approach-level findings paint a picture of pay practice convergence between firms competing for both product and labour. At these two levels, pay is seemingly being used strategically.

At the level of the pay *design*, defined as the formulation of specific and technical pay policies designed to fulfil the strategic aspirations stated in the pay approach, the findings begin to reveal a more complex picture of pay determination within the case study firms. Prima facie, all of the case study firms have adopted very similar profiles of pay practice in the form of market-linked base pay, a significant proportion of the base pay being linked to individual performance and performance-based base pay progression. All firms make extensive use of variable pay programmes, both long term and short term, and place largely comparable portions of employee pay at risk, based upon combinations of individual, team and company performance, across all functions and levels. All firms also offer a comprehensive range of benefits, and emphasize the value of individuals' choices over benefits received. Moreover, all of these multiple elements of pay are bundled within coherent pay packages and, with varying degrees of success, are integrated with non-financial rewards such as career progression, opportunities for personal development and then labelled as total rewards. Again, the portrait of case study company pay practice is one of conformity to industry trends and the prescriptions of best practice strategic pay. Such startling convergence of case study firm pay practice around very specific norms suggests the existence of some powerful forces informing the outcomes of the pay determination process. However, it is at this point that the picture of conformity ceases and a new, more complex perspective of case study company pay practice emerges.

While there is clearly evidence of convergence of the types of pay system selected by each of the case study firms, some notable differences emerge between the case study firms concerning *how* these same pay interventions are managed. In three of the seven case study firms, the determination of the pay design is devolved primarily to line management and supported by line HR and representatives of the central pay function acting as roving consultants. In the remaining four firms, the determination of the pay design (pay policy to all intents and purposes) is more centralized, with two firms determining pay on a geographical regional basis and two firms determining pay policies on a global basis. A crucial distinction between the case study firms, therefore, is centralized and decentralized design of pay systems.

In those case study companies where determination of the pay design is largely decentralized to business units, the pay approach in the form of strategy serves as a guiding framework and establishes loosely the parameters of the scope for pay determination. In the case of centralized pay design/pay policy formulation, such policies, when cascaded throughout the organization, are often perceived as reflecting a poor fit for local business units. These often represent a source of conflict and tension, by imposing potentially a high cost base on line units with responsibility for their own profit and loss and, equally significantly, constraining their opportunity to develop bespoke organic systems. Clearly, there are advantages and disadvantages to both approaches, and it is at the level of pay operation that the implications for pay systems' effectiveness, and associated pay outcomes experienced, become obvious.

The final level of analysis, the pay *operation*, reveals the realities of strategic pay systems in practice. What is intended in the form of pay policy is, for a variety of reasons, not necessarily achieved as operational practice. Irrespective of the saliency of the design, although often manifestly, in part, because of the selected pay policy reflecting a poor fit for the organization, the relative inability of organizations to enact, implement and operationalize pay systems as intended is a core barrier to pay systems' effectiveness and, in turn, results in unintended pay outcomes that have a negative impact on organizational value, creation and performance. Seemingly, a key contributor to pay system effectiveness and the outcomes experienced, be they positive, neutral or negative, is the degree to which pay determination is centralized or decentralized. In those case study firms where pay design and management is decentralized, pay is typically aligned to local targets and, as desired centrally, pay determination is largely autonomous. Where local management have the discretion and autonomy to manage pay as they see fit, pay, including variable pay, typically takes the form of post hoc reward for performance and effort. Pay systems are neither used, nor do they act, as levers promoting desired employee behaviours over others. The systems do not possess strong motivational qualities, but rather reinforce the best efforts of local management to inspire, lead and manage their people on a day-to-day basis.

The findings highlight that, where used, variable pay is not used as an incentive, often being purposefully disconnected from individuals' objectives for reasons of manageability. Moreover, incentive payments are linked typically to business unit, team or divisional performance overall, and are often awarded retrospectively, and at the discretion of local management, on the basis of perceived performance and not according to any system of formal appraisal or metric. In these cases, pay is devolved and takes the form of typically post hoc rewards that support local management and bind employees to their business unit over the organization as a whole. Operationally, bonus systems are managed less as incentives and more as rewards.

In the case of those case study firms where pay determination is centralized, however, the operational experience of those same pay systems is again quite different. A variety of reasons motivate the firms to manage pay centrally, not least seemingly the desire for corporate control in the case of company5, company4 and company7. In company6, however, the motivation is less about control, but more a matter of governance, and the view of paternalistic senior management that the interests of employees are best served by direct intervention, over their terms and conditions, by a professional pay function – 'mother knows best', in effect. Nevertheless the centralized determination of pay creates difficulties for those for whom the arrangements are binding – both managers and employees. The centralization of pay requires that those who have choice over pay options, and responsibility for the design of pay practice and policy, understand what is required in terms of both business need (corporately and locally) and the firm's human capital, and tailor the pay system design to those conditions. As Chapter 6 illustrates, however, decision makers are rarely able to operate on the basis of such information, with the result that their decisions may reflect a poor fit for the conditions in which they are applied operationally, and all of the negative outcomes that then may be produced.

Thus, the multi-level approach and framework adopted reveals a complex process of pay practice *formation* within seven leading firms, and presents a portrait of pay practice as it is perceived by the multiple stakeholders involved at all levels of the firm – senior management, the pay function, line management and employees. What is clear is that all of the sample case study firms attempt to use pay strategically, deploying very similar profiles of pay practice. However, as noted, they all experience quite different outcomes, principally as a result of their different approaches to the management of those same pay practices. Whether determined centrally or devolved to local management, the pay systems used do clearly fulfil some strategic aims: the attraction and retention of desired labour and talent; symbolically communicating to employees what is organizationally important; supporting and reinforcing attempts to promote high-performance cultures corporately; and, lastly, reducing fixed wage costs. But the findings do not indicate that the so-called strategic pay systems used achieve all of the aims that they are supposed to, and arguably do not achieve those stated aims most important from a strategic perspective.

The evidence does not confirm that using pay strategically promotes alignment of employees to the interests of the business through line of sight, nor are the motivational benefits of pay obvious, with pay being viewed by many as a 'hygiene factor' and not something that promotes either effort or desirable behaviours. Nor is there a clear, or demonstrable, link between the use of strategic pay practices and improved company performance. Definitions of pay system effectiveness are (the experience of the case study firms would suggest) highly problematic, as are any attempts to apply meaningful measurement (Figure 8.1).

What is demonstrable and manifest, especially within three of the seven case study companies, are the negative outcomes associated with

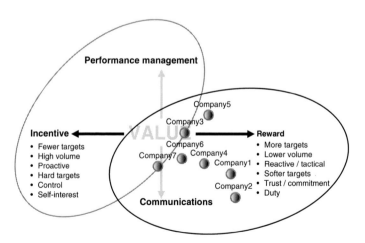

Figure 8.1   The basis for case study company incentive pay in practice

attempts to use pay strategically. A significant number of case study firms experience negative *pay* outcomes, as they are perceived operationally, as a result of the pay systems used. Contrary to expectations, it is apparent that pay systems can serve to diminish motivation, misdirect behaviours undesirably, consume managerial time and effort, misallocate pay spend and produce various other outcomes that are quite contrary to what it is supposed to happen, and potentially consume and destroy more value than is created. Moreover, if pay is indeed a value-adding activity, then the value created is seemingly impossible to measure in the way that is most often financially desired. The inability to assess and measure quantitatively the financial value-added contribution of pay is a perennial frustration for all those with a vested interest in pay – particularly senior management and the pay function. Clearly, all firms are struggling to get pay 'right', and some are failing to the degree that, arguably, they are getting it 'wrong'. Nevertheless some companies do experience better outcomes than others – what are they doing differently?

The gap between what is desired, intended and achieved

Pay determination is manifestly a complex process and results in outcomes potentially neither desired nor intended. Unlike standard theory, the case study findings do not confirm that pay, when used strategically, produces outcomes that benefit the organization in terms of company performance and competitive advantage. Rather, the findings challenge much of the received wisdom of strategic pay, by illustrating the profound difficulties encountered by all of the case study companies when attempting to use pay strategically, and the unpredictability of outcomes as a result. The findings confirm that the case study companies are attempting to use pay strategically, but all struggle to manage effectively their 'strategic' pay systems. The case study companies respond to these challenges by approaching the management of pay in different ways. The operational outcomes experienced suggest that some manage their strategic pay systems better than others. As a result of ineffective management, in a number of cases, pay is non-strategic and potentially achieves, operationally, the opposite of what was originally desired strategically and, or, intended as policy.

> If you ask companies, 'do you *manage* pay strategically', most of the organizations we talk to will say, 'of course we do'. Most practitioners are very sensitive to the idea that they are doing anything that is not

'strategic', and saying things like 'we are aligning pay with performance' is motherhood and apple pie in the HR community at the moment. I do work with companies where, in unguarded moments, HR people will say 'quite frankly, we don't do any of this stuff', but the aspiration is clearly there.

(management consultant, consult1 – emphasis added)

The 'gap' between what is desired strategically (the pay approach) intended as policy (the pay design) and achieved as pay practice (the pay operation) is an important recognition of the fallibility of strategic pay, which again is not sufficiently recognized in the literature. The ability of firms to enact pay policies, as intended, varies manifestly between firms and even within the same firm. A key finding of the research, and one overlooked by theory, is the importance of *how* the case study companies approach the management of strategic pay systems. A key distinction, covered in more detail in subsequent sections, is the degree to which pay determination is centralized or devolved. In all cases, however, whether centralized or devolved, local business unit leaders grapple with the complexity and challenges seemingly inherent within the pay determination process and attempt to make centrally imposed pay policies 'work' (Figure 8.2).

At the heart of strategic conceptions of pay (and HRM) is the value chain illustrated in the literature review. The problematic linkage between practice and outcomes, identified in the literature, remains a key challenge to standard theory. However, the findings illustrate clearly that the linkage between strategy and realized practice is also

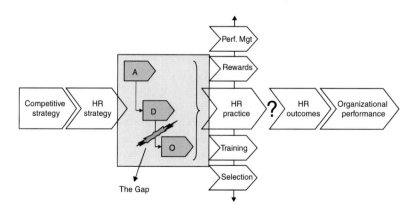

Figure 8.2   The revised value chain and the gap between strategy and execution

inherently problematic – an issue largely neglected by standard theory. All classical conceptions of strategic management assume that intent translates directly into action (Wright and Nishii, 2004; Whittington, 1997). The findings illustrate clearly, however, the pervasiveness of the gap between pay strategy, policy and execution in a number of the case study companies. The implication is that, irrespective of strategic desire or the saliency of the design, ineffectual execution results in ineffectual pay practice, which then impacts negatively upon the pay outcomes experienced as a result. While mainstream studies continue to investigate the nature of the relationship between practice and performance (illustrated in Figure 8.2 by the grey question mark), such studies are moot if 'realised' pay practice differs from the 'espoused' (Mintzberg, 1978). The neglect of the gap between strategy and execution is therefore a critical weakness of strategic theories of pay.

The multi-level review of practice and the exploratory nature of the research affords us this perspective where traditional methods would not, merely capturing perceptions of practice effectiveness from one stakeholder group (the pay function, for example) and not all. What firms believe that they do corporately is shown, in four of the seven cases, to be far from the reality as it is perceived operationally within front line business units. Thus, firms aspire to use pay strategically (approach), and design elaborate systems in order to fulfil that aspiration (design), but fail to realize the ambition because of difficulties encountered at the point of execution, and those systems are not implemented as intended (operation).

> It's entirely counterproductive. We are a classic case study of how *not* to do it at the moment, absolutely classic.
>
> (senior general manager, company4)

This distinction between intended and actual practice is largely omitted from strategic management literature. Very little of the research underpinning standard theories of strategic pay recognize that 'not all intended HR practices are actually implemented, and those that are may often be implemented in ways that differ from the initial intention' (Wright and Nishii, 2004), and the findings clearly lend support to this. Despite rational planning at the design stage, selected pay systems are rarely perfectly applied or enacted by those charged with implementation – typically line management – for a variety of reasons, which are elaborated in later sections. In the language of Gerhart and Rynes (2003), functional pay strategies are neither successfully implemented nor executed.

If you're asking a load of reward people, you might get a different answer from the people who are actually dishing it to people day to day, the line managers. And, therefore, that kind of link is something we've pushed a bit harder in the surveys as far as we can, just to start trying to find out how do people perceive that link, are the line implementing the policies as planned, and so on.

(professional association representative)

The strategic pay literature reviewed in Chapter 2 noted that standard theory assumes implicitly that management is collectively united in intent in the interests of achieving shared goals – economic maximization. It assumes consensus within the management function in relations to goals, expected and desired outcomes, and the methods by which these outcomes are best achieved. The case study-based evidence would lead one to question whether this is indeed true. In place of unitarism, pluralism of interest characterizes not only the relationship between employer and employees, but also between the managerial stakeholder groups involved at the various levels and stages of the pay determination process (Fox, 1971; Kochan et al., 1986).

Using the multi-level framework of pay practice approach, design and operation, it is possible to discern multiple rationales influencing the formation of pay practice. Each distinct stakeholder group involved in the pay determination process (the pay function, for example) holds differing expectations of the ideal role, contribution and form of pay practice. Moreover, each stakeholder group is responsible for shaping the practice when they encounter it, and take ownership of it, which is at different stages of the process and at different levels – for instance, line management is primarily involved at the implementation stage and not design. Thus, the managerial group most involved in any given level bears the greatest influence on the desired and expected outcomes.

At the level of approach, the desire for *alignment* is the key rationale driving the use of pay practice. The stakeholder population primarily involved in the determination of the pay approach is senior management, assisted by external expert help in the form of advisers, professional services and consultants. Alignment is the primary rationale because, it is perceived, it is through alignment that the business need for the maximization of financial outcomes will be best achieved. Accordingly, the practice approach consists of, primarily, aspirational values that senior management feel serve best to align the organization with the interests of shareholders, such as a performance-based culture promoted through performance-based individual pay.

At the level of design, both *legitimacy* and personal *credibility* become key drivers of the determination of the pay design. The pay function, assisted by external experts, design pay practices they feel best align with the espoused pay approach. In theory at least, this act of compliance ensures that pay policies, in technical content and form, fulfil the aspirations set forth in the pay approach and support the overall strategic direction of the organization.

However, while alignment clearly influences the pay design, the need to establish both functional legitimacy and the personal credibility of those within the pay function also serves to influence the shape and formation of pay practice at the level of design. In the interests of establishing legitimacy, and in doing so satisfying professional need, those that design pay practices extensively (a) reference the practices of peer companies; (b) use external consultants and advisers; (c) participate in industry peer groups, and share company practice; and (d) engage with the research community. In a related vein, the need to either establish, promote or maintain personal credibility within the organization renders those within the function especially prone to the influence of external fashions and fads. Furthermore, the desire for professional status and personal credibility may, the findings indicate, encourage pay function staff to seek to mollify and please the many 'customers' of the function. In place of designing pay systems and practices that best fulfil the needs of the organization, as they are understood by those that prescribe the approach and those that construct the design, the temptation is to furnish the business (line managers) with what is vocally stated as acceptable and desired.

Indeed, a weak pay function is constrained explicitly by what the business (line management) state they will accept and, implicitly, what might prove popular and status-enhancing. As a result of this perceived need to establish and/or consolidate personal status within the organization, the pay function may seek to satisfy their peers internally, and engineer pay policies to that end. This is not necessarily a conscious or articulated intention, indeed almost certainly not in the context of the case study company findings, but one might expect it to be a feature of a weak function in search of professional legitimacy and personal credibility. At the level of design, the rationale is, primarily, if not explicitly, centred on satisfying professional and personal need, and not the business need. There is thus an opportunity for a natural disconnection between the practice approach and the practice design because of differing managerial motivations. The outcome of such a disconnection is a design that does not 'fit' the espoused values and philosophy of the practice approach, which renders the approach both abstract and redundant, with the aspirations of senior management ultimately frustrated.

> Within the remuneration function, probably by the way your peers in other remuneration functions react ... in other companies ... I think it just reflects the professional expertise, professional pride I think that there is about doing remuneration well. That is not necessarily a test of how well it serves the organization's purpose at all.
>
> (country reward manager, company7)

At the level of operation, the desire for *equity* is the key managerial interest driving the management of pay. Generalist line management, supported in some cases by line HR, but not all, are expected to enact the intended pay design and continuously improve the pay practice in the long term to reflect the changing business. Enactment requires the line manager to balance the introduction of new pay practice(s) in a way that is congruent with the intended design *and*, necessarily, the local operating environment. As the findings indicate, line management interpret differently how pay policy is enacted most effectively within the context of local operations, and with the least amount of disruption. However, the introduction of a new pay system is rarely without disruption or controversy, pay being a highly emotive subject, and any change being viewed potentially as a threat to the established status quo.

> It goes off into loads of different directions because whether these are linear or not, they all exist and they will exist whether they're aligned or whether they're joined up, and whether they're positive they will still exist. What you're trying to do is find a way of lining them up and making them causative. I defy anybody to do that because I suspect the line manager is a fixture here. He will be managing his team while the strategists and the designers are long gone but he knows that and he will continue to manage.
>
> (country reward manager, company7)

In a number of the cases, but especially company5, at the operational level and when required to comply with the introduction of a new pay system, it was evident that local line management were driven mostly by the desire to maintain equity, despite changes to pay, and, in doing so, promote harmony and limit conflict. In the interests of keeping disruption to a minimum and promoting workplace harmony and stability, line managers sought to promote practice conformity to local pay norms. These pay norms typically include expectations of levels of pay and the pay systems by which employees are remunerated (such as bonus schemes) and the degree to which those systems are perceived as fair and equitable. Thus, the enactment of the intended design is subverted purposefully by line management, as illustrated in a number of the case study companies, in the interests of ensuring workplace harmony.

> I think the intent when this was done was quite clear. I think for a whole variety of reasons, and they are primarily, you know, sometimes people's rather malicious desire to interpret things differently, but because of a lot of these things, that's not what we ended up with.
>
> (senior reward director, company7)

Such a multi-level perspective is not without resonance in existing commentary. When reviewing a strategic choice perspective on industrial relations, Kochan et al. (1986) divide the activities of management, unions and government into three tiers, including '(1) a top tier of strategic decision making; (2) a middle, functional tier, of collective bargaining or personnel policy making; and (3) a bottom, or workplace level tier where policies are played out and affect individual workers, supervisors, and union representatives on a day to day basis' (ibid.). The three tiers correspond broadly to the three levels of practice used in the framework for this study – approach, design and operation. Practice approach at tier (1) involves both high-level decision making and the formulation of an overall strategy. Practice design at tier (2) is more policy orientated than strategic, involving the designation of appropriate reward systems/industrial relations systems: 'the middle tier [tier number 2] encompasses the most traditional terrain of industrial relations, since it focuses on the practice of collective bargaining and personnel policy formulation' (ibid.). Practice operation, and tier number 3, is orientated around the day-to-day implementation of industrial relations/HR policy at the level of the workplace, by generalist line management, supervisory staff and employee representatives.

Pay systems, especially those that are centrally determined, are in a number of cases substantially adapted, rejected or subverted by line management in favour of maintaining the status quo, or adopting an alternative system, either known or unbeknown to the pay function. Indeed, the findings are replete with examples of emergent operational pay practice that to varying degrees is discordant with the espoused principles of the pay approach in each of the case study companies. A number of the large, well-resourced, high-performing and prestigious multinational companies comprising the case study sample do not achieve, operationally, what is both desired strategically and intended as policy in pay terms. Pay is non-strategic operationally. Nor are the outcomes of attempts to use pay strategically manifest in the value-added performance terms of standard theory. Outcomes, positive, neutral and negative, are often not obvious except, perhaps, in retrospect. Even then, the benefits of strategic pay systems are often greatly outweighed by the perceived disadvantages encountered, many of which have long-term and lasting effect – employee retention, for example. It is alternative management practice, at the interface between the manager and the managed (line manager and employee, in effect), that seems to matter most and, in particular, strong leadership. Far from adding value, pay is often perceived as a barrier to effective local leadership because it compromises the ability of line management to manage their staff as they otherwise would.

Despite the nihilistic tone of the findings thus far, there are some manifest positive outcomes of the pay systems used within the case study companies. Like 'old pay', strategic 'new pay' remains an important element of the ability of the case study companies to attract and retain valued talent. While it is only emphasized formally by one case study firm, company6, all the case study companies aspire to present themselves as 'employers of choice' and view the recruitment of high-calibre employees as a vital element of company performance and competitive advantage. The degree to which all firms extensively benchmark against the external labour market, in the interest of competitiveness, is evidence of this. Pay is also a powerful tool for communicating what is valued by senior management to employees and serves to promote a sense of shared culture that is valued by line management and employees. Strategic pay, especially in company2 and company1, *supports* non-pay managerial measures.

Less publicized are the benefits of financial flexibility and risk sharing that the use of broad-based company-linked incentives confer upon the organization. The driver for adopting pay interventions such as incentives remains, in rhetoric at least, the desire to establish a line of sight between employee performance and reward for motivational purposes, as prescribed within the literature. The discreet benefits of enhanced financial flexibility and reduced risk are also recognized as important corporately, however.

I think it's ... if I'm being completely honest, I think it's the latter [for the purposes of attraction and retention]. I think there are reasons ... there are other reasons, business reasons, why I would want to pay bonuses. One being I would not, if I think we're being competitive, because you can go at this two ways, you could up your base, and take out your incentives. Companies have done this. And therefore you know, you're not worried about it year in year out. The trouble I have with that is that you've artificially raised your fixed costs. But it also allows you to have a cost structure that is variable with your business results. So the business side of me says, of course I'd want a bonus structure, because it's more effective in terms of our ability to pay when things aren't going so well, and to pay more when things are going great.

(global rewards director, company5)

As with other cases, the use of broad-based, company performance linked incentives in company5 is not purely, or even primarily, to derive greater value from the firm's human capital, but to introduce financial flexibility into a rigid, and traditionally fixed cost structure that is a risk in times of poor company performance. In this sense, pay does achieve its objective, but the objective was not primarily 'value adding' in the strategic sense. While financial flexibility is of obvious benefit to the firm, using incentive systems as a means to divest the firm of fixed costs and thereby place the risk upon employees, it is not without consequences as, in addition to other unintended consequences, the following sections illustrate.

The risk of centralizing pay determination

A key theme running throughout all levels of the findings is the convergence of pay practice between the case study companies. Such convergence might be considered, prima facie, further empirical support for the notion of best pay practices around which firms are conforming purposefully. At the firm level of the findings, this assertion might be justified on the grounds that all of the case study companies are market-leading and employ the same pay practices. The convergence may also reflect, in part, the contingent nature of pay practice upon contextual factors such as employee base, industry, company size and company stage in the life cycle, emphasizing the importance of context. All of the case study companies are similar in this broad respect.

It is argued here, however, that there is a level of complexity not encompassed by explanations of best practice alone. There are numerous examples from the case study company findings of divergence between the intended pay design (policy) and achieved pay operation (practice). Pay practice varies both *within* the case study companies (for example, between business units) operationally, and *between* the case study companies overall, despite their shared pay practice aspirations and policy intentions. There is, as a result, an acute convergence of companies' approaches to pay, but significant variation of actual pay practice because what is intended is not always what is achieved operationally. Irrespective of strategic intent or desire, a good deal of operational pay practice is, as the findings indicate, emergent – perhaps inevitably.

The centralization of pay determination is an emerging trend within the case study firms with implications for pay trends more broadly. The findings would suggest that the greater the degree of centralized pay determination, the greater the likelihood of unintended consequences. Similarly, the greater the degree of decentralization in pay determination, the greater the likelihood that operationalized pay practice is *emergent* from a corporate perspective, being locally determined and not the result of centralist prescription in the form of formal policy.

Each case study firm represents a degree of centralized pay determination upon the continuum between centralization and decentralization, and between intended versus unintended consequences. Emergent practice is not mutually exclusive with unintended consequences, emergent practice itself being something, especially in the case of company5, that is considered undesirable and unintended. However, in the case of company1 and company2, emergent practice is recognized as necessary – or inevitable – from a corporate perspective – indeed even desirable – as long as it is within the parameters of the guiding framework established within the pay approach and communicated in the form of pay strategy. In the case of company3, where, again, pay determination is largely decentralized, the lack of communication regarding the pay approach, and its failure, therefore, to act as a guiding framework for the determination of pay with local business units, results in the emergence of practice that is considered undesirable by those at the centre. As a result of being discreet, the pay approach fails to inform pay determination operationally.

The qualitative findings point to a relationship between the degree to which pay practice is centrally determined, and the degree to which pay system outcomes are unintended. In the majority of the case study firms, where pay is by decree determined centrally, the resultant pay systems do not achieve operationally what is intended. In addition, negative outcomes are also in evidence, with the case study firm with the greatest degree of centrally determined pay, company5, experiencing the greatest number and severity of negative pay outcomes, such as employee disengagement, employee turnover and misdirected behaviours.

Where pay determination is largely decentralized, the findings suggest that from a corporate perspective pay practice is largely emergent, being locally determined and informed primarily by local and not corporate contextual conditions, managerial objectives and local management capabilities. In all cases of decentralized pay determination, pay is used as a supporting measure complementing local leadership and people management. Such a use of pay is an interpretation of the espoused pay approach, but not one that is of concern to those responsible for the determination of pay at that level (senior management, for example), and reflects an ethos of pay contrary to that of those firms attempting to prescribe pay practice regionally and corporately.

Significantly, no one case study firm attempting to prescribe pay practice regionally or corporately achieved pay system execution, or pay system outcomes, operationally that were intended. Moreover, as a result of attempting to manage pay systems centrally, a range of negative outcomes were experienced. Quite simply, the greater the degree of centralization of pay determination, the greater the likelihood of pay system ineffectiveness, when judged by the terms of the espoused approach, intended design and negative outcomes experienced. Those firms attempting to use pay strategically, through central planning and coordination, experience the greatest number of negative outcomes, with pay being responsible for employee disengagement, demotivation, misdirected behaviours and other negative outcomes. Might other factors be responsible? Undoubtedly. However, controlling for all the factors that might result in unintended consequences and negative outcomes is beyond the gift of this study. The evidence points clearly, however, in each of the cases, to the centralization of pay decision making, and to a lesser extent administration, as being highly significant.

A key question is why are the case study firms experiencing these outcomes? Why does the experience of the case study firms seemingly suggest that strategic pay systems *cannot* be centrally determined and achieve both what is intended and, in turn, what is desired strategically? What is intended as the pay design is achieved in those firms where pay determination is largely decentralized, company1 and company2 in particular, but arguably their aspirations in pay practice terms are more modest than in those firms where pay determination is centralized. Indeed, are company1 and company2 attempting to use pay strategically in the same terms as the other case study companies? They espouse the same values and broadly desire the same outcomes, and exhibit similar profiles of pay practice such as the use of variable pay systems, but their approach to the management of those same pay systems is that much more democratic. Operationally, pay is not perceived by line management as a strategic intervention but rather an important element of the overall employee proposition, and is more akin to the 'old pay' approaches rather than 'new pay'. Thus far, the findings portray a somewhat pessimistic perspective of pay practice in reality, one that does not sit well with prescriptive theory and practice.

The unintended consequences of attempting to use pay strategically

Given that the centralization of pay decisions increases the likelihood of unintended consequences, what are the risks of attempts to use pay strategically? As noted, the unintended consequences experienced are often negative, yielding outcomes that are the opposite of what was desired strategically and intended as policy. Strategic pay systems, in those instances, are not merely ineffectual in realizing outcomes of strategic value, but damaging. As illustrated in the previous chapter, obvious examples of negative outcomes include instances where mismanaged incentives either resulted in employee disengagement or incentivized wrong behaviours. In each instance, the incentives used communicated the wrong message to employees about what was valued by management. More pressingly, they presented employees with unattainable targets and penalized the failure to achieve those targets. Clearly, the mismanagement of incentives, and other forms of performance-based pay, go hand in hand with perceptions of fairness, with implications for employee morale, motivation and ultimately retention.

> And that's the biggest issue, in fact, funnily enough I was just doing one of my 'War and Peace' emails before you called on exactly this subject, which is we have got right now a *huge* morale and retention issue. And it is for the most part related to bonuses, not because people – and I'm going to repeat what I said earlier on – not because people are saying, you know, I was banking on going on a fancy holiday this year, you've [swindled] me out of it, I'm a few thousand pounds down – but because people are effectively formally being told that

collectively they have failed, when actually, I'm damned, in certain areas, where I can't see how we could have done anything else.

(senior general manager, company4)

The case study findings do not support the contention that broad-based performance pay systems promote desirable employee behaviours. Where such behaviours were in evidence, it was perceived to be for reasons other than pay, for example, additional motivational factors such as inspiring leadership. The findings are, however, replete with examples of cases where, when attempting to drive positive behaviours, pay systems have resulted instead in negative behaviours and dysfunctionality.

> You'd find some ... particularly towards the end of the year, one or other senior manager trying to get something done which you were thinking has nothing much to do with me, why does he want all this work done, and you find out by a bit of digging that it's one of his bonus objectives. Well, I'm not getting anything out of this, it's not contributing to my objectives, why am I being bullied and pushed and so on to get this work done so that somebody else can collect their bonus.
>
> (rewards practitioner, company1)

In the case of company3, the designation of targets at a regional level, and the configuration of pay systems locally around the achievement of those targets, results in a number of undesirable behaviours at the individual market level. The regionally determined targets, within the context of local market conditions, are relatively unachievable as they do not take into account changes within the local market, such as environmental disasters, nor are they sensitive to market challenges beyond the control of incentivized staff. Specifically concerning the South American company3 operation, the regional sales and profit target setting, and the lack of clear sales channels at border distributors and wholesalers, results in the Mexican sales staff competing directly for market share with other company3 sales forces in surrounding countries. As a consequence, each country representing company3 within the region is forced into price competition with each other, in addition to external competition, with the result that revenue and profit targets (especially the latter) are reduced. Sales staff are incentivized to behave in such a way but, in turn, are negatively impacted as they are penalized financially for their relative inability to meet increasingly unrealistic performance targets – targets that have been determined centrally. Moreover, the absence of a clearly articulated pay approach means that both managers and staff fail to understand clearly the rationale for the pay systems deployed. However, this experience of incentives was not confined purely to company3:

> I would say we've got a real mixed bag. I would say 50 per cent of the time they are genuine incentives, we've got it right, we've got the incentive whether it be behaviour or result lined up, and people are actually thinking, yeah, you know what, I can actually see if I do this, do that and do the other, I'm really going to earn that this year, get highly motivated. Other people look at it and say, 'Boy, they've got it wrong, I can't do any of these things, so I'm just switched off, I get what I get at the end of the year.'
>
> (senior operational manager, company4)

Negative outcomes resulting from the use of strategic pay systems are not purely confined to unintended *behavioural* consequences – employee disengagement, demotivation and misdirected behaviours. The introduction and operation of strategic pay systems, especially those that are performance-based, require a large degree of managerial input and were, in all cases, viewed as highly labour intensive both for those managed and managers. Base pay progression and annual incentives are, in all cases, linked to performance management outcomes that require inputs in the form of the assessment of employee performance against annual personal and team objectives. The formal processes of performance management used in all cases are elaborate systems of measurement and are highly labour intensive, requiring considerable preparation by both employees and management.

> Well, the risk I think is the distraction from the business, the amount of time you have to spend doing it. So, to just very briefly explain some of what we're doing, in the past you would do objectives at the beginning of the year, you'd do two, three, four reviews during the year ... what's the word I want, um, not obligatory, what's the word, discretionary ... discretionary. So, I mean it's taken me an hour's meeting with each of them to go through it, and I have a tiny, tiny team of four people. Imagine if you've got a team of 20? And that worries me.
>
> (reward director, company4)

Moreover, while linked to annual pay awards, in all cases, such assessment exercises can take place more frequently throughout the year, even on a quarterly basis. Performance management is not simply based on measures of productivity, but also measures of technical and behavioural competence within the role, requiring a subjective assessment according to predefined, but broad, criteria. The volume of work required to provide meaningful and robust assessments of performance means that, potentially, a great deal of managerial resource is consumed.

An additional negative outcome of attempts to use pay strategically is reputational risk for the pay function in terms of its perceived role, value and status and, accordingly, its ability to fulfil the mandate expected of it by senior management. Strategic theories of employment, pay and HRM generally all stress the importance of a strategic component in the traditional reactionary and administrative role of the employment function. Ulrich's typologies (1997) of the SHRM function – strategic partner, change agent, employee champion and administrative expert – all stress the strategic contribution of the function to company performance. In attempting to promote the use of pay strategically, the pay function has to itself act strategically.

The difficulties encountered by human resource functions within firms when attempting to fulfil the prescribed strategic role are well documented (Sisson, 1995; Truss et al., 1997). Clearly, as much as there is an imperative to use pay strategically, and for the function to act strategically, neither is accepted necessarily by the organization. One explanation for this may involve the nature of the endeavour itself. Value derived from human resources is notoriously hard to define and equally hard to measure, as noted (Fitz-Enz, 2000). In standard accounting terms, the contribution of the HR function (pay function included) is especially hard to quantify and express as a financial return. Pay spend, when viewed as a strategic investment, is especially problematic but remains a core criterion by which the value of corporate activities is measured to the detriment, largely, of the function and its status. While the 'value-add' of the function is difficult to establish in non-qualitative terms, the costs of HR and pay interventions are readily apparent and more easily expressed in standard accounting terms. The relative inability of the function to illustrate numerically its value and its role combined, therefore, leads to it being perceived poorly.

I was very rude to the HR guys about the whole performance management objective setting process, because I basically said to them, 'Your objective, being polite, is "roll out performance management across Europe" in inverted commas. Mine is "take the biggest loss-making business we've got globally and fix it". Okay, who's got the harder objective?' And they just kind of looked at me and said, 'What's your point?' – at which point it just proved everything I've ever thought about HR people.

(senior general manager, company4)

A consistent theme running throughout the interviews with non-pay functional management and employees was the lack of understanding of the contribution of the pay function. The function and functional activities were commonly perceived as 'overheads' and not sources of value creation. For all of the case study firms, like the majority of both private and public service-based organizations, the cost of employing labour – wage costs – constitutes the single greatest operating cost. As a consequence, cost minimization, in the absence of more relevant and robust measures, is used to measure the effectiveness of the pay functions in each of the case study firms. Costs, and not the return on investment (ROI) on valued-added strategic interventions, are clearly a source of tension, as pay function staff are measured against costs and not value added, although the latter is the purported contribution of their role. Such challenges to the role of the function are exacerbated by the perceived ineffectiveness of the interventions for which they are viewed as being responsible. In this respect, the findings of this study are an important contribution to the debate on the status of the HR function. If ineffective operationally, pay systems not only produce negative outcomes, such as placing a burden upon line management for which the pay function will be viewed as responsible, but pay strategies themselves become marginalized as mere rhetoric and are not regarded as a strategic endeavour to be taken seriously.

The problem is that people keep taking reward in isolation ... reward is the bit that everyone loves to hate, because, they will always blame it for whatever. Even if someone who's very highly paid leaves, it's because we didn't ... we couldn't give them more. I'd have given them more if I had more budget. It was the reward system that stopped me. If our bonuses had paid out last year, we'd have kept all these people. They didn't pay out because ... we didn't deliver. And an interesting thing is that actually reward just reflects some of the business philosophies, or the business 'health'.

(senior reward director, company4)

In those cases where pay is largely decentralized, the function is necessarily low profile as a result of the devolved locus of pay determination.

The formal pay function fulfils an advisory role in the three cases where headquarters provide good practice guidance on upholding minimum (governance) standards, but do so on a 'light touch' basis. This involvement is limited, however, and relies upon line management approaching the pay function for assistance in the first instance. Thus, the involvement of the pay function is limited by the degree to which their input is perceived as valuable by those who manage. From the perspective of the line units, especially in the cases of company1 and company2, the central pay function is seen as distant, and its role and potential contribution ambiguous. Consequently, the demand for pay-related 'advice', and the degree to which devolved pay determination benefits from the critical mass of pay system experience and technical knowledge, is debatable.

> I would say for probably 70 per cent of our organization, HR is still just seen as an administrative support.
>
> (HR function practitioner, company5)

What becomes realized as effective pay practice operationally is, in part, contingent upon the degree to which the central pay function, operating in each of the case study firms, is able to position itself as a valuable resource to be used in the pay determination process; and the degree to which those who manage deign to use that resource. It is, however, those cases where pay system determination is centralized where the findings would suggest there is the greatest degree of potential reputational risk for the pay function.

> I think there are individuals within HR who are very highly regarded. I think as a generalism, HR is regarded as being very old-fashioned, very much the kind of gatekeepers of policy ... policy police and gatekeepers as well. So they police policy, we kind of own the keys to all sorts of salary adjustments, company cars, and so on. I think we're seen as being too bureaucratic, I think we're seen as being top heavy in terms of too many senior people, you know, too many chiefs and not enough Indians, and I think we're seen as being relatively ineffective. Now, there are lots of reasons as to why that is, but I think that people tend to, when they comment on HR, they tend to say, 'Well, there are some individuals who do a fantastic job as individuals, but it's more to do with them as individuals than the fact that they're part of HR.' So as a general function, we don't win a lot of praise.
>
> (line unit HR manager, company4)

Given the findings of the case studies, has the nature and role of the pay function (those responsible for pay) changed dramatically as a result of the companies' attempts to use pay strategically? It is undeniable that pay functions within the case study companies aspire to occupy a strategic role and have organized the function accordingly. What is less clear is the degree to which they have succeeded in adopting this role in practice. They are often not perceived by line management within the case study companies as a strategic function with a value-creating contribution, and the legacy of a reactive administrative function persists that consumes value in the form of unnecessary overheads.

The value of 'not getting it wrong'

In light of the findings, is it worthwhile thinking afresh about the relation of pay and value? Is it reasonable to continue to presume, on the basis of the evidence of standard theory that is perhaps less rounded than that presented here, that pay is something companies can get right and, in doing so, benefit from in terms of company performance and sustained competitive advantage?

> Well, you never do [know you have it right], because ... is the simple answer. Because the world keeps changing, people keep changing, people's expectations keep changing. I don't think you ever do know that and you can't make an absolute science out of this, you know, at the end of the day, we manage people, and I say there is no science in doing that.
>
> (senior operational manager, company4)

> But it is something that's hard to ... it will always be something that ... it's always going to be something that's hard to quantify. It does sometimes come down to ... you can quantify it in HR statistics about retention, about leaders, about sort of how many people are performing and you can do all that. But to c-o-n-c-r-e-t-e-l-y say it's being successful, it can really only come down to whether we're doing this or that. There again there are other variables. It is a really hard one.
>
> (corporate rewards manager, company1)

Is it just a case of not having sufficiently sophisticated measures of the effectiveness of pay systems? The evidence is that it is something more fundamental to the nature of the endeavour itself.

Have we always got to be changing, can we ever win? No, we can never win, because it is always changing, and we will hear that, you know, one sector went off and did something completely different. And so we've got to bring them back into the fold, literally. Or, that somebody else did it, but did it very reluctantly, so we've got to go back out and train again, or whatever. And the trouble I have with it is to stay positive long enough. I can be enthusiastic and positive for a bit, and then I go, 'Why do I bother?' and you kind of give up after a while.

(reward director, company4)

Such statements suggest that effective pay is less about getting pay right than about not getting it wrong. The penalties for getting pay wrong are acute and manifest themselves in a way that positive linkages between pay practice and company performance do not. As an outcome, conflict is immediate and obvious and does not abate without resolution or reconciliation achieved through careful management. This brings us to a point where perhaps a redefinition of performance, and the relationship between pay and company performance, is required.

If a redefinition of the contribution of pay to company performance is required, being seemingly not a value-adding activity that rational decision makers acting strategically should attempt to optimize (get right), but rather an activity that is very much easier to get wrong and, thereby, destroy value, what does *not getting it wrong* look like? A key assumption of the standard literature is that there is a tangible causal link between practice and performance. The evidence itself would presumably take the form of consistently enhanced financial performance of companies using pay and other HR interventions over those that do not, all things being equal.

I'm fond of using the plumbing analogy: when was the last time you thought about the plumbing in your house? It was when the sink got blocked. You didn't think about it before then. You didn't think about it afterwards. When it stopped working, the smell came, you were suddenly very concerned with the plumbing. When it's working properly you don't give it a moment's thought.

(rewards practitioner, company1)

This remark, indicative of many remarks expressed by others, tells us something perhaps of the true nature of pay and how it is viewed in practical terms within the context of ongoing, day-to-day operations of the complex case study companies. The findings indicate that pay is not an activity at the forefront of corporate strategy, nor is it something that managers attempt to manage proactively. Rather, it is something that requires tactical, reactionary intervention when it goes wrong. The emphasis is on tactical and not strategic attention, requiring reactive and not proactive management, which is characteristic of 'old pay' rather than 'new pay'. Moreover, when effective, pay is not something that delivers tangible and demonstrable returns, unlike many other 'value adding' activities.

> Oh God ... I think because you don't [know if it is right] ... because you don't even notice it. Nobody notices it, nobody talks about it, because this is an area when the pendulum is wrong, it causes friction and tension, and so I think it's the *absence* of something that you know you've got in the right place, to be honest. I know that's not very ... strategic!
>
> (senior HR practitioner, company6)

Why is this so? Getting pay right is clearly inherently problematic given that firms universally struggle to do so. Is it perhaps because, as suggested earlier, the reality of the utility of pay is not what we might be led to believe it is by standard theory? When well managed, pay seemingly removes many of the obstacles to value creation, acting as an enabler, but the evidence would suggest it is not a source of value creation in itself. Pay merely 'greases the wheels', as one interviewee remarked. This conceptual misalignment of orthodox theories of pay taps into the very heart of a wide-ranging and important debate about the nature of HRM, its role and its contribution to the success or failure of the firm.

Strategic pay and the troublesome relationship with value

Does pay matter at all, then, from a strategic perspective? Orthodox strategic theories of pay, like classical or rational actor accounts of strategic management, assume a linear relationship between strategy and strategic decisions, as independent variables, upon which company performance, the dependent variable, is contingent. The critical reflections on the strategic orthodoxy highlighted in the literature review point to possible failings in the way in which strategy, performance and the relationship between the two are conceptualized. No study has yet conclusively established the causal relationship between strategy and performance, despite progressive attempts to unpack the 'black box'

(Becker and Huselid, 1998). The findings presented here do not, as one might have predicted (and positivist commentators might argue could not because of the choice of methods) confirm any sort of relationship between the attempts of case study companies to use pay strategically and case study company performance.

This study did not set out to establish any such linkage, however. The case study sample was selected purposefully on the basis of their superior financial performance in comparison to the industry average. Exploring the use of pay within case study companies, selected on the basis of their 'dependent variable' (company financial performance), shifted the emphasis of the study away from the typical approach of establishing correlations between company practice and company performance. Superficially, such a correlation does indeed exist. All firms are financially successful by the standard definitions of company performance. All are market-leading and all aspire both to use pay strategically and deploy specific forms of pay interventions, considered as best practice by strategic pay theorists, to those ends. However, the findings go beyond such a superficial relationship and expose a complex set of processes, determinants and outcomes that ultimately influence the shape and formation of pay practice at different levels throughout the firm that would challenge the notion of such a causal relationship. More pressingly, the experiences of the practice of pay within the case study companies would, in direct contrast with strategic theories of pay, cast doubt over the value-adding capacity of pay.

> So you do see organizations at the top level cascading down to the first couple of levels and really trying to align the shareholder, the business objective with compensation. You can see that and you see companies maybe doing more of it than they would have done in the past, but that might not. ... I'm not even sure that that's entirely true. If you look down into employee compensation, I see very little evidence that that really is making a difference.
>
> (remuneration consultant)

Pay in the case study firms is universally viewed as important, but it is not, as opinion would suggest, the source of value creation purported by strategic pay advocates. Representative of a wide cross-section of opinion, such a remark is indicative of practitioner expectations of pay. However, the pay outcomes within the case study companies are not universally positive, nor are they the outcomes desired, nor even those intended.

I don't wholly subscribe to it. I think it's very important that your reward initiatives *support* the other initiatives that the company is trying to do, and don't get in the way of it.

(rewards practitioner, company1)

Initiatives can, however, often be negative and serve to diminish value and/or be a barrier to those organizational activities that do fulfil the value-adding role, for example informal managerial interventions, such as inspirational leadership, challenging work, communication and aspects of people management.

I think non-alignment is obviously not hygienic. Alignment is hygienic. It would really be silly to say what we see as important is customer service and all your reward is based on cost. That is non-alignment, but having alignment I don't think will necessarily drive that forward to the same extent as other management practices would do.

(country reward manager, company7)

Where pay is deemed to work well, it is when it has been integrated closely with other interventions, such as careers, communication and so on, and used as an *enabler* of these interventions and not as a primary source of value creation itself.

Does pay drive performance? No. It doesn't. I truly believe that all that reward does is act as an enabler, so I don't really believe blissfully that it drives performance. The way that it can be an enabler as enhanced performance is by the combination of a tidily designed plan, which I'll talk to in a minute, and great communication and great management, using it as an effective tool to make the management communication more effective by having something riding on it.

(senior reward director, company3)

Why, then, do we have the expectation that pay can, and should, deliver value-adding outcomes and can do so largely as a standalone intervention? It may be that the pervasive evidence upon which such assertions are based, outlined in the literature review, developed through precisely those large cross-sectional, co-relational studies that attempt to isolate independent variables, such as HR practices, in order to assess their effect on individual dependent variables. Again, it is perhaps our conceptions of strategy, practice, performance and linear relationships between those variables that are promoting a frame of reference out of kilter with the diffuse, complex and often opaque reality of pay determination in practice. As such, the findings do not confirm any such positive relationship, but challenge it and suggest further that pay is not a source of value creation but rather a risk with the potential, if managed poorly, to diminish and destroy value rather than creating it.

> I think it can be a terrible brake, I don't think it can be a terribly good accelerator.
>
> (rewards practitioner, company1)

In light of the findings, then, should firms be attempting to use pay strategically, given that the evidence would suggest that it cannot be so used? Or maybe, pay can be used to achieve some outcomes that are felt to be of strategic value to the firm, namely attraction and retention of desired labour, contributing towards the creation of a positive working culture and so on, but realistically not for the purpose of driving performance through enhanced productivity and behaviours. Attempts to achieve the latter are destined to potentially end in failure, with serious consequences, ultimately, for the continued motivation, engagement and behaviours of staff. Is it the case, then, at this juncture, and on the basis of what we have learnt from our experiences of attempting to use pay strategically over the past decade, that we need to rescale our expectations of what pay can achieve organizationally? Pay does not do what it is supposed to do because it is unrealistic to expect it to do so. Are we at the tipping point of another reform to the use and management of pay of a similar magnitude to that witnessed with the boisterous emergence of strategic theories of pay? If so, what can and should practitioners do differently as a result, given that reform will have to be, in the absence of once-purposeful societal groups such as trade unions, largely managerially driven? Given the findings, it is perhaps incumbent upon practitioners to seek widely a shift in the ideology of pay currently and, within their own organizations, to promote a new mode of pay usage and practice that reflects a more realistic set of objectives and deliverables.

> I think that, you know, definitely for us as senior people, senior HR people, it's quite a challenge because it's not, as you and I both know, it's not ... bonuses can't rescue organizations, they can encourage and reinforce behaviours if they're very well designed, and if you've got other things in place like a good performance management system and good education for managers and so on, but, you know, I think

people tend to see it as just if you put something in you get something out, it's like a sausage factory, but it's not that simple.

> (senior rewards practitioner, company1)

This may require an acceptance that pay is not strategic, in the sense advocated by proponents of strategic pay. Neither is pay a source of value creation in and of itself, but rather a powerful supporting activity that acts as an enabler of other organizational activities. While pay may act as a motivator to some degree, it is not the sole motivator, and is arguably less capable of motivating staff towards the achievement of objectives than other measures within the domain of managerial discretion.

No, it isn't [a driver of performance]. It comes low down in the list of things that motivate people. Leadership is up front, which is why the emphasis is on leadership and why the reward system is trying to support the leadership initiatives and ... I can do it from memory, leadership is in there, feeling of belonging, the chance to do something, make a difference, which we get the impression company1 is quite good at, giving people responsibility and some room to get on with it.

> (rewards practitioner, company1)

Neither can pay be used as a crutch for weak leadership, nor should it be a means through which management seek to exert corporate control over increasingly diverse, fragmented and complex global organizations in which innumerable pressures resist any such effort.

The thing that really changes what happens is what we do as leaders. And we tend to use it [pay] as a crutch for leadership. ... I think it's a clumsy attempt to do something which by definition you can't do, and that is to impose culture. I think we're trying to impose cultural change and behavioural change, by setting the bonus scheme to do it, rather than taking on the leadership challenge of changing it.

> (senior general manager, company4)

Above all, it is perhaps most important to abandon, or, at the very least, revise the expectation that pay is something it is incumbent upon strong leadership to 'get right'.

I think you get it as right as you can. You cannot afford to get it wrong.

> (senior reward director, company4)

When you look at companies that have achieved more than they forecast that they would do, compared with companies who only achieve what they forecast they would do, it isn't pay that's made the difference, it's leadership. Pay again is way down the list. So it's back to my plumbing analogy, isn't it? Pay can have a very destructive effect on the business but is not much help in making a positive atmosphere. It certainly is no substitute for all the things that *do* make a positive atmosphere.

(rewards practitioner, company1)

But the research also provides an insight into the changing context in which pay is being used, and is consistent with other empirical studies, which have reviewed pay and HR in practice. Strategic pay, if improperly managed, can be a source of corporate disadvantage (Purcell, 1999). The findings illustrate clearly that firms can get pay wrong, and the implications for company performance and value creation are significant. And yet, despite the negative outcomes highlighted within the findings, the lessons are not captured corporately for the betterment of future pay decisions. Operational experiences of pay, both positive and negative, are for a variety of reasons largely localized.

You get very senior people talking at conferences about what best practice is and what happens in their organization. It bears no relationship to what actually happens.

(country reward manager, company7)

With the exception of crisis situations necessitating corporate intervention and mediation, the 'everyday' experience of pay, as the case study findings indicate, is not easily measured or conferred, and thus rarely ever captured comprehensively at the corporate level. Consequently, the basis upon which future pay decisions are made, and what is understood corporately regarding the effectiveness of pay systems, does not necessarily reflect operational experiences but rather the perceptions of a removed senior management and/or the pay function. There is a rhetoric of pay espoused by the companies that is discordant with the realities of pay in practice.

I mean, you look at these organizations again, you can look at the private sector, the bonus, it's all about, you know, we want to enhance business performance, we want to communicate change, we want to reward high performers. But again I suppose it's to say you do that, they say that they're doing this for these reasons, but actually are they doing it for those particular reasons? We know what they say they do, but do they do what they say? And I suppose that's always an issue, isn't it?

(professional association representative)

At the levels of approach and design, all of the case study firms do use pay strategically. The two levels are, it is argued here, reflections of what is desired strategically (the approach) and what is intended as policy (the design) and not ultimately the reality of pay practice (the operation). As the interviewee referenced earlier asks: are firms doing what they say they do? The findings illustrate a number of instances where case study company pay practice is not what was desired or intended. Companies clearly do not always do what they say they do in relation to pay as a result of the gap. All of the case study companies are market-leading and prestigious in their own right, however, and are cited frequently as examples of pay 'best practice' within the practitioner community. The implication for other firms with similar aspirations is that they might also benefit from following the example of these 'excellent' firms. The value of strategic pay, as it is perceived by those removed from the operational reality, forms a rhetoric that influences others that desire the same.

Is there such a thing as best practice? Well, there is. Is there such a thing as a right model, you know, an absolute correct solution to all of this? I don't know. I suspect not. I mean there's always problems with every solution in this area, because at the end of the day it's people we're dealing with and you cannot make people behave in a certain way at all. So I don't think there is an absolutely right model. I just think we believe that because of the needs of the FMCG market-place, you know, the 'P&G' model seems to have more attraction than the 'Unilever' model.

(senior operational manager, company4)

Such rhetoric takes the form of 'inspiring' stories of corporate success and is propagated through a number of channels by consultancies, peer groups and professional associations. These success stories become, by degree, corporate lore and reflect not the often chaotic reality of strategic pay in practice, but an idealized version, further divorcing the reality of strategic pay from the rhetoric.

Summary

The research has lifted the veil on pay determination within seven market leading multinational FMCG firms and reveals pay practice in stark contrast with the prescriptions of standard theory. All firms have attempted to use pay as a managerial means of achieving the managerial ends of aligning employees' interests to those of the company, encouraging desirable behaviours and attracting and retaining valued talent. Performance-based pay systems are also used implicitly to achieve financial efficiencies and flexibility, which, along with those outcomes already mentioned, standard theory posits will benefit the company through enhanced performance and competitive advantage. The case study companies are all similar in both organizational profile and performance, and deploy, prima facie, the same pay interventions for the same categories and levels of professional, technical and managerial employee. They manage those same pay systems in a variety of different ways, however, and experience significantly different outcomes as a result. Despite convergence around the *types* of pay systems deployed, there is wide divergence between firms regarding *how* and *how well* those same pay systems are managed.

The findings do not confirm that the pay systems used within the case study firms operationally achieve all the strategic outcomes that they are supposed to do. Moreover, it is apparent that all of the cases, to varying degrees based upon their expectations of what pay *should* do, experience profound difficulties when attempting to use pay strategically. There is frequently, in the majority of the case study companies, evidence of a gap between what is intended as pay policy and what is actually achieved operationally as pay practice. Pay is often, operationally, *non-strategic* and thus strategic aspirations go unrealized as a result. This is not necessarily appreciable to senior management, or the pay function, however, and a rhetoric of pay practice may persist that is quite divorced from the operational reality and experience of pay in practice.

Pay remains, clearly, an important component of the ability of the company to attract and retain desired labour; it is a powerful communication tool symbolically conveying the performance and behavioural expectations of the executive to employees; and, by using variable pay extensively based upon company performance, reducing fixed costs of the wage bill and removing what would otherwise be a risk to profitability. Pay, however, is not perceived to be the means by which those outcomes of greatest strategic value are elicited: for example, workforce motivation, productivity, performance and desired behaviours.

Moreover, in attempting to use pay to achieve such outcomes, and if managed improperly, as illustrated in Chapters 5, 6 and 7, a number of negative outcomes may result, ultimately diminishing company performance and destroying value in place of creating it. Experience of case study company practice would suggest that attempting to use pay strategically carries with it a number of risks, not least the possibility that the strategic pay systems deployed achieve largely the opposite of what they are supposed to, and that success, when experienced, results in modest organizational outcomes. Strategic pay systems rarely, if ever, seem to do what they are supposed to do.

The findings raise a number of important questions. The difficulties encountered by the case study companies in managing strategic pay systems effectively is a recurrent theme within the findings. Critically, *why* do strategic pay systems fail to achieve all that they are supposed to in the terms of standard theory?

9
Can Pay Be Strategic?

Fulfilling one of the key aims of this study, the findings present a grounded perspective on strategic pay in practice, one that in many respects is in stark contrast to the prescriptions of standard theory. Pay within the case study companies is universally valued as a managerial tool for securing competitive advantage, through enhanced company performance. To that end, the case study companies all aspire to use pay strategically. All firms deploy pay practices that would be characterized as both strategic and best practice by conventional standards. However, all of the case study companies have encountered significant difficulties when attempting to use strategic pay systems, with the result that they were perceived often as ineffectual and, in operational terms, *nonstrategic*. A key finding of the study is a gap, in a significant number of the case study companies, between what they aspire to do strategically, what they intend as policy and what they achieve operationally as pay practice. As a result, pay systems do not necessarily do what they are supposed to do. Why?

The review of case study company pay practice suggests that it is the ineffective *management* of strategic pay systems that results in the gap observed, with clear implications for the outcomes – positive, neutral and negative – experienced as a result. The implication is that, despite their best attempts, the case study companies are not managing their strategic pay systems effectively, or as standard theory would prescribe. Drawing further upon case study data, this chapter contrasts and compares the reality of pay management in the case study companies with the core assumptions of standard theory and reveals a number of inconsistencies between the two. It is argued here that the assumptions upon which strategic pay theory is based are not sufficiently grounded in the messy reality of pay determination – especially within the context of complex, fast-moving organizations. Alternative theories are suggested that better reflect the reality of case study company pay practice.

The orthodoxy of strategic choice and pay

Espoused theories of strategic pay are all predicated on the notion of *strategic choice*. Choice in the strategic sense involves decision makers selecting those pay strategies and systems that are judged optimal. Opinion is divided about the basis upon which pay practice should be chosen to ensure optimality. Should it represent best practice or should it represent best fit with the company's strategy? Pay determination is, nevertheless, informed by managerial choice. The influence of managerial choice on the shape and formation of pay practice is firmly rooted in the voluntarist tradition of free will and choice free from limitation. Rational actor accounts of strategy, 'rationalists', view leadership as the primary moderator of organizational behaviour (Whittington, 1997). Managers choose pay strategies and dictate a path of action, while removed from the process of implementation. The parallel often drawn is that of a general directing the course of battle from atop a hill, but not personally taking up arms in combat. The presumption is that managerial decree equals corporate action. The organization is in mission, design and performance, because it has been chosen to be so (Gerhart and Milkovich, 1990).

Key for rationalists is the assertion that causal conditions preceding choice (for example, deterministic pressures emanating from the environment) are not, of themselves, sufficient to produce that outcome (de Rond and Thietart, 2004). There exists an array of potential choices, within any given situation, each with merits and disadvantages, and therefore more or less attractive as a result. In the language of the rationalist, the process of differentiating between options is one of preference ordering, and it is the ability to discern that which is most preferable, or optimal, that renders the decision maker as rational. In the context of pay determination, selecting the optimal means of supporting the achievement of corporate goals is using pay strategically (Lawler et al., 1995). The presumption of managerial ability to choose pay strategies and practices that result in predicted positive outcomes is a core belief of the prescriptive literature on strategic pay. Simplistically, the manager, as decision maker, reigns supreme.

In a related vein, de Rond and Thietart (2007) note that the *libertarian* viewpoint on choice and free will is relevant for contemporary strategic management, because it (a) provides a justification for the belief that we have choices available and that we are free to deliberate rationally over our choices; and (b) our beliefs and impulses, which sometimes conflict (when there is incongruence between what we think and feel), would not make sense except for the existence of the gap and the freedom to choose. Similarly, the rationalist viewpoint promotes individuals' responsibilities, and accountability for choices made and actions pursued, precisely because of the ability and freedom to choose. However, if the action determined is beyond the control of the individual, then individuals cannot be truly held accountable for the resultant success or failure, and vice versa. This is consistent with the current emphasis placed upon the contribution of leadership and their accountability for corporate performance. The libertarian viewpoint allows us to: '(a) hold companies and individuals morally responsible for their strategic actions; (b) it helps legitimise deep-seated attitudes (for example, resentment or appreciation); (c) it explains the experience of freedom when deliberating about strategic choices (for example, by assigning relative importance to various reasons for, or against, a particular strategic decision); and (d) it emphasizes the importance of anticipation, or the belief (central to our discipline) that strategic choices have causes as well as consequences' (de Rond and Thietart, 2004).

What does this mean in light of the findings? Have the strategic pay systems in each of the case study companies failed to achieve what they are supposed to do, and worse, because of the poor quality of managerial decisions? Are management, therefore, responsible? Standard theory would affirm that decision makers are accountable, given their rational capacity for strategic choice. However, the findings bring into question the validity of a number of the core assumptions underpinning strategic theories of pay, in particular notions of strategic choice. The following sections of this chapter review critically the core assumptions underpinning strategic pay theory in the context of the findings, and where appropriate, suggest alternative theory more reflective of contemporary pay practice.

Constrained choice and pay

The first challenge to the strategic choice of pay selection is *deterministic* constraints on the scope of managerial discretion. A number of factors serve directly to constrain what managers would otherwise do if they were free of such constraints. In this sense, managerial choice is contingent upon the constraints they face, and there are many constraints as the findings indicate. Firstly, each level of the pay determination process – the approach, the design and the operation – is formed in response to different and distinct contextual properties. The context in which the approach to pay was formed was characterized by primarily external, competitive and institutional pressures, to which senior management were the most prone as they face both industry and economy-wide pressure.

At the level of design, the context of pay determination, as perceived by the pay function, is characterized primarily by institutional 'best practice' norms and internal structures. At the level of operation, the context of pay determination is characterized by internal, structural and institutional pressures. Thus, the three elements of pay are determined in response to different contextual pressures operating at different levels of the company. The properties that comprise the context in which pay is determined are broader than standard theory would suggest. A key finding is the pervasiveness and influence of institutional pressures at all levels of the pay determination process. This will be discussed in later sections of this chapter.

The context in which pay is determined is not therefore the 'closed system' assumed by standard theory, but a fluid *open system* of a variety of contextual properties acting at multiple levels of the company and influencing, profoundly, the outcomes of the pay determination process at the three levels of approach, design and operation. A graphical depiction of the open system of pay determination within the case study companies is illustrated in Figure 9.1. Four categories of pressure are present, including external competitive, external institutional, internal structural

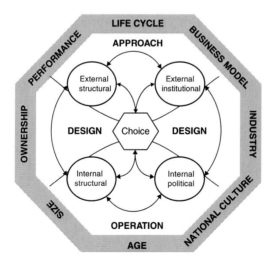

Figure 9.1   The 'open systems' context of pay determination

and internal institutional. The pressures, as shown, all have influence at all levels of the pay determination process, but are more influential at some levels than others. Thus, the context for the determination of pay at the operational level is primarily characterized by internal structural and internal institutional variables pervasive at that level.

The outcomes of the pay determination process (practice) are, therefore, contingent upon the context in which pay determination occurs, which has implications for pay outcomes experienced as a result. This observation finds traction with contingency theory. Contingency theory, as defined, extends to include 'any variable that moderates the effect of an organizational characteristic on organizational performance' (Pugh, 1973). Related to the model above, contingency theory clearly has application because, firstly, there is an explicit association between contingency and organizational structures; secondly, contingency serves to determine the organizational structure, and if an organization changes its contingency, then the structure will change accordingly; thirdly, there are degrees of fit, or congruence, between the organization's structure and contingency variables.

The contextual characteristics of the organization are treated as independent variables upon which the organization's structure is dependent (Lawrence and Lorsch, 1973). The labour employed by the firm has been identified as a 'first order' variable upon which pay system choices are contingent (Gerhart and Milkovich, 1990). The external labour market has come to replace collective bargaining and internal labour markets as the basis upon which pay levels are determined (Brown, 2001). Additional research has addressed this phenomenon directly, and termed it *competitive isomorphism*. The central tenet of competitive isomorphism is that to compete is to conform, and the greater the degree of competitive pressure the greater the degree of conformity (DiMaggio and Powell, 1983).

> No, what I think I'm saying is these companies make their compensation and reward decisions less because of the business strategy and it's more the external factors, you know, the socio ... the labour market compensation benchmarking and what they've done in the past, those factors are I think much more significant than the idea of 'we have a business strategy and a business goal and we will try to align all of our compensation towards this business goal'. (remuneration consultant, consult1)

Other 'variables' such as firm size (Donaldson, 2001), organizational life cycle (Balkin and Gomez-Meija, 1987) and company performance also influence pay system choices. Obvious case study examples of the contingent nature of pay include the effect of the industry in which the firms operate. All the companies encounter similar challenges in relation to technology, raw materials, product demand and pricing (Mahoney, 1979).

> Even if you don't feel you're limiting yourself because of what might be constraints, I mean the reality is you are, aren't you, just by your whole? I think you have to discipline yourself to say what is right, okay? Now that's the right thing to do. Now is that possible? Well, not really and, therefore, where are you going to compromise a bit without losing the whole? If you compromise too far you might as well not change anything. So I think the reality is you're always ... you're always going to be bound to some extent by what is possible.
>
> (senior rewards practitioner, company1)

All of the case study companies are large, complex multinationals employing thousands of employees, at numerous locations throughout the world, fulfilling a variety of functions and tasks. Each represents an extremely complex organizational entity and, arguably, this places severe limits on strategic pay decisions.

> You've got seven different businesses with no synergies, which is their fundamental business problem, how *would* you design reward for that and I'm not sure, you know, if you haven't got a single business strategy, if flowing from that you haven't got talent able to move from one business to another very easily, because the skill sets aren't very easily transferable, you know, you're in a very different ball game in terms of, you know, what are you trying to achieve as a business and how would reward fit. And I truly don't know whether you could put in a consistent framework in that kind of business or what it would look like.
>
> (senior reward director, company3)

Large organizations, such as the case study companies, are necessarily more decentralized, with specialized departments and specialized division of labour, which attract higher levels of pay within the external labour market (Donaldson, 2001). All of the case study companies are market-leading in terms of brand value and financial performance, which is also positively linked to higher levels of pay (Gerhart and Milkovich, 1990). As a result of competitive isomorphism, and the additional contextual factors encouraging conformity of practice, prototypical clusters of pay practice emerge that may be responsible for the norms observed within the industry-level data. In their continued quest to secure competitive advantage, however, companies perpetually seek to differentiate their position vis-à-vis the competition through innovation and change. Competing organizations are engaged, therefore, in inventing and reinventing pay to ensure competitiveness. Innovative organizations enjoy the benefits of little or no competition, through having capitalized on niche market opportunities. However, this period of dominance is usually short-lived owing to the rapid replication of those innovative practices by others. This is very much in evidence within the industry-level findings. Thus, new pay practices become the norm very quickly within FMCG companies.

Similarly, evolutionary theories of strategic management share a deterministic leaning by emphasizing the importance of market forces in shaping company behaviour, rather than solely relying on rational planning on the part of management. Irrespective of the methods (strategy) that management adopt, a process of 'natural selection' will ensure that only the best performers survive (Whittington, 1997). Evolutionists, fundamentally, contest the ability of managers to negotiate the range of competitive pressures through 'detached calculation'. Survival through competitiveness is a constant struggle, in which there will always be winners and losers for reasons other than the formulation of, merely, sound strategy. Even when the organization is in a privileged position of advantage over the competition, the process of natural selection still serves to condition the shape, formation and intent of the organization. It is markets and not managers that choose the prevailing strategies within a particular environment (Whittington, 1997), such as the FMCG sector. This clearly has a bearing on the pay trends observed within the industry-level findings.

> One of the real dangers of organizations looking at aligning performance, organizational performance with reward is you can do it in a small room and you can come up with some really clever ideas. And as consultants we're often very guilty that we come up with a good idea and say 'oh well, let's do this', and then if you don't think about how other companies have done it, part of that gives you a discipline to understand whether it would be feasible or not because quite frankly there's not a lot of new things that can be done in terms of paying people.
>
> (remuneration consultant, consult1)

The emphasis of evolutionary theory is one of market fit. In order to survive, companies must adhere to the conditions of the 'market' by observing changes both in terms of market demand (say, for product) and market composition. While theory has focused mainly on product market competitive pressure, market fit applies equally to all areas of capital, including innovation, technical capital and, not least, labour. By definition, to survive is to be successful. Competitive pressures within markets naturally weed out weak performers and deselect them as part of the ongoing struggle of survival of the fittest (Whittington, 1997).

Is contingency, and not choice, responsible for the degree of convergence of pay practice evident within the industry-level dataset? Are FMCG firms merely conforming to type and a shared operating environment? Hard determinists are of the view that all (in this case organizational) actions are causally determined by events preceding our own (the subject's) existence, which are beyond our control (de Rond and Thietart, 2004). If one were able to understand all of the deterministic influences shaping action, one could accurately explain and predict outcomes in any given situation (Reid, 1987). Hard determinism dictates that we (humans) are not free, because our choices are fixed by circumstances beyond our control and, perhaps, our understanding (de Rond and Thietart, 2004). Contingency theory, however, does not discount rationality and choice, nor is practice formation viewed as an entirely determined outcome (Donaldson, 2001). Rather, contingency theory rejects the purist notion of universality, and redefines rationality as the choice of those strategies that *best fit* the organization and its context, in addition to mission and strategy – sentiments that find traction within the case study company findings and more broadly (Armstrong and Brown, 2001; Brown, 2001). In one sense, this is the essence of strategic alignment.

Rationality, therefore, is not defined within the context of the case study companies as the selection and adoption of universal best practice but the selection and adoption of *best fit* practices. With few exceptions, all of the case study firms are superficially very similar, as noted in Chapter 3. All firms compete in FMCG and, if not for product directly (for example, beverage versus confectionery), they all compete for the same labour. All are large, mature in life cycle terms and multinational. There is minor variation in terms of ownership and organizational structure, with one being a subsidiary of a larger parent company and another being structured as a holding company. However, variation between firms, where it does exist, is much more in relation to management styles, culture and structures, all of which are firm-specific and path-dependent. As a result, the evidence suggests that one size cannot fit all and one pay system applied as standard will not best fit the multiple local organizations comprising the larger whole of either the multi-divisional or multinational firm overall. This may in part explain why centrally determined pay systems fail to achieve, in practice, what is desired strategically, or intended as policy, and result instead in unintended consequences, many of which are negative. This is an important implication for evolutionary theorists. Failure to select a best fit pay system, resulting in misalignment, leads to sub-optimal performance, and ultimately deselection (Nickerson and Silverman, 2003; Whittington, 1997).

Choice, therefore, continues to play an important role in the determination of pay. It is important to recognize that pay choices are bound by context, the influence of which, however, should not be discounted to the degree that it is within standard theory. The implication is that FMCG companies are converging around pay norms because, in the face of contextual and competitive constraints, they have little choice but to do so. Managers are, therefore, not entirely free to choose optimal pay systems as theory assumes. Nor should they, it is argued here, attempt to adopt universal best practices. What works for others will not necessarily (perhaps inevitably) work for them. The options that are available to pay decision makers are largely predetermined and confined to those available. Moreover, of those available, only those that represent a best fit for the complex operating environment of large multinational fast-moving organizations should be chosen.

Impaired choice and pay

Even from a reduced 'menu' of options, are management able to discern what constitutes best fit? The findings, again, challenge the assumption that management is able to make informed pay decisions in the standard sense. The causal means–ends relationship of pay practice and pay outcomes is, by its nature, discreet and largely immeasurable, especially a priori (Wright and Gardner, 2000). As a result, management is denied the information necessary to make strategic pay decisions in absolute terms. Moreover, the ability to choose pay systems strategically is further impaired by the innate bounded rationality of decision makers (Simon, 1957) and compounded by the complexity of operating environments of all of the case study companies.

'Maximizing' theories, such as strategic pay, can be criticized on the grounds that they are based upon an implausible form of 'super-optimization' in which 'all relevant costs and benefits are precisely known, global comparisons of all alternatives are made, and actions are taken which move one (the unitary firm) immediately to an equilibrium position' (Reid, 1987). Is 'super-optimization' realistic within the context of determining pay in large diversified multinational firms?

> No, I think lots of people think they want a rewards strategy and all that, and I don't think they know what that means or really understand it, or really want it. I think it's a frequently used, you know, header but the reality behind it might not be the case because people don't understand what it means or do it, or even have a good enough idea of their own business strategy to be able to make sure that their reward strategy is aligned with it.
>
> (senior industry analyst, consult1)

Three main limitations serve to impair strategic choice in the terms of standard theory. Firstly, decision makers have an imperfect knowledge of their environment. However, standard economic theory assumes no information problem: 'We know only a fraction of the things we need to know.' This lack of information about the environment prohibits a decision maker from achieving objectives through optimal means (Simon, 1959). Secondly, decision makers, owing to limited calculative ability, are incapable of anticipating and considering all options to solve a problem. Standard theory assumes that all actors have unlimited cognitive ability to capture, coordinate and process information. Thirdly, decision makers are limited in the amount of attention that they are able to marshal for the capturing and processing of information. If one were to assume that decision makers had the computational ability to acquire and process all relevant data, they would be limited to considering the data piecemeal, and not holistically (Forest and Mehier, 2001).

Moreover, decision makers do not simply choose from a range of manifest options, as assumed by standard theory, but are required to formulate the options in the first place. By virtue of the necessary division of labour in large multinational companies, such as the case study companies, collective organizational learning is achieved only with great difficulty. Experience and learning are largely transient, and confined to the few and not the whole. If true, how are the case study companies coping with these challenges? One such coping mechanism is incremental decision making, which resonates with many of the sentiments expressed by pay specialists within the pay function (Jones, 1999). In light of their cognitive limitations, though not expressed as such, and given the complexity of the environment and the ambiguity of outcomes, decision makers will benefit from: (a) moving away from problems, rather than moving towards solutions; (b) such movements are small; and (c) be responsive to feedback from the environment (ibid.).

> I think you've got to be careful not to substitute 'I wouldn't do it this way' for 'unhappy with' because there's no silver bullet and correct answer, so any bonus policy you have is quite likely to sit comfortably in the market place but is not necessarily the one I'd have chosen. They're fine. You can't make all the decisions. Sometimes you have to implement other people's decisions. You hopefully get to influence people not just on specific stakeholder interviews, or whatever, but just by generally your observations about the market, what's happening, what your belief and reward philosophy is, then that will or will not influence the final decision. But in the end, a decision on what reward policy to follow is based on somebody's belief that it will achieve. It's a *belief* not a fact.
>
> (country reward manager, company7)

The notion of incremental decision making is clearly relevant and corresponds with developments in pay within the case study companies. In particular, the management of base pay increases is an incremental process, which encompasses movement around an established base, such as the market median. Despite the increasing availability and sophistication of market data, it is never complete or absolute in its accuracy. Given that wage costs are the single largest cost for all of the labour-intensive case study companies, mismanagement of pay determination profoundly weakens a company's financial performance. Incremental decision making is necessary, therefore, in order to contain the unavoidable risks associated with pay management.

Far from seeking the optimal pay practice, leading to the optimal pay outcome, pay function staff seek to negate the impact of pay risks by directing action through incremental and measured activity. An additional difficulty is accommodating uncertainty within strategic pay planning. Rationalist accounts of strategic management assume crudely, in light of the findings, that decision makers operate in a stable and observable environment. The company-level findings illustrate that this is far from characteristic of the multiple environments, at multiple levels, in which pay is determined.

> That's why I say it'll never be perfect, so it will be more than satisfactory, but it will never be perfect, because what's a perfect thing for

this year, we're not actually putting it in until April next year. So things will have changed. I mean, even just talking about inflation is, you're never there, because it's moved on again by the time you actually put it in place. And I think what you're doing is trying to get the best compromise, with some elements better than compromise. Because especially if you're looking globally, you can never have a perfect global system, you cannot, because of the very different approaches in the country. So, it can't *be* perfect because there are external influences which are *positively* not under our control.

(senior reward director, company4)

In the face of such limits, decision makers necessarily adopt a 'satisficing' path that permits attainment of needs at some satisfactory (reflexively specified by self) level (Simon, 1957). The fundamental characteristics of the satisficing 'organism', as defined by Simon, include: (a) a limitation on the ability to plan long behaviour sequences, the limitation being imposed by the bounded cognitive ability of the organism as well as the complexity of the environment in which it operates; (b) the tendency to set aspiration levels for each of the multiple goals that the organism faces; (c) a tendency to operate on goals sequentially rather than simultaneously because of the 'bottleneck of short term memory'; and (d) satisficing rather than optimizing search behaviour (ibid.).

The findings would support the critique of rationality, by the likes of Simon, and suggest further that pay system choices *cannot*, therefore, be strategic in the orthodox sense, owing to the cognitive limitations of decisions, compounded further by the increasing complexity of the operating environment. However, that does not prevent decision makers from attempting to use pay strategically, and continuing to choose on the basis of optimality and choice-determining outcomes. In attempting to do so, pay decision makers face the prospect of considerable frustration and uncertainty of the sort much in evidence within the case study companies. In place of optimization they necessarily settle for those pay systems that seem most satisfactory.

Optimization in pay practice conceptually implies that there is one best way – an optimal outcome is an absolute outcome. Optimization in this sense plays well to notions of pay best practice for which there is compelling evidence (Lawler, 1990; Pfeffer, 1998). However, a conceptual limitation associated with rational agency is that, given the exact same circumstances, no two decision makers may make the same decision, despite intending to reach an optimal outcome (Falzon, 1987). Within the context of the debate on contingency, and the complexity of the environment in which pay is determined, an equally plausible alternative to optimization is the concept of *equifinality* (Doty et al., 1993). Equifinality holds that there are multiple unique patterns of action for achieving the same outcome (ibid.). There is no one best way, rather a number of different methods, each of which carries equal weighting in terms of value derived from the achieved outcome. In terms of pay decisions, the findings do not support the notion of one best way given the importance of context, but multiple unique patterns of action leading to outcomes considered *satisfactory* in lieu of uncertainty concerning what is optimal.

> Well, you never do [get it right], because ... is the simple answer. Because the world keeps changing, people keep changing, people's expectations keep changing. I don't think you ever do know that and you can't make an absolute science out of this, you know. At the end of the day, we manage people, and I say there is no science in doing that.
>
> (senior operational manager, company4)

Processualist accounts of strategic management share the same lack of confidence about the ability of rational planning by management to secure profit maximization (Whittington, 1997). Unlike purely economic perspectives of the sorting effect of market forces, processualists equally lack confidence in the ability of competitive markets to secure profit maximization (Cyert and March, 1963). Both management (representative of the rational planning process) and markets (representative of competitive pressures) are 'messy', from which 'strategies emerge with much confusion and in small steps' (Whittington, 1997). Indeed, it is imperfections present within the market generally, and other organizations specifically, to which managers owe their success.

For processualists, recognition of the complexity of internal states of organizations is key. They reject both rational actor and evolutionary (market forces) accounts as efficiency optimizers, and embrace two radical departures from the received wisdom: the cognitive limitations of rational action, already discussed, and the 'micro-politics' of organizations (Cyert and March, 1963). The micro-political view of the company rejects unitarist notions of companies comprising a single entity, but views the company and the management structure instead as comprising groups and individuals each with their own interests. As a result, no strategy is ever developed fully in accordance with the aspirations of everyone within the company, but reflects instead a 'set of joint goals more or less acceptable to them (the decision makers) all' (Whittington, 1997).

For processualists, an articulated strategy is at best the result of bilateral compromise: 'Although strategy is typically conceptualised as a macro field, what actually happens in an organization (strategy execution) depends on a great number of decisions made by individuals at the micro level, as well as their ability to execute those decisions. *Successful strategy execution depends on choices and actions taken at all levels of the organization'* (Gerhart and Rynes, 2003 – emphasis added). This contrasts with one of the core assumptions of standard theory, namely that management act collectively in relation to pay because of their shared interest in economic maximization. The findings, however, suggest that this assumption does not hold true in practice. There exist a number of different states of practice within any one company, reflecting the various life cycle stages of practice adoption (strategy determination, policy determination and practice determination). Within such constraints, cognitive and micro-political, the pay function must necessarily accept and adopt that which is satisfactory and not that which is optimal.

Informed choice and pay

What is satisfactory in the context of global FMCG companies? How do management within the case study companies define what pay *should* do, and on what basis is pay practice selected as a result? In light of the impaired rationality of decision makers, institutional theory offers an additional compelling explanation for the conformity observed at the industry level, and between the case study companies and their desire to use pay strategically. In the face of uncertainty about what constitutes an appropriate pay strategy, decision makers are likely to reference the experiences of 'influential others' and, in doing so, become prone to a range of internal and external social and political pressures that serve to encourage expected forms of behaviour (DiMaggio and Powell, 1983). Institutionalists counter rationalist assertions by claiming that the 'formal structures of many organizations in post-industrial society dramatically reflect the myths of their institutional environments instead of the demands of their work activities' (Meyer and Rowan, 1991). Pay practice is not, therefore, necessarily the result of rational deliberation.

For institutionalists, organizational actors are motivated by normative social and political pressures and not purely by economic rationality, as standard theory would suggest (Kessler, 2001). Social pressures such as norms, rules, rituals and beliefs impact upon organizational behaviour at a number of levels: at the individual level, in terms of informing the values of decision makers; at the firm level, the culture and politics of the organization; and through regulatory pressures and industry-wide norms at the inter-organizational level (Kessler, 2001; Oliver, 1997). The impact of these pressures is profound, but also discreet in the form of taken-for-granted rituals, scripts and norms (DiMaggio and Powell, 1991). Measuring the impact and effect of institutional pressures is, for this very reason, problematic (Donaldson, 2001).

Relatively little work has explored the influence of institutional pressures upon the outcomes of pay determination. And yet, research on the institutionalization of organizational forms would suggest that they might have an important impact upon the nature and outcomes of pay determination (Kessler, 2001). In their seminal paper DiMaggio and Powell (1991) ask: 'Why is there such startling homogeneity of organizational forms and practice?' One might ask the same question about FMCG sector pay. The industry-level findings highlight such a 'startling' homogeneity of practice. In addition to those already discussed, evolutionary explanations for example, attempts to understand more clearly the trend towards conformity of pay practice should consider, in light of the findings: 'what kinds of social pressure arise from these three levels [of institutional pressure] to affect pay practice and how do these pressures affect the nature and pace of change in approaches to pay?' (Kessler, 2001). Consistent with the predictions of institutionalists, the findings indicate that institutional pressures within the FMCG sector are encouraging conformity, or *isomorphism*, of practice among FMCG firms. Significantly, institutional pressures are deterministic in nature and induce firms to behave for reasons other than purely economic interest. This means that the resultant pay systems are, again, non-strategic in the terms of standard theory.

The structuration of UK FMCG sector pay

Institutionalists contend that organizations are embedded in 'organizational fields' pervaded by social and political values (DiMaggio and Powell, 1991). In order to understand the institutionalization of organizations, it is necessary to understand the institutionalization and 'structuration' of the 'network' or 'population' (Hannah and Freeman, 1977) of the field in which they are embedded (DiMaggio and Powell, 1991). The organizational field affects how organizations select models for emulation; where they focus information-gathering energy; which organizations they compare themselves with; and where they recruit personnel (DiMaggio and Powell, 1991). The institutionalization of a field consists of four elements, namely 'an increase in the extent of interaction among organizations in the field; the emergence of sharply defined inter-organizational structures of domination and patterns of coalition; an increase in the information load with which organizations in a field must contend; and the development of a mutual awareness among participants in a set of organizations that they are involved in a common enterprise' (DiMaggio and Powell, 1991).

The UK FMCG industry fulfils all of these criteria. All organizations contained within the sample are members of an industry peer group. This group is a club of firms that compete in the FMCG market operating in the UK. Membership is limited to FMCG firms, and participation within the club is on an 'invitation-only' basis. Each firm makes a financial contribution to the running costs and organization of the group. It is managed by a rotating committee comprising three or four nominated company representatives, and changes yearly. Involvement from member firms typically includes representation by compensation professionals who have a remit over the management of pay at a UK, European and/or global level.

In the majority of cases, the firms comprising the group membership are large multinational FMCG companies with operations, manufacturing, R&D, distribution, marketing and sales within a number of countries throughout the world. The level of membership is limited in practice to approximately 30 firms. Informally referred to as the 'club', it fulfils a number of purposes for its membership. It provides a network through which member firms can 'safely' benchmark against the competition, via FMCG sector-specific labour market surveys. Each member firm provides benchmark data across roles, functions and levels of managerial, professional and technical employees. The pay surveys are administered by a specialist firm of consultants who are tasked with survey design, data collection, analysis and dissemination. The data are used by member firms to inform pay level decisions on an annual basis.

In addition to pay level benchmarking, the group is also used, as the name suggests, as a forum for dialogue and discussion between compensation professionals in FMCG companies on issues of mutual and professional interest. It also conducts informal research among the membership and engages consultancies for more formalized research. On a twice-yearly basis, the group meets to discuss the results of the pay survey and invites presentations from member organizations, consultancies and academics, on a range of issues considered, by the incumbent committee, to be of general interest to the membership. There is, therefore, a wide-ranging and in-depth flow of information regarding company practice between competing firms. These formal opportunities for knowledge sharing are supplemented by informal discussions and networking between the membership. As a result of the stringent membership requirements, the tenure of participation of those involved is quite high.

As a key feature of the UK FMCG organizational field, the group ensures that the context of the observed pay norms becomes more obvious. The social and political pressures acting upon the pay determination process at all levels – industry, firm or individual – also become clear, which encourages conformity of pay practice between the participating FMCG companies. The variety of institutional pressures encouraging conformity of practice are numerous and disparate, and most usefully clustered into three forms: coercive, normative and mimetic (DiMaggio and Powell, 1983, 1991).

Isomorphic processes encouraging conformity

FMCG firms are converging around *perceived* pay best practices. The FMCG pay norms of performance-based pay, for example, are powerful and encourage firms to converge around specific configurations of pay practice. Strategic pay is clearly a powerful movement within practitioner circles as a result of its propagation by advocates – academics, consultants and practitioners – all of whom are able to offer compelling stories of success. These success stories enter the collective consciousness as examples of best practice and come to reflect what is perceived as being *legitimate*, and consequently worthy of emulation, by aspiring others.

> This is what everybody is doing. This is what you should be doing [the norm]. The conventional wisdom is that you need to bonus people, whether it's right, wrong or indifferent [for the firm] doesn't matter. The conventional wisdom is you should be doing it.
>
> (UK rewards practitioner, company1)

Mimetic processes resulting in organizational isomorphism reflect those pressures arising from the desire to emulate the legitimate practice of 'influential others' owing to *uncertainty* (DiMaggio and Powell, 1991; Kessler 2001). Organizations may emulate others in order to mitigate the inherent uncertainty in selecting a pay system, where the benefit of adopting a particular pay strategy over another is largely unknown a priori. To inform choice and mediate risk in the form of failed change, reward specialists reference the experiences and practices of others, often emulating what is considered successful elsewhere. An impaired understanding of the likely outcomes of pay decisions encourages decision makers necessarily to emulate 'influential others', resulting in isomorphism of pay practice. Senior management (non-pay function) within FMCG firms also have a significant input into pay determination. For many of the FMCG companies participating in the industry peer group, the UK is neither the headquarters home of the company nor the country where senior management reside. Thus, institutional pressures influence the determination at a number of levels, irrespective of location.

> This happens so many times, you know, the CEO picks up *Business Week* or a magazine, calls up the SVP of HR and is like 'we need to have pay for performance, it says in this article everybody else has pay for performance', you know, and then the SVP of HR says to his reward director 'okay, implement pay for performance because that's what the CEO wants'!
>
> (management consultant, consult2)

Susceptible to the diffusion of institutional pressures as a result of their desire (or requirement) to emulate 'influential others', and mediate the risks of their own uncertainty, pay decision makers draw primarily upon two sources – external expertise and 'influential others' within their own profession and/or organizational field. In terms of external expertise, management consultants and professional bodies stand out in terms of influence. Operating internationally, management consultancy firms offer advice and solutions to domestic and multinational firms on a range of pay and compensation issues. Despite marketing a tailored approach, the consultancy advice, methodologies and technical solutions are standardized. This is because bespoke development of a solution is time and labour intensive and therefore less profitable. A number of major compensation consultancies advise FMCGs. All seven FMCG firms within the case study sample use one or more of these consultancies when determining pay, and often do so simultaneously. At some point, they have used all of these consultancies and continue to maintain an ongoing relationship, if not a formal engagement.

> Part of it is just the ... I will hold my hand up ... is the consultant's fault! Because like when broad banding came out right? You know, we went out and, you know, we went out and talked to a lot of companies and held seminars and it kind of became the 'flavour of the month' as we call it. And so everybody was like 'oh my gosh, we have to move to broad banding, we have to get away from the Hay system, the Hay system doesn't work, it's antiquated'.
>
> (management consultant, consult2)

All of the case study firms have participated regularly in the industry-wide FMCG pay club survey conducted by two of the consulting firms who participated in this study. The consultancy firms assist with the shape and formation of pay strategies, systems and practices, and also administer the surveys of the FMCG labour market, upon which all of the sample FMCG case studies base, in part, their pay-level decisions.

> They're always looking for the next product to sell, they're no different from any other industry, and they will leap on to a bonus scheme design, or have a share incentive scheme, or have something like that, that they can hawk around us, as often willing victims, because, yeah, we are all looking for the Holy Grail! (laughs).
>
> (senior HR generalist, company4)

External professional associations also serve to encourage conformity of pay practice. The Chartered Institute of Personnel & Development (CIPD) is the largest professional association for personnel and human resources specialists in the UK, with over 130,000 members. It provides codes of best practice relating to all aspects of employment management, including remuneration, guidance for practitioners on effective employment management in the form of conferences, seminars and workshops and, perhaps most significantly, an extensive range of taught courses and qualifications. The implicit assumption is that the adoption of these practices results in superior performance. The transparency of financial markets highlights 'winners and losers'. Winners, as previously mentioned, are regularly illustrated as 'best practice' organizations, losers the opposite. Winners therefore become objects for other aspiring organizations to emulate, and institutions such as CIPD facilitate such a process.

Normative institutional pressures are those that encourage isomorphism primarily as a result of the *professionalization* of the organizational field (DiMaggio and Powell, 1991). Professionalization is the collective attempt by members of a profession to define the conditions, methods and outcomes of their work, and in doing so, establish occupational legitimacy, autonomy, power and influence (Larson, 1977). A number of factors contribute to the normative isomorphic outcomes of professionalization. Firstly, formal education encourages the development of organizational norms and shared rules among professionals, which thus naturally pervade the organizations in which they are employed. Secondly, developed professional networks typically span organizations and provide a mechanism through which new models, rules and norms are diffused on an inter-organizational basis. The net result of professionalization is 'a pool of almost interchangeable individuals who occupy similar positions across a range of organizations and possess a similarity of orientation and disposition that may override variations in tradition and control that might otherwise shape organizational behaviour' (DiMaggio and Powell, 1991). The professionalization of a particular organizational field, such as UK FMCG companies, means that professional pay function personnel are hired from firms within the same industry.

> Part of it too is, I feel, the movement of people within the HR function within company to company ... sometimes the movement happens so often that the person who came there and started the initiative is no longer around to see it manifest itself.
>
> (management consultant, consult2)

There is a great deal of labour mobility between FMCG firms, with industry-specific experience considered a prized commodity by employers hiring pay function personnel. Indeed, HR and rewards personnel within firms with perceived 'leading practice' are often targeted specifically for their experience and expertise and the legitimacy they confer upon the hiring organization through their appointment. In addition to practitioners, pay and/or FMCG industry specialist consultants often transfer out of the consultancy sector to take up full-term practitioner roles or in-house project-based roles. Thus a great many of the unique characteristics of companies are transferred with staff when they move between firms. While the appointment of a new director of pay and remuneration may, in the first instance, create conflict through the sometimes painful and protracted process of reconciling social rules, norms, expectations and rituals between the incumbent individuals and the collective status quo, conflict is eventually reconciled through the internal reorganization of the firm, or the departure of the individual. This process may also change the firm in relation to peer (competing) organizations, thus allowing the disparate social properties of firms to permeate through the institutional field, resulting in greater homogeneity.

Conformity of FMCG sector pay practice

The most obvious outcome of the structuration of UK FMCG company pay is isomorphism of pay practice. As a result of its formal structures, wide-ranging knowledge-sharing activities, longevity and restricted membership, the industry peer group is highly structured. The isomorphism of pay practice within the FMCG field has some implications for participating firms. Isomorphism implies that organizations: '(a) incorporate elements which are legitimate externally, rather than in terms of efficiency; (b) they employ external or ceremonial assessment criteria to define the value of [internal] structural elements' (Meyer and Rowan, 1991). Despite competition for both product market share and labour, it is apparent that participation in the industry peer group, and other such industry and professional peer groups, encourages the cross-fertilization of knowledge, shared experience and education and, crucially, a generic framework for negotiating industry-wide challenges and pay-related issues.

Consciously and unconsciously, participation within the industry peer group necessarily serves to inform decision makers' knowledge of pay and pay management. It also serves as a source of innovation; defines perceptions of effective and/or legitimate practice; and in addition, may also confer or reinforce feelings of professional status and authority (DiMaggio and Powell, 1991). Given the emphasis placed on HR and pay as a means of securing competitive advantage by advocates of strategic pay/SHRM, it is interesting to observe that within this sample of largely leading firms, those tasked with responsibility over rewards confer regularly with peers in competing firms. The outcome of participation within the industry peer group, and other groups like it, is the creation of common frames of reference – *professionalization*, in effect. These include generic styles of management, performance expectations and perceptions of legitimacy in those that make reward-related decisions, necessarily encouraging conformity of practice selection and adoption – isomorphism. The implication of institutional isomorphism in the case of UK FMCG companies is that organizations are embracing the institutionally sanctioned notion of strategic pay and adopting related practices.

> So we believe that we [company6] must pay the best salary or differentiate ourselves quite significantly from the rest that we can tell candidates, look at this, maybe you'll get the same anywhere else but we have this in particular, yeah? So it's *uniqueness* that should come through, yeah? Now this is a bit of a contradiction because you look at uniqueness but you look also exactly at what others are doing, yeah? And then they [senior management] tell you why don't you do what they are doing? And they're always responding yes, but does it mean we are losing our own [company6] way of doing business, and I have to say more and more my senior managers respond 'so what, let's do this'.
>
> (senior rewards practitioner, company6)

Far from providing evidence for strategic choice, as evinced by the selection of best practice reward programmes, the conformity of company pay practice illustrated within the quantitative pay data may be evidence of the degree to which participating firms have become institutionally structured. In other words, institutional structuration might be responsible for the high degree of conformity of practice between competing firms.

> It [the reward change process] becomes a little bit of a cookie-cutter exercise, because what happens is you come in and then people say 'well, I'm P&G, so what are Diageo doing, what does the Unilever structure look like, Nestlé structure look like?' Okay, so they're all done, they only have five bands; I wonder why they only have five. Well, it's because of this, this and this reason, because of the industry and *da de dah de dah*. Okay, I guess we should have five bands too.
>
> (management consultant, consult2)

FMCG firms are, therefore, adopting pay practices that reflect externally sourced *legitimate* norms and not practice that is necessarily best fit for the vision, values and strategy and internal state of the organization.

The conditions necessary for institutional structuration

Why are organizations prone to isomorphic pressures emanating from the institutional environment? The conventional institutionalist argument is that, necessarily, organizations are embedded in institutional fields that comprise networks, relationships, rules, rituals and norms, that are both consciously appreciated and taken for granted and manifest in collective behaviour such as practice conformity. However, are all organizations equally prone to institutional pressure? Are some organizations more likely to conform to the norm than others? If so, what does that reflect about the organization, the management and their capacity for choice and discretion over the organizational form that manifests as pay practice? DiMaggio and Powell (1991) highlight three key factors that explain the degree of structuration of organizational forms – they specify uncertainty, professionalization and legitimacy. There was clear evidence that *uncertainty* is a large factor determining the degree to which companies reference external practice.

> Well, I think that's the answer isn't it. *It's your confidence, yeah?* The big companies tend not to have that entrepreneurial spirit, especially if they're a paternalistic company like us. So, if you're in a paternalistic

company and you've have been bought up in it and you've got to leadership [a leadership position] through it, you will be saying, 'What do other people do, we don't want to be doing anything silly.'

(senior rewards practitioner, company4 – emphasis added)

Company6 had for many years deliberately chosen to disregard market pay practice and enjoyed, it is perceived, superior HR outcomes as a result, including the attraction and retention of key staff and greater organizational performance than that of competitors. However, a worsening of the financial fortunes of the company owing to the maturation of core markets and limits of expansion and revenue generation, prompted management to reference more greatly the practice of peer organizations:

We have been, for many, many years, disconnected from the market. We didn't care; we were not interested in what was going on. We did our thing, we were very successful, and all the markets were growing – fine. Now the growth levels, particularly in the mature markets in the West, have quite significantly reduced, yeah? Some markets are stagnating, so people say fine, what are we doing wrong? Let's have a look at what's going on somewhere else, maybe we can learn something from there. And that's why, more and more are interested in knowing what's going on outside. So it's a bit of a lack of confidence.

(senior rewards practitioner, company6)

Consistent with the literature, *uncertainty*, and/or a lack of *confidence*, as expressed here, renders decision makers prone to institutional pressures: 'You know, part of it is the … is the pressure *to* conform and the risk aversion of creating something that's too different' (management consultant, consult3). In the case of company6, a large, well-established brand leader with a history of strong corporate performance, recent poor performance had led the organization to change its long-standing policy of using base pay as the cornerstone of their pay offering and introduce instead broad-based variable pay, based upon company performance. The rationale for changing the existing structures lies not, interviewees within the firm might argue, in choosing a system that best promotes value-adding employee activity, but one of emulating 'important others' in their peer group. Bucking the normative trend within industry is something to which decision makers are averse.

They're afraid of being different, I think. I think they're afraid of being different because if they get … sometimes you might have someone in senior management who says 'well, this is so different from what everybody else has', you know, 'why would we want to be so different, is that a good thing?'

(remuneration consultant, consult1)

The discussion of uncertainty relates also to the role, status and influence of the pay function as a profession. The industry peer group unites representatives of competing firms in collective endeavour, such as benchmarking and the sharing of information, where there would otherwise be little or no interaction. Despite rules guarding the proprietary ownership and sensitivity of information such as companies' pay data, the industry peer group might be viewed as an example where a *profession* has transcended the organizational boundaries established by competition, resulting, among other things, in collaboration, and the formulation of mechanisms for formal knowledge transfer. Does the industry peer group and professional peer clubs like it serve another function, however?

In addition to organizational outcomes, participation also confers positive outcomes on the pay profession. Is it professional interest driving participation within the peer group and the outcomes, therefore, of pay determination? However, it is apparent that institutional pressures apply not only to those with direct responsibility for the management of rewards. Additional stakeholders in the pay determination process may also be susceptible to the perceived successes of other normative trends and a desire for practice that confers legitimacy. In the case of senior management, this was evident in a number of case study FMCG organizations.

Let's be more like the competition, yeah, which is a bit worrying because that tells me that my senior managers have lost a bit of faith in how [company6] used to do business and are trying now to copy a bit what others are doing, yeah?

(senior rewards practitioner, company6)

In all of the FMCG companies participating in the case study element of the research, senior management ultimately sign off proposed changes to the company's reward structures. This includes changes to the level of pay (budgetary approval), and changes to the basis of pay. Similarly, senior management, including functional representation from the director of HR, may define the broad direction of rewards, such as the use of performance-based pay, while not necessarily defining the mechanics of such an approach. Ultimately, in attempting to comply with the wishes of senior management, there is evidence that the rewards function will choose those practices that conform best to the stated expectations and perceived aspirations of business leaders, and not those that are necessarily most appropriate for the organization.

> Because it's sort of like ... again it's the perception too. You know, the CEO reads the business pages and says 'well, why aren't we doing broad banding, why are we still on the Hay method? I hear that that's not the way to go and it's horrible and broad band's the way to go and it's much easier to administer and people understand it', and *da de dah de dah*. And then, again, because of the resource issue, it doesn't get implemented the way it should.
>
> (management consultant, consult2)

Tied in with the notion of uncertainty, being itself a determinant of the degree to which decision makers are prone to institutional pressures, either through a conscious lack of knowledge and the desire to benefit from the experiences of others, or the unconscious susceptibility to take for granted norms, rules and rituals, is the status, power and capability of the HR and rewards function. The ability of the function to represent what is technically best for the firm, despite institutional pressures acting at all levels of the firm, is greatly diminished when the function is perceived as weak internally (Sisson, 1995).

> I used to have a joke where the marketing director used to rush into the managing director's office and say 'I've got this brilliant new idea, nobody has ever thought of it before, we're going to' And the managing director says '*go* for it, yeah!' And then the HR director tries the same thing and he says 'are you *sure* we should be doing this, *if nobody else is doing it, is it right for us?*' Just because it's an HR initiative.
>
> (rewards practitioner, company1 – emphasis added)

The experience of the case study companies would suggest that it is precisely the inability to understand a priori, or even in hindsight, the means–ends relationship between pay and HR practice and performance that may be responsible for the function being viewed in such poor terms. It is extremely difficult for the function to demonstrably prove its worth financially. In lieu of a demonstrable financial return a priori, the perceived legitimacy of strategic pay practice is used as the basis for selecting pay systems. For example, the literature would suggest that performance-based pay, as a basis for pay progression, is currently perceived as more legitimate than pay for tenure. Whether the greater competitive advantage desired through enhanced organizational performance is the result of performance-based pay systems is not clear in standard financial terms, but the perception remains that it is the optimal means available and is, therefore, selected over alternatives.

In the face of uncertainty, institutionalists contend that institutions provide 'dependable and efficient frameworks for economic exchange', overcoming the uncertainty inherent in the transaction as a result of the aforementioned challenges (North, 1988). Institutions are therefore of benefit when determining pay, because it conditions others to behave in a non-opportunistic manner and compensates for the bounded rationality of actors by imposing templates of established behaviours, codes and rules. The properties that comprise pay institutions serve to reduce the uncertainty inherent in pay determination: 'It is quite inappropriate to conceive of firm behaviour in terms of deliberate choice from a broad menu of alternatives that some external observer considers to be "available" opportunities for the organization. The menu is not broad, but narrow and idiosyncratic; it is built into the firm's routines, and most of the "choosing" is also accomplished automatically by these routines' (Nelson and Winter, 1982).

Nevertheless the consensus over the role of institutions as a positive influence on the mediation of uncertainty is not universal. Opportunistic behaviour is seen by some (see Williamson, 1986) as the greatest constraint on the achievement of optimum outcomes, whereas others (see Matthews, 1986; North, 1988) view the information asymmetry of monitoring costs and cognitive limitations as the primary source of cost and, therefore, risk (DiMaggio and Powell, 1991). Exactly *what* institutions serve to mediate is also not without controversy. Institutions, in this context, are seen as an optimal response to a social need. This raises some significant questions about the status of institutions, their nature and their role in the economic process, which have not yet been developed comprehensively within the literature.

Do pay-related institutions, such as those observed within the FMCG sector, arise and persist only when they confer benefits (such as frameworks for emulation, legitimacy and conferred status) that are greater than the cost of creating and sustaining them? Can firms even attempt to use pay strategically without them? Similarly, are institutions purely instrumental in nature, their role being to facilitate a predominantly economic process? While new institutional economics attempt to reflect the complexity of 'optimising behaviour', and in doing so recognize satisficing behaviour and the influence of institutions on economic process, it focuses on the 'more formal and fixed aspects of the political process' to the neglect of the importance of institutions and their influence (DiMaggio and Powell, 1991).

The findings indicate, however, that institutions and institutional pressures do clearly have a great deal of influence on the determination of pay. Standard theories of strategic pay do not recognize the importance of the role of institutions, nor the degree to which choices are informed by institutional forces, both consciously and in ways that are taken for granted. In practice, the greater the uncertainty under which decisions are made, the greater, it seems, is the likelihood that decision makers reference practice externally and become by degree, therefore, prone to the isomorphic institutional pressures pervasive within their organizational field. The implication is that pay system choices are not driven by purely economic interests. Institutional pressures are primarily social and political and not economic, which places the reality of pay determination at odds, again, with that assumed by standard theory. Pay systems are selected for reasons other than for purely economic maximization.

The implications for theory

The discussion of preceding sections suggests that some revision is required if pay theory is to become more grounded in the reality of pay in practice and, therefore, more robust theoretically. Several key areas of tension were identified and the core assertions of standard theory contrasted with the reality of pay practice presented through the findings. A running theme to emerge throughout the findings is the weakness of the *managerial* assumptions underpinning strategic pay, such as choice and unity of managerial intent. Consistent with some of the claims of critical theorists, the misconceived foundation assumptions render what is now standard pay theory vulnerable to criticism. Alternative theories lying outside of the mainstream strategic management and strategic pay movement find greater traction with the findings, including contingency theory, bounded rationality and, of particular relevance, institutional theory. The findings presented here do not directly invalidate or diminish the value of those additional theories underpinning strategic pay – motivational theories, for example. The findings do, however, illustrate clearly that the reality of pay determination is far from the prescribed ideal of standard theory – a case in point being the limited scope and impact of strategic choices on pay determination outcomes.

If it is not solely strategic choice in the standard sense, what is influencing pay determination? Contrary to the assertions of proponents of strategic pay, managers do not operate on the basis of comprehensive, much less perfect, information about the internal and external environment of the organization, or the nature of pay and the nature of the business need. This problem is, of course, exacerbated within the context of large diverse global organizations, where the variables – managerial, technical, political and social – requiring consideration are proportionately that much greater than in smaller, less structured organizations. Neither can pay decision makers have an accurate understanding of the likely outcomes of decisions they make a priori, as the nature of pay means that it defies prediction, and even probability of outcome, in many cases.

The findings indicate that pay decisions over the optimal *form* of pay are, therefore, often little more than elaborate guesswork on the part of management, based upon past experience, rudimentary data that can be gathered about a process and series of outcomes that are largely intangible and, therefore, largely immeasurable by standard conventions. This is challenging given the turnover of those involved and the relative lack of shared experience available as a result. In the face of such *uncertainty*, decision makers have little option but to reference practice externally, to consider the experiences of others who are perceived as legitimate. Indeed, pay decision makers, especially those dedicated pay specialists within the pay function, are encouraged to do so as the other powerful generalist stakeholders involved in the pay determination process, such as senior management, demand justification in the form of benchmarks (Figure 9.2).

Pay decisions are *informed* by institutional norms prevalent within the organizational field in which the organization resides. The global and

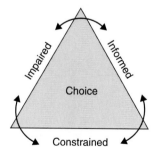

Figure 9.2 A grounded perspective on pay choices

UK FMCG markets are one such organizational field, and a number of institutional mechanisms present within those fields, such as industry peer groups and consultants, promote and facilitate the dissemination of pay practice between like firms especially, but even between not so like firms on the basis of 'best practice sharing'. Far from being best practice in *absolute* performance terms, the pay norms observed in the industry-level findings represent perceived best practice in *institutional* terms. Such best practices do not confer enhanced financial performance on the adopting organization but, rather, confer enhanced legitimacy in the eyes of interested stakeholders, both internal and external to the organization. Firms are, therefore, converging isomorphically around specific pay norms in the absence of knowing what else to do. Pay systems, therefore, do not arise purely as the result of managerial discretion. Rather pay systems are *formed*, being the result of myriad different pressures acting upon the pay determination process and influencing pay determination outcomes, of which managerial choice is but one.

What are the implications of the findings for our understanding of issues such as choice? Within the context of the open system of determinants identified, with multiple pressures – competitive, institutional and structural – bearing influence on the pay determination process at each of the three levels, what remains of the contribution of managerial choice in pay determination? Choice continues to feature, clearly, but it is one of many inputs and is evidently less influential than others in certain circumstances. This is especially the case when, in addition to the constraints observed, the ability of pay decision makers to choose strategically is also impaired by uncertainty over the means–ends relationship – the outcomes of their decisions. The 'right' course of action in relation to pay is often not obvious, especially a priori, thus necessitating the referencing of external practice and resulting in choice being informed deterministically.

Despite these manifest challenges to managerial choice as the sole determinant of pay practice, firms continue to attempt to use pay strategically. They do so within constraints, as noted, but the view persists that management is free to manage pay as they see best in the interests primarily of economic gain – a core tenet of standard theory. The findings challenge this view and suggest that much of the freedom that management enjoy unilaterally to determine pay is more perceived than real. This is consistent with the notion of *soft determinism* (de Rond and Thietart, 2004). Soft determinists take the viewpoint that when making decisions, one experiences a sensation or feeling of freedom. Our will is no less bound by the deterministic influence of circumstances beyond our control, much in the same way that causal laws regulate the physical world, but we remain convinced of our ability to choose nonetheless. This ability to choose is in fact an illusion permitted by our ignorance of the determinants shaping managerial will.

Freedom is defined by soft determinists as 'the power to do what one wants', even if one's desires are themselves wholly predetermined (de Rond and Thietart, 2004). Pay decision makers, particularly those responsible for determining the pay approach and design, are prone to institutional forces that inform their decisions directly in ways that are consciously appreciable, but also indirectly through the form of taken-for-granted rules and norms that are not consciously appreciable. The right pay decision is not that which is optimal, but that which is perceived as being optimal and is judged often on the basis of the external reference experienced. This is not necessarily consciously appreciated, nor is it a realization easily accepted by incumbents. Clearly, this resonates closely with the notion of 'structuration' and 'systemic' accounts of strategic management (Giddens, 1979; Whittington, 1997).

The findings indicate that the role of strategic choice and the licence it confers upon decision makers by rationalists is misconceived and not reflective of the reality of pay choices in practice. These conclusions are not without traction in the literature. In addressing similar themes, Whittington (1997) asks pointedly: has orthodox strategic management failed, and what are the alternatives to the orthodox approach of strategic choice? The useful framework of choice, chance and determinism illustrated by de Rond and Thietart (2004) maps well on to the findings and, when applied, provides a platform from which the determinants influencing the formation of practice might be better understood. Constraints on choice serve to influence practice formation in a way that could be considered deterministic. Similarly, decision makers are prone to institutional pressures encouraging conformity to established patterns of legitimate practice in ways that are not consciously appreciable. While their choices and related actions are not 'wholly' predetermined, the findings suggest clearly there is not as much freedom in the pay decision process as standard theory assumes, but decision makers nevertheless continue to operate under the illusion of their own ability to choose free from interference – something reminiscent of soft determinism.

The implication for contemporary pay management is profound. If pay decisions are not – cannot be – rational in the classical sense, can they be strategic? If pay practices are informed by factors other than purely managerial choice, are they strategic? Indeed, pay is seemingly not formulated, but *formed*. Pay decision makers operate under the illusion of *complete* choice over pay determination and formulate policy on that basis; but it is rhetorical and not substantive, which may explain why, operationally, pay practice fails to achieve what was desired strategically, and what was intended as policy. Pay strategies and policies are not grounded sufficiently in the complexity of the organization at the level of operation, indeed could not be, given the limits on rationality, and thus can never be achievable by the absolute terms of standard theory. Clearly, this does not sit well with standard theory as it brings into question the viability of strategic pay in practice and its theoretical value.

Summary

This chapter sought to understand why the reality of pay practice is discordant with the prescriptions of standard theory. It reviewed and contrasted a number of the key assertions and assumptions of standard theory with the case study company findings. In light of the findings, many of the assumptions of standard theory arguably lack grounding in the complex reality of pay determination. As noted in the previous chapters, it is the failure to *manage* strategic pay systems effectively that results in their not achieving outcomes of strategic value and, worse still, unintended consequences. An important question is: why do firms struggle so when attempting to use pay strategically? Is it purely because they manage pay poorly and, if only they were to manage it better, they would secure competitive advantage from pay outcomes of strategic value, such as behaviours, for example?

It is true that some firms manage pay better than others and do, we presume, benefit as a result. The findings indicate that they experience a fewer number of unintended consequences. The implication of such a view is that strategic pay conceptually and theoretically is robust and relevant when applied as practice. The problem is that companies have not yet developed the necessary managerial competence to derive fully the value-added benefit from their strategic pay systems. Such a view would hold that it is practice, and not theory, that is responsible for the outcomes experienced by the seven companies reviewed in this study. Implicitly, therefore, strategic pay, when applied, would yield the promised strategic outcomes if only companies were to use it properly.

Or would it? The findings reviewed in this chapter suggest that there is something more fundamental at fault that explains why strategic pay often fails to yield outcomes of strategic value. Many of the core assumptions of strategic pay theory do not, in light of the findings, reflect the reality of pay determination in complex organizations. The findings suggest that strategic pay advocates overestimate the level of choice available to decision makers in pay system design and selection and, as a consequence, the expectations of what pay systems are able to achieve are unrealistic. Senior management, and the pay function, do indeed exercise both choice and control over pay systems' determination. That choice is limited in numerous ways, however, by pressures acting directly and indirectly upon both the organization and decision makers. The practical implications are that (a) firms aspire to use pay strategically; (b) managers operate under the illusion of a choice over pay systems design; (c) choice is often constrained in the first instance; (d) choice necessarily constitutes a best guess in the face of uncertainty; (e) choice, therefore, is often little more than emulation of 'influential others'; (f) the rationale driving pay determination is not economic maximization but institutional legitimacy; (g) outcomes are necessarily satisfactory and not optimal; and (h) outcomes are, ultimately, often unknown and indeed unknowable, a priori, except when negative. Many of these observations lend empirical support to the claims of critical HRM theorists.

Thus considered, can pay be strategic? It is argued here that by the absolute terms of standard theory, it cannot. Strategic pay theory is not sufficiently grounded in the complex reality of pay determination to be achievable in the standard sense. Strategic pay theory makes unrealistic assumptions about the nature of managing pay within the context of contemporary organizations and is, therefore, an unrealistic ideal. As a result, many of the prescriptions of strategic pay theory, which have come to represent the 'received wisdom', are unachievable in practice. This may help explain the limited success that organizations (even the leading case study companies) have experienced when attempting to use pay strategically. In attempting to do so, the case study companies have exposed themselves to a greater likelihood of failure than success, and the risks associated with failure are significant in value terms.

Difficult to get right and seemingly easy to get wrong – is attempting to use pay strategically worth the risk? The implication is that a revision to standard theories of strategic pay is required to reflect more clearly the reality of what organizations can do, and therefore should do, in relation to pay. Despite the strong language employed here, it is not being argued that pay cannot be strategic in any sense, but that a redefinition of the potential of a strategic contribution of pay may be required.

10
Conclusion and Implications

The most recent development in pay theory proposes that pay, when used strategically, is a powerful means through which companies are able to secure competitive advantage. As a management tool, the advocates of what is now standard theory position pay as a lever through which management might enhance company performance and secure competitive advantage by attracting and retaining valued labour, driving effort and performance and encouraging desired behaviours among the broad-based workforce. Economy-wide pay trend data reviewed in Chapter 2 – the literature review – indicates that a significant number of employers have embraced a strategic approach to pay, especially within the private services sector. A review of pay trend data specific to the UK FMCG sector indicates an even greater inclination towards the use of strategic pay systems among companies.

A small but vocal body of critical opinion, however, questions the robustness of some of the prescriptive, normative and conceptual foundations of strategic pay theory. Empirical data supporting strategic pay theory is most typically derived from large-scale quantitative studies investigating the relationship between individual pay practices and company performance and confers few insights about the reality of strategic pay in practice. Grounded commentary on exploring strategic pay, in practice, is undeveloped as commentary despite the academic and practical potential worth of such an approach. Against the backdrop of what has become received wisdom in practice and the new orthodoxy of theory, and given impetus by critical commentary and the dearth of understanding of strategic pay in practice, this study has sought to explore the following issues: are leading firms attempting to use pay strategically, and if so, on what basis and for what purpose? What is the nature of these strategic pay systems in practice and how effective are they?

Within the context of the industry-wide trend towards the use of strategic pay, the case study findings reveal that individual companies are attempting to use pay strategically and formulate strategies and select largely the same pay systems to that end. However, all firms encounter significant difficulties when attempting to implement strategic pay systems with the result that, in the majority of cases, what is realized operationally as pay practice is neither what was desired nor intended strategically. As a result of the *gap* between intended policy and achieved practice, between the espoused and the realized, pay within a number of the case companies does not fulfil the strategic objectives of motivating managerial, professional and technical employees to work harder. It does not engender commitment or loyalty as outcomes, nor does it equip management with the behavioural 'lever' promised by standard theory. Despite the best efforts of leading companies, and the rhetoric of their espoused pay practice, pay practice is operationally non-strategic.

Moreover, attempting to use strategic pay systems, such as incentive pay, often results in unintended consequences and negative outcomes that destroy value and not create it. The case study company findings are littered with examples of strategic pay systems producing outcomes precisely the opposite of what was desired strategically, such as employee demotivation and disengagement, misdirected behaviours and conflict. In process terms, strategic pay systems are also administratively time-consuming, placing significant demands on managerial time and effort operationally, but also to reconcile the tensions that arise often as a by-product. Strategic pay can, therefore, represent a significant organizational risk if managed improperly and is, in many cases, a far cry from the value-added means of securing competitive advantage envisaged by strategic pay proponents.

Why do firms struggle so when attempting to use pay strategically and why do these systems not always do what they are supposed to do? The literature review highlighted a number of core assumptions underpinning strategic theories of pay. The previous chapter critically reviewed many of these core assumptions and compared and contrasted them to the reality of pay practice manifest in the case study findings. The result was to challenge much that is taken for granted in standard theory – notions of rationality and strategic choice, for example. In direct contrast with the foundation assumptions of theory, pay systems are not solely determined as a result of managerial choice. Rather, a variety of institutional and contextual factors act upon the various stages of the pay determination process and contribute to the formation of pay practice – of which managerial choice is but one input. What firms do in relation to pay, therefore, does not necessarily reflect choice in the strategic sense, but is a tactical compromise within the confines of context and managerial capability. Similarly, the assumption of collective managerial intent, and unity of managerial interest, is again, in light of the findings, misplaced. Such assertions are challenges to the perceived strategic role of the pay function which, along with their brethren in other sub-functions of the HR function, are labelled frequently as 'strategic partners' and 'change agents' contributing to organizational performance *and* accountable therefore, to shareholders (Ulrich, 1997).

Failure to manage strategic pay effectively results in the gap observed in a significant number of the case study companies between what is desired strategically, what is intended as policy and what is achieved operationally. The gap renders both strategic desire and intent, manifest in all cases in the form of strategy and policy, as so much *rhetoric*. The *reality* is that pay is operationally, the findings suggest, frequently non-strategic in nature and therefore does not yield outcomes of strategic value. Moreover, the poor management of pay can produce unintended consequences and negative outcomes that diminish value and not create it. The issues identified in the previous chapter highlight some, but not all, of the reasons why firms fail to achieve operationally strategic pay in practice. The implication is that theory is out of step with reality and represents a largely unattainable ideal in practice.

Is this true? Are the managerial limitations identified in all of the case study companies insoluble? The case study companies were purpose-fully selected on the basis that standard theory would predict that, as market-leading firms, they would be using pay strategically. A review of strategic pay in practice within those firms reveals that operation-ally they do not do so, however, despite their best attempts. If leading companies cannot manage pay strategically, what hope is there for anyone else?

Can pay be strategic, therefore? By the absolute terms of standard theory, the findings discussed here indicate not. It would be overly pessimistic and wrong, however, to conclude that pay cannot be stra-tegic in *any* sense because of the managerial limitations identified. It is argued here that a revision and not an abandonment of strategic pay is required. Clearly, attempting to use pay strategically is not as straightfor-ward as prescriptive commentary, or advocates of strategic pay, suggest. Despite the difficulties encountered by all, some case study companies clearly experience better outcomes than others – in large part because of their approach to the use and management of strategic pay systems.

Two such obvious examples are those case study companies where pay determination is largely decentralized. Pay in those cases is universally perceived to be of value, and the gap between what is desired strategically and what is achieved operationally is much less than in the other five remaining cases. Pay is of strategic value in company1 and company2 when it is supporting the business by removing constraints towards the achievement of outcomes of strategic value. Pay acts as an *enabler* of the achievement of these outcomes through additional means, and is not itself a driver of performance or the 'behavioural lever' of standard theory. In particular, pay is of strategic value when it allows the firm to recruit and retain valued talent, and when it is used as a communication tool and reinforces, culturally, a corporate sense of identity and shared purpose. The aspiration for alignment is less a matter of maximizing unity of interest between employer and employees, but reducing the inherent conflict of interest within the employment relationship – the persistence of pluralist relations. Thus considered, the expectations of company1 and company2 and what pay, when used strategically, can and should deliver are modest in comparison to the other firms in recognition, perhaps, of the challenges involved.

In light of the findings, firms should approach the prescriptions of strategic pay advocates with caution and adopt more modest expectations of the desired pay outcomes. A key implication of the research is that standard theory has established an ideal with little practical grounding that is, as a result, inherently challenging to achieve. Moreover, practitioners not only cannot avoid achieving only limited success, but also run the risk of incurring negative outcomes as an unintended consequence of attempting to use pay strategically, by the terms of standard prescriptions. The findings of this study challenge many key aspects of standard theory and provide the basis for a grounded reorientation of the pay literature to reflect more closely the reality of contemporary pay practice. One such theoretical development might include a revision of the assumptions of the manageability of pay systems. Equally, the current focus on the practice and performance linkage to the neglect of the potential gap between strategy and execution is another such area requiring revision. If sensitive to such issues, a revised approach to strategic pay would necessarily be less ambitious in terms of promised outcomes as a result of the limitations identified in the previous chapter.

While challenging a compelling and enduring corpus of literature, this view is consistent with some of the most recent commentary on strategic pay. Armstrong and Brown (2001), formerly two of the most vocal advocates of strategic pay, having produced over nine practitioner-orientated books between them alone, reflect on developments to strategic rewards (strategic pay by another name) and call for a 'new realism' in our approach to pay:

> When mostly North American concepts of strategic HRM and reward first entered into management thinking and practice in the UK we were some of their most fervent advocates, writing and advising individual employers on the benefits of aligning their reward systems so as to drive business performance. We helped articulate strategic plans and visions, and to design the pay and reward changes that would secure better alignment and performance. ... Some 20 years later, we are a little older and a little wiser as a result of these experiences. We remain passionate proponents of a strategic approach to reward management ... but in conducting this work *we have seen some of the risks* and opportunities ... at times *there has been an over-ambition and optimism in terms of what could and couldn't be achieved by changing pay and rewards arrangements.*
>
> (Armstrong and Brown, 2001, emphasis added)

In principle, strategic pay remains a laudable ambition. Companies continue to aspire to use pay strategically and, despite the challenges encountered, show little sign of deviating from their current trajectories, nor of adopting alternative approaches. Indeed, alternative approaches are not obvious such is the pervasiveness of standard approaches. Can firms move beyond the orthodoxy of strategic pay? Any change to the prevailing status quo would necessarily have to be incremental, given the inertia of company practice, the taken-for-granted associations developed in the minds of decision makers and the norming effects of a labour market where so-called strategic pay interventions are not simply commonplace, but benchmarks to which both firms and employees attach great value. The findings prompt a call for a fresh perspective that better reflects the reality of strategic pay in practice.

From old pay to new pay to *something in between?*

What might a fresh perspective look like? While having concluded that even leading companies struggle to manage strategic pay effectively with the result that pay is often non-strategic operationally, the research does not in any way contest the continued importance of pay. The findings suggest that an alternative approach to the use of pay systems *in support* of strategy is required: one that acknowledges the relative limits on the ability of companies to manage pay strategically by the terms of standard theory, and incorporates provision for a redefined contribution that would better serve the aim of securing competitive advantage.

The use of pay was not always thought of, or practised, in strategic terms. As discussed within Chapter 2, pay within post-war Britain was determined primarily as a result of collective bargaining conducted at multiple levels – occupational, industry and multi-employer. Such centralized pay determination served to take wages out of competition between employers. Management was neither free, in principle, nor empowered, in practice, to determine pay unilaterally for the achievement of purely managerial ends. Pay represented a 'cost of doing business' or, more particularly, the cost of hiring the labour necessary to do business.

The philosophy underpinning the employment relationship differed too, emphasizing the pluralism of interest between employer and employee. Bargaining arrangements were focused predominately on the avoidance of conflict through negotiation. The risks of not reaching a mutually acceptable settlement included strikes and other forms of well-publicized industrial action. While not expressed in such terms, industrial action, in its various forms, represented a significant business risk. Pay was not, itself, used to secure competitive advantage, but was considered to be a critical risk that required careful management to avoid the crippling effects of industrial conflict. The value-added outcomes of pay are hard to define and equally difficult to measure, but the negative consequences of 'getting pay wrong' are all too obvious.

In this vein, this study sought to redress what was perceived by the author to be an imbalance in theory and practice towards strategic notions of pay. In doing so, it highlighted some of the weaknesses of what is now standard theory and, importantly, the implications for contemporary pay practice. The relevance of additional theory was exposed, as well as a number of avenues of rich empirical research hitherto neglected, all of which merit further development academically. In attempting to move beyond the dominant logic of strategic pay, future research might best focus on exploring further the role that neo-institutional pressures play in shaping pay practice. Furthermore, little work known to the author has sought to integrate these neo-institutional pressures with other powerful environmental forces that also serve to constrain and inform managerial choices, and understand therefore the dynamic interplay of forces that the shape and formation of firms' pay practices. The model illustrated in Figure 9.1 in Chapter 9 was an attempt – necessarily limited by word and time constraints – to do precisely that. This study benefited from – indeed, would not have been possible without – the use of a robust multi-level framework. The segmenting of pay practice into the three states of approach, design and operation, now has a proven track record and would benefit future research aimed at investigating the subjects suggested above. It is recommended that the framework be both developed further and deployed through future research. The methodological approach adopted here – in many ways a departure from mainstream approaches – has, it is hoped, proven its validity and its utility. In addition to the multi-level framework, therefore, future research might seek to develop our understanding of pay-related phenomena by deploying the same or similar methods. An obvious direct development of this study would be to combine more quantitative methods within the predominantly qualitative approach in the interests of yielding an even richer empirical portrait of pay in practice.

How should one define 'development' of the subject, however? It is perhaps the resonance of the findings with the reality of contemporary pay practice, and the resultant grounding of theory, that is the most valuable contribution of this book. Perhaps the single greatest opport unity for the development of theory is not the forging of new ground empirically, or asking 'what's next?', but reflecting on what we already know of pay from past practice. In trying to move beyond the dominant logic of strategic pay, do we perhaps need to reflect on what pay was – old pay?

Many of the features of old pay continue in practice to pervade the operational management of pay, strategic or otherwise. Despite the underlying ideology of strategic pay being one of unitarism, the management of pay operationally continues to be characterized by pluralist relations between employer and employee, and by pluralism within the management structure itself. Given these, and other challenges, involved our definition of what constitutes strategic pay might be rescaled to reflect more clearly the reality of pay in practice. The strategic contribution of pay should not be to maximize value, given the constraints on the ability of companies to do so, but to minimize the inherent risks associated with pay, whether used strategically or not. Indeed, what is maximization in pay determination? In practice, pay professionals are not 'strategic partners', but risk managers, and continue to fulfil a great number of the tasks and activities characteristic of old pay, such as conflict resolution. Effective pay management, in practice, is effective risk management and attempts to manage it on any other basis are inherently, and inevitably, problematic.

It is recognized that such a revision will not prove popular with large sections of the pay profession, remuneration and management consultants, academics and others with a vested interest in the success of strategic pay conceptually and prescriptively. They will find it overly negative – pessimistic perhaps – and may challenge the conclusions drawn from the findings by citing numerous counter-examples and stories of success. The methods used here, necessary to gain the 'deep' insights presented as findings, may also be criticized on those same grounds that relegate qualitative studies of pay as secondary in terms of importance to dominant positivist studies – namely reflexivity, lack of generalizability and other such acknowledged limitations. As such, this book was not written aiming to reform the opinion of the 'faithful', but to put forward an alternative perspective garnered as a result of *grounded experience*. It is hoped that, ultimately, these findings and conclusions will resonate most with those for whom attempts to use strategic pay systems prove the most problematic – a frustrated and often much-maligned pay function, long-suffering line management and disgruntled employees.

Notes

2 From Old Pay to New Pay

1. Sample of 466 organizations across all industrial sectors with a coverage of over one million employees.
2. Their survey report titled 'Effectively Managing Global Compensation & Benefits' (2006–7) involved 275 multinational organizations employing over 10 million employees.

3 The Study

1. Fast moving consumer goods are non-durable, retail products, purchased on a regular basis, ranging from food and beverages to tobacco, health, hygiene and luxury personal care products. FMCG is a value-added business, being mostly comprised of large multinationals, operating multi-billion dollar sub-industries throughout the world. The global food, beverage and tobacco industry has experienced low growth over the past few years, particularly tobacco and alcoholic beverages sales. The food, beverage and tobacco industry group reached a sales value of $3974.6 billion in 2004, representing a compound annual growth rate of 2.7 per cent since 2000. Over the major regional markets, Europe (the largest market) accounts for $1410.3 billion, and 35.5 per cent of the total global market value. This compares to the Asia Pacific region, with $1144.7 billion, and 28.8 per cent of the global market share, and $817.4 billion, and 20.6 per cent, from the US (Datamonitor, 2005).
2. Job matching involves each participating firm matching their incumbent roles to a generic job description, for a specific role and level of employee. The matching performed by the participating firm is further validated by a representative of the administrating consultancy firm, and cross-checked against matching performed by other participating firms. The matching process requires a reconciliation between the generic descriptions of the survey roles and equivalent roles within participating companies. Job matching is highly labour intensive and time-consuming, but it is used as an industry standard in pay benchmarking as the best means of ensuring like-for-like comparison of pay levels and practice between companies participating in pay surveys.
3. This is done by typically uploading payroll information from their human resource information systems (HRIS) into a custom-built, standardized database provided to each participant by the administrating consultancy firm. The following pay data is reported by role by each firm (a core requirement of participation):
   - Base pay
   - Target bonus (expressed as a percentage of base pay)
   - Actual bonus (aggregate average of position matched to survey benchmark role)

- Benefits (broken down to individual elements, such as value of pension, medical, and so on)
- Value of total benefits
- Ad hoc cash allowances
- Value of long-term incentives (common valuation methodology, 'Black Scholes', applied to all cases allowing for direct comparison between firms)
- Total remuneration.

4. A copy of the standardized interview structure is included as an appendix.
5. Each interview lasted typically over an hour, but in the case of interviews with case study stakeholders, or key pay specialists, where it was requested by the interviewee, the interviewer allowed more time. All interviews were conducted by the author and were recorded digitally. Where possible, all interviews were transcribed, although both technical and language barriers did not allow for the transcription of all interviews. Of the 140 interviews, 86 were transcribed.
6. The majority of the face-to-face interviews were conducted in the UK, at company headquarters and business unit sites. Some face-to-face interviews were also conducted internationally, in the Far East, North and South America and Europe, on successive fieldwork trips. Where travel prohibited face-to-face interviews, digitally recorded telephone interviews were carried out, which permitted the widest possible coverage of staff based throughout multiple locations in the UK and internationally.

Appendix 1
Semi-Structured Interview Questionnaire

Name of interviewee:
Role title:
Function/department:
Company/business unit:
Location:
Telephone number:
E-mail:

About the role holder:

- Scope of role/position within organizational structure
- Responsibilities and accountabilities
- Length of tenure
- Past background and experience

Business strategy/organizational context

1. *Strategy, business model, vision:* How is value created? What is the customer value proposition? Long-term strategic goals? – financial and non-financial.
2. *Prevailing structure/design of the organization:* Multi-divisional, holding company.
3. *Culture:* What are the core values of the business? Are these values articulated?
4. *Global vs local:* Does strategy, vision, culture, and so on, differ across divisions and/or countries?

Existing reward practices/systems

1. What are the most critical reward practices and processes for driving value (please describe)?
   - Base pay management
   - Bonus/short-term incentives
   - Long-term incentives
   - Benefits, including pensions
   - Non-financial rewards

Positional questions – **pay practice** (what and why):

1. What is the overall reward philosophy/strategy of the organization? (for example performance-based, customer-focused, fairness/equity, innovation)
2. What is the reward philosophy/strategy intended to achieve?
3. In response to what? At your level, what drives reward management?

- Business strategy, vision, mission and goals
- Institutional pressures – external influence
- Organizational conditions/context

4. To whom/what is it applied – are reward strategies standardized across the organization?
5. With what is the reward strategy/philosophy integrated?
6. What are the key reward management priorities going forward?

Functional process questions – **pay practice** (how):

1. What is the process through which a reward philosophy/strategy is formulated?
2. How is the reward philosophy/strategy disseminated/communicated throughout the organization?
3. How are reward strategies implemented and coordinated across boundaries, for example geographical or business unit/divisional?
4. Is HR and rewards, functionally, as you understand it, organized effectively to deliver the reward strategy?
5. What functional capabilities (for example skills and competencies) are required for effectiveness?
6. How would you characterize the role of the people management function?
7. Is there a process of continuous improvement – both process and practice? If so, how does it work? Is this a coordinated, articulated process? Or, ad hoc process?

Effectual questions – **pay practice** (how well):

1. What do you define as reward philosophy/strategy effectiveness?
2. How do you measure reward philosophy/strategy effectiveness?
3. How effective (or successful) is the current reward philosophy/strategy?
4. What feedback do you get from the organization?
5. What should be changed, if anything? What could be changed? How could it be changed?
6. Are there any temporary and persistent challenges and/or barriers to enhanced effectiveness? If so, what are they? Are they shared across the organization, or specific to your remit/area?
7. How effective are reward policies? Examples? By what criteria would you make that judgement?
8. How effective is reward management operation? Examples? By which criteria would you make the judgement?
9. Are there any questions/issues/points for discussion you feel should be raised?

Appendix 2
Research Requirements Brief

Research resources required

For participating companies, case study research methods would ideally include:

1. Semi-structured interviews:
    Interviews with 20–25 staff, including senior management, middle (line) management, specialist HR function staff and sales professionals to establish a holistic stakeholder perspective on reward management. The sample of interviewees will ideally consist of:

Level	Function	Area of investigation
Senior management – head of function / department	• Performance & reward director • HR director • Business unit leader(s)	• Establish a broad overview of business goals and strategic direction • Critically evaluate the perceived contribution of HR to the achievement of business success • Explore the pressures, external and internal, serving to influence the shape and formation of strategy and policy • Establish the processes by which senior management make decisions in relation to reward systems • Establish what constitutes reward systems success for senior management • Gauge the alignment of specialist HR staff to the organisation and its goals • Explore how this impacts upon the design of rewards systems
Specialist HR staff	• Performance & Reward Manager	• Review additional pressures influencing the shape and formation of reward system design • Elaborate on the processes by which reward systems are designed and disseminated throughout the organization • Establish parameters of success for the specialist reward function
Line HR staff	• HR Directors • Business unit account managers	• Gauge the alignment of line HR staff to the broader organisation (e.g. group) and the local (line) organisation and their respective goals • Explore the role and responsibilities of specialist line staff and their contribution to both policy design and practice implementation • Explore the processes by which line specialist assist line management with the interpretation and implementation of reward policies and strategies

Level	Function	Area of investigation
Line management	• Generalist line managers	• Assess the degree to which intended reward policies 'fit' the local organization • Review the impact of local context and local / line business objectives on the management of rewards • Explore the processes by which reward policies are implemented and continuously improved over time • Assess the implications for reward system effectives and organisational performance more broadly • Understand better the 'line' perspective on the management of rewards and inconsistencies with those of other key stakeholder groups
Management level employees	• Junior to senior managerial employees • Reward system 'customers'	• The end user (employee) experience • Develop an employee centric perspective on the purpose, content and processes of the reward management systems • Explore and review perceived strengths, weaknesses and alternatives • Understand better the outcomes / impact of the reward management system and its link to organisational performance

- Each interview is expected to last no more than 1.15 hours.
- The interviews will follow a broad format established by the semi-structured interview questionnaire, but the interview may deviate from the established structure in order to capitalize upon the unique expertise, experience and interests of the interviewee.
  - Each interview, unless specified otherwise, will be recorded. The recording is purely for the benefit of the researcher, and will not be shared or disclosed with another party.
  - Each interview will be considered privileged and confidential.
2. Company data analysis (used in confidence and where permissible):
  - Organizational (financial) performance data – mostly available in the public domain.
  - Divisional performance data (for example, financial performance data for the divisions represented within the sample).
  - Organizational charts and corporate publicity/information, company background.
3. HR and reward data:
  - Reward and related HR policy documents
  - Internal communication materials
  - Presentations, for example, position papers, consultation documents
  - Pay data, including salary scales, job families, incentive scheme rules, performance management/appraisal guidelines
  - Employee demographic information – how many employed where?

Appendix 3
Research Solicitation Brief

Research brief

Currently, there is little published literature on the processes that companies use to manage rewards and determine pay, both practices and levels. In an attempt to redress this dearth of research and understanding, I propose to examine, through doctoral research, the determinants of reward management approach (strategy), design (policy) and operation within a sample of high-performing fast moving consumer goods (FMCG) organizations.

The first area of investigation will focus on the process of reward strategy decision making in relation to influences both within and without the business. The notion is that, for firms operating in the same product market, a combination of inter-firm pressures may encourage conformity of *approaches* to reward management, thereby resulting in a convergence of approaches to pay between similar organizations. The second area of research will focus upon the processes by which firms *design* reward policies, within the framework of the overall reward strategy, and in response to the internal contextual conditions of the organization. The third, and final, focus of the investigation is on *implementation* of reward management policies, and will focus on the extent to which unique firm structures influence the ultimate shape and formation of pay practice, independent of the firm's original pay design (policy) and approach (strategy).

Key themes addressed through the research

Pressures within and without the firm serving to influence the shape and formation of reward management at the levels of strategy, policy and practice:

- The (vertical) relationship between corporate strategy and reward strategies
- The (horizontal) relationship between reward practices and other human resource interventions, organizational processes, systems and structures
- The implementation and long-term operation of reward strategies across decentralized and devolved organizational structures – barriers to successful implementation
- Implications for the role and status of the people management function – line and specialist reward architects.

What am I asking of you?

In order to undertake this research I am seeking to do some in-depth company investigations into reward management practice in a number of FMCG companies. Over a period of one (plus) month(s) the case study research methods will include:

- Semi-structured interviews with HR senior management, middle (line) management and HR function specialist staff. Possibly a total of 10–15 people.
- Company data analysis (assuming the data is available and non-sensitive): organizational (financial), performance data (organizational and employee), management structures, HR structures, pay spend data, benchmark pay data (labour market analysis), employee demographics, policy documentation and performance management scheme rules.
- Observation of policy formulation and policy implementation and enactment, where practically permissible and of relevance to the study, for example performance appraisal.

What is in it for you?

Much of the quality of the research depends on the quality of the access granted by participant companies. In recognition of research access, the following would be provided to participants:

- Access to thematic findings, analysis within a report distributed upon completion
- Participant-specific analysis of their reward management and processes
- Feedback of results through a seminar to interested participant personnel, and wider audience, should it be desired, in either Cambridge or a location convenient for the participant.

By gaining a better understanding of the drivers of pay management policy, strategy and processes, it is hoped that participating organizations will be able to develop these areas to improve efficiency of pay spend and the attraction, motivation and retention of employees.

Bibliography

Ansoff, I. (1965) *Corporate Strategy*. New York: McGraw Hill.

Armstrong, M. and Brown, D. (2001) *Strategic Rewards: Making it Happen*. London: Kogan Page.

Armstrong, M. and Murlis, H. (1998) *Reward Management*. (4th edn). London: Kogan Page.

Armstrong, M. and Murlis, H. (2004) *Reward Management: A Handbook of Remuneration Strategy and Practice (5th edition)*. London: Kogan Page.

Amstrong, P (1995), 'Accouting for Personnel' in Storey, J. (1995), *Human Resource Management: A Critical Text*. London: Thompson.

Arthur, J. B. (1992) 'The Link between Business Strategy and Industrial Relations Systems in American Steel Mini-Mills', *Industrial and Labor Relations Review*, 45: 488–506.

Arthur, J. B. (1994) 'Effects of Human Resource Systems in Manufacturing Performance and Turnover', *Academy of Management Journal*, 37: 670–87.

Baird, L. and Meshoulam, I. (1988) 'Managing Two Fits of Strategic Human Resource Management', *Academy of Management Review*, 13 (1): 116–28.

Balkin, D. and Gomez-Meija, L. (1987) 'Toward a Contingency Theory of Compensation Strategy', *Strategic Management Journal*, 8: 169–82.

Barney, J. (1991) 'Firm Resources and Sustained Competitive Advantage', *Journal of Management*, 17: 99–120.

Barney, J. (1995) 'Looking inside for Competitive Advantage', *Academy of Management Executive*, 9 (4): 49–61.

Bartel, A. P. (1994) 'Productivity Gains from the Implementation of Employee Training Programs', *Industrial Relations*, 33: 411–25.

Becker, B. and Gerhart, B. (1996) 'The Impact of Human Resource Management on Organizational Performance: Progress and Prospects', *Academy of Management Journal*, 39: 779–801.

Becker, B. and Huselid, M. A. (1992) 'The Incentive Effects of Tournament Compensation Systems', *Administrative Sciences Quarterly*, 37: 336–50.

Becker, B. E. and Huselid, M. A. (1998) 'High Performance Work Systems and Firm Performance: A Synthesis of Research and Managerial Implications', in *Research in Personnel and Human Resources Management*, 16: 53–102.

Beckert, J. (1999) 'Agency, Entrepreneurs, and Institutional Change: The Role of Strategic Choice and Institutionalized Practices in Organizations', *Organisational Science*, 20 (5): 777–99.

Beer, M., Spector, B., Lawrence, P., Mills, D. and Walton, R. (1984) *Human Resource Management: A General Managers Perspective*. New York: Free Press.

Bergman, T. and Scarpello, V. (2002) *Compensation Decision Making*. New York: Thomson Learning.

Bonoma, T. V. (1985) 'Case Research in Marketing: Opportunities, Problems, and a Process', *Journal of Marketing Research*, May, 199–208.

Boselie, P., Paauwe, J. and Jansen (2001) 'Human Resource Management and Performance: Lessons from the Netherlands', *International Journal of Human Resource Management*, 12: 7.

Boselie, P., Paauwe, J. and Richardson, R. (2003) 'Human Resource Management, Institutionalization and Organizational Performance: A Comparison of Hospitals, Hotels and Local Government', *International Journal of Human Resource Management*, 14 (8): 1407–29.

Bowen, D. and Ostroff, C. (2004) 'Understanding HR – Firm Performance Linkages: The Role of 'Strength' of the HRM System', *Academy of Management Review*, 29 (2): 203–21.

Boxall, P. (1999) 'The Strategic HRM Debate and the Resource-Based View of the Firm', in Schuler, R. and Jackson, S. (eds) *Strategic Human Resource Management*. Oxford: Blackwell.

Brewster, C., Sparrow, P. and Harris, H. (2005) 'Towards a New Model of Globalizing HRM', *Journal of Human Resource Management*, 16 (6): 949–70.

Brown, D. (2001) *Reward Strategies: From Intent to Impact*. London: Chartered Institute of Personnel and Development.

Brown, W. and Walsh, J. (1994), 'Corporate Pay Policies and the Internalization of Markets', in J. Niland, R. Lansbury and C. Veveris (eds) *The Future of Industrial Relations: Global Change and Challenges*. London: Sage Publications.

Cannell, M. and Wood, S. (1992) *Incentive Pay: Impact and Evolution*. London: Institute of Personnel Management and National Economic Development Office.

Cascio, W. F. (1991) *Costing Human Resources: The Financial Impact of Behaviour in Organizations*. Boston: PWS-Kent.

Chandler, Alfred D. (1962), *Strategy and Structure*. Cambridge, MA: MIT Press.

Chartered Institute of Personnel and Development (2007) *Reward Management Survey 2007*. London: Chartered Institute of Personnel and Development.

Coase, R. H. (1937) 'The Nature of the Firm', *Economica*, 4: 386–405.

Cully, M., Woodland, S., O'Reilly, A. and Dix, G. (1999) *Britain at Work*. London: Routledge.

Currie, G. and Procter, S. (2001) 'Exploring the Relationship between HR and Middle Managers', *Human Resource Management Journal*, 11 (3).

Cyert, R. and March, J. (1963) *A Behavioral Theory of the Firm*. Englewood Cliffs: Prentice Hall.

Danford, A., Richardson, M., Stewart, P., Tailby, S. and Upchurch, M. (2004) 'High Performance Work Systems and Workplace Partnership: A Case Study of Aerospace Workers', *New Technology, Work and Employment* 19 (1): 14–29.

Datamonitor (2005), Company Report, www.datamonitor.com

de Rond, M. and Thietart, R. A. (2004) *Chance, Choice and Determinism in Strategy*. Judge Institute of Management Studies, working paper series.

de Rond, M. and Thietart, R. A. (2007) 'Choice, Chance and Inevitability in Strategy', *Strategic Management Journal*, 28 (5): 535–51.

Delaney, J. T. and Huselid, M. A. (1996) 'The Impact of Human Resource Management Practices on Perceptions of Organisational Performance', *Academy of Management Journal*, 39 (4): 949–69.

Delaney, J. T., Lewin, D. and Ichniowski, C. (1989) *Human Resource Policies and Practices in American Firms*. Washington, DC: US Department of Labor, Bureau of Labor-Management Relations and Cooperative Programs.

Delery, J. E., and Doty, D. H. (1996) 'Modes of Theorising in Strategic Human Resource Management: Tests of Universalistic, Contingency and Configurational Performance Predictors', *Academy of Management Journal*, 39: 802–35.

Delery, J. E., Gupta, N. and Shaw, J. D. (1997) *Human Resource Management and Firm Performance: A Systems Perspective*. Atlanta: Southern Management Association Meeting.

DiMaggio, P. J. and Powell, W. W. (1983) 'The Iron Cage Revisited: Institutional Isomorphism and Collective Rationality in Organizational Fields', *American Sociology Review*, 48: 147–60.

DiMaggio, P. J. and Powell, W. W. (1991) 'The Iron Cage Revisited: Institutional Isomorphism and Collective Rationality', in W. Powell and P. DiMaggio (eds), *The New Institutionalism in Organizational Analysis*. Chicago: University of Chicago Press.

Donaldson, L. (2001) *The Contingency Theory of Organizations*. Auckland: Sage.

Doty, D. H., Glick, W. and Huber, G. (1993) 'Fit, Equifinality, and Organizational Effectiveness: A Test of Two Configurational Theories', *Academy of Management Journal*, 36: 1196–250.

Dyer, L. and Holder, W. (1988) 'Toward a Strategic Perspective of Human Resource Management', in L. Dyer (ed.), *Human Resource Management Evolving Roles and Responsibilities*, ASPA/BNA Handbook of Human Resource Management, vol. 1.

Dyer, W. G. and Wilkins, A. (1991) 'Better Stories, not Better Constructs, to Generate Better Stories: A Rejoinder to Eisenhardt', *Academy of Management Review*, 16 (3): 613–19.

Eisenhardt, K. (1989) 'Building Theories from Case Study Research', *Academy of Management Review*, 14 (4): 532–50.

Falzon, P. (1987) 'Les activités de conception: l'approche de l'ergonomie cognitive', 222–9.

Feagin, J. R. and Orum, A. M. (1991) *A Case for the Case Study*. San Francisco: Jossey-Bass.

Ferguson, D. H. and Berger, F. (1985) 'Employees as Assets: A Fresh Approach to Human Resource Accounting', *The Cornell HRA Quarterly*, 25 (4): 24–9.

Fitz-Enz, J. (2000) *The ROI of Human Capital: Measuring the Economic Value of Employee Performance*. New York: Amacom.

Flannery, T., Hofrichter, D. and Platten, P. (2004) *People, Performance and Pay*. New York: Free Press.

Forest, J. and Mehier, C. (2001) 'John R. Commons and Herbert A. Simon on the Concept of Rationality', *Journal of Economic Issues*, No. 3, September.

Fowler, J. (1988) 'New Directions in Performance Pay', *Personnel Management*, 20 (11).

Fox, A. (1971) *A Sociology of Work in Industry*. London: Collier-Macmillan.

Freund, W. and Epstein, E. (1984) *People and Productivity: The New York Stock Exchange Guide to Financial Incentives and the Quality of Work Life*. New York: Dow Jones Publishing.

Frombrun, C., Tichy, N. and Devanna, M. (1984) *Strategic Human Resource Management*. New York: Wiley.

Galbraith, J. K. (2001) *The Essential Galbraith*. New York: Houghton Mifflin Books.

Gerhart, B. and Rynes, S. (2003) *Compensation: Theory, Evidence and Strategic Implications*. New York: Sage.

Gerhart, B. and Milkovich, G. T. (1990) 'Organizational Differences in Managerial Compensation and Firm Performance', *Academy of Management Journal*, 33: 663–91.

Giddens, A. (1979) *Central Problems in Social Theory: Action, Structure and Contradiction in Social Analysis*. California: Berkeley Press.

Gilman, M. (1999) *Performance Related Pay in Practice: Organisation and Effect* (unpublished Ph.D. thesis), University of Warwick.

Goodhart, H. (1993) *Rewards for Top Performers*. Financial Times, November, 3, 16.

Guest, D. E. (1997) 'Human Resource Management and Performance: A Review and Research Agenda', *International Journal of Human Resource Management*, 8: 265–76.

Guest, D. E., Michie, J., Sheehan, M., Conway, N. and Metochi, M. (2000) *Effective People Management: Initial Findings of the Future of Work Study*. London: Chartered Institute of Personnel and Development.

Gummerson, E. (1991) *Qualitative Methods in Management Research* (revised edition). Newbury Park: Sage.

Hammer, N. and Champy, J. (1993) *Re-Engineering the Corporation*. San Francisco: Jossey Bass.

Hannah, M. T. and Freeman, J. (1977) 'The Population Ecology of Organizations', *American Journal of Sociology*, 82: 929–64.

Hendry, C. and Pettigrew, A. (1990) 'Human Resource Management: An Agenda for the 1990s', *International Journal of Human Resource Management*, 1 (1): 17–23.

Herzberg, F. (1975) *One More Time, How Do You Motivate Employees?* Harvard Business School: Harvard Business School Press.

Huselid, M. (1995) 'The Impact of Human Resource Management Practices on Turnover, Productivity and Corporate Financial Performance', *Academy of Management Journal*, 38: 635–70.

Huselid, M. and Becker, B. (1995) 'High Performance Work Systems and Organizational Performance', Paper presented at the annual meeting of the Academy of Management, Vancouver.

Hussey, J. and Hussey, R. (1997) *Business Research: A Practical Guide for Undergraduate and Graduate Research*. Basingstoke: Palgrave Macmillan.

Itami, H. (1987) *Mobilising Invisible Assets*. Boston: HBS Press.

Jackson, S. and Schuler, R. (1995) 'Understanding Human Resource Management in the Context of Organisations and their Environments', *Annual Review of Psychology*, 46.

Jones, B. (1999) *Politics and the Architecture of Choice: Bounded Rationality and Governance*. New York: Sage.

Keenoy, T. (1999) 'HRM as a Hologram: A Polemic', *Journal of Management Studies*, 36 (1): 171–88.

Kersley, B., Bryson, A., Alpin, C. and Forth, J. (2006) *Inside the Workplace: Findings from the 2004 Workplace Employment Relations Survey*. London: Routledge.

Kessler, I. (1994) 'Performance Related Pay: Contrasting Approaches', *Industrial Relations Journal*, 25 (2): 122–34.

Kessler, I. (2000) 'Remuneration Systems', in S. Bach and K. Sisson (eds), *Personnel Management*. Oxford: Blackwell.

Kessler, I. (2001) 'Reward System Choices' in J. Storey (ed.), *Human Resource Management: A Critical Text*. London: Thomson Learning.

Kessler, I. and Purcell, J. (1992) 'Performance Related Pay Objectives and Application', *Human Resource Management*, 2 (4).

Kirk, D. and Miller, M. (1986) *Reliability and Validity in Qualitative Research.* New York: Sage.

Kochan, T. A., Katz, H. C. and McKersie, R. B. (1986) *The Transformation of American Industrial Relations.* New York: Basic Books.

Larson, M. (1977) *The Rise of Professionalism: A Sociological Analysis.* Berkeley: University of California Press.

Lawler, Edward E. (1990) *Strategic Pay.* New York: Jossey-Bass.

Lawler, E. E. (2000) *Rewarding Excellence: Pay Strategies for the New Economy.* San Francisco: Jossey-Bass.

Lawler, Edward E, Mohrman, S. A. and Ledford, G. E. (1995) *Creating High Performance Organizations: Practices and Results of Employee Involvement and Total Quality.* New York: Jossey Bass.

Lawrence, P. and Lorsch, J. W. (1973) 'High Performing Organizations in Three Environments?' in D. S. Pugh (ed.), *Organization Theory* (1997). London: Penguin.

Legge, K. (1995) 'HRM: Rhetoric, Reality and Hidden Agendas', in J. Storey (ed.), *Human Resource Management: A Critical Text.* London: Routledge.

Legge, K. (2001) 'Silver Bullet or Spent Round? Assessing the Meaning of the High Commitment Management/Performance Relationship' in J. Storey (ed.), *Human Resource Management: A Critical Text.* London: Thomson Learning.

Lewis, R. (1991) 'Performance Related Pay: Pretext and Pitfalls', *Employee Relations*, 13 (4).

MacDuffie, J. P. (1995) 'Human Resource Bundles and Manufacturing Performance: Flexible Production Systems in the World Auto Industry', *Industrial Relations and Labor Review*, 48: 197–221.

Mahoney, T. (1979) *Compensation and Reward Perspectives.* Homewood: R. D. Irwin.

Marler, J. H., Woodward Barlinger, M. and Milkovich, G. T. (2002) 'Work Attitudes: Research and Practice in Human Resource Management', *Human Resource Management Journal*, 9 (2): 50–63.

Marsden, D. (1986) *The End of Economic Man?* London: Harvester Wheatsheaf.

Matthews, R. (1986) 'The Economics of Institutions and the Sources of Growth', *The Economic Journal*, 96: 903–18.

McKelvey, R. D. and Page, T. (1999) 'Taking the Coase Theorem Seriously', *Economics and Philosophy*, 15 (2): 235–47.

Mercer Human Resource Consulting (2004) *Compensation in Leading Companies.* Consultancy Report.

Meyer, J and Rowan, B. (1991) 'Institutionalised Organizations: Formal Structure as Myth and Ceremony', in W. Powell and P. DiMaggio (eds) *The New Institutionalism in Organizational Analysis.* Chicago: University of Chicago Press.

Miles, M. B. and Huberman, A. M. (1994) *Qualitative Data Analysis: An Expanded Source Book.* (second edition). Thousand Oaks: Sage.

Miles, R. and Snow, C. (1978) *Organisational Strategy, Structure, and Process.* New York: McGraw Hill.

Milkovich, G. T., and Newman, J. M. (1999) *Compensation* (6th edn). New York: Irwin/McGraw Hill.

Milward, N., Bryson, A. and Forth, J. (2000) *All Change at Work? British Employment Relations 1980–1998, as Portrayed by the Workplace Industrial Relations Survey Series.* London: Routledge.

Mintzberg, H. (1978) *The Structuring of Organizations: A Synthesis of Research.* New York: Prentice Hall.

Mintzberg, H. (1990) 'The Design School: Reconsidering the Basic Premises of Strategic Management', *Strategic Management Journal*, 11: 171–95.

Napathiet, J. and Ghoshal, S. (1998) 'Social Capital, Intellectual Capital and the Organizational Advantage', *Academy of Management Review*, 23: 242–66.

Nash, D. (2003) *Determinants of the Use of Financial Incentives in Investment Banking.* ESRC Centre for Business Research, University of Cambridge, working paper no. 256.

Nelson, R. and Winter, S. (1982) *An Evolutionary Theory of Economic Change.* New York: Belknap Press.

Nickerson, J. and Silverman, B. (2003) 'Why Firms Want to Organize Efficiently and What Keeps Them from Doing So: Evidence from the For-Hire Trucking Industry', *Administrative Science Quarterly*, 48: 433–465.

North, D. (1988) *Institutional Change and Economic Performance.* Cambridge: Cambridge University Press.

Okuno-fujiwara, M. (2002) 'Social Relations and Endogenous Culture', *Japanese Economic Review*, 53 (1): 1–24.

Oliver, C. (1997) 'Sustaining Competitive Advantage: Combining Institutional and Resource Based Views', *Strategic Management Journal*, 18 (9): 697–713.

Parkhe, A. (1993) 'Strategic Alliance Structuring: A Game Theoretic and Transaction Cost Examination of Inter-Firm Cooperation', *Academy of Management Journal*, 36: 794–829.

Pendleton, D. (1992) 'Performance Related Pay in British Rail', in S. Vickerstaff (ed.) *Human Resource Management in Europe: Text and Cases.* London: Chapman and Hall.

Penrose, E. T. (1959) *The Theory of the Growth of the Firm.* New York: Wiley.

Pettigrew, A. M. (1990) 'Longitudinal Field Research on Change: Theory and Practice', *Organization Science*, 1 (3): 267–316.

Pfeffer, J. (1994) *Competitive Advantage through People.* Boston: HBS Press.

Pfeffer, J. (1998) *The Human Equation.* Boston: HBS Press.

Porter, M. (1980) *Competitive Strategy.* New York. Free Press.

Porter, M. (1991) 'Towards a Dynamic Theory of Strategy', *Strategic Management Journal*, 12, 95–117.

Pugh, D. S. (1973) 'Does Context Determine Form?' in D. S. Pugh (ed.) *Organization Theory* (1997). London: Penguin.

Purcell, J. (1999) 'Best Practice and Best Fit: Chimera or cul de sac', *Human Resource Management Review*, 8: 311–31.

Purcell, J. and Ahlstrand, B. (1994) *Human Resource Management in the Multi-Divisional Company.* New York: Oxford University Press.

Reid, G. (1987) *Theories of Industrial Organization.* London: Blackwell.

Reward Management Annual Survey Report (2007). London: Chartered Institute of Personnel Management.

Robertson, P. L. and Langlois, R. N. (1994) *Institutions, Inertia and Changing Industrial Leadership.* Oxford: Oxford University Press.

Rumelt, R. (1984) 'Towards a Strategic Theory of the Firm', in R. Lamb (ed.) *Competitive Strategic Management.* Englewood Cliffs: Prentice-Hall.

Rynes, S. L. and Gerhart, B. (2000). *Compensation in Organizations.* San Francisco: Jossey-Bass. Edited Volume. Frontiers of Industrial and Organizational Psychology series.

Scapens, R. W. (1990) 'Researching Management Accounting Practice: The Role of Case Study Methods', *British Accounting Review*, 22: 259–81.

Scarpello, V. and Theeke, H. A. (1989) 'Human Resource Accounting: A Measured Critique', *Journal of Accounting Literature*, 8: 265–80.

Schmidt, F. L., Hunter, J. E., McKenzie, R. C. and Muldrow, T. W. (1979) 'Impact of Valid Selection Procedures on Work-Force Productivity', *Journal of Applied Psychology*, 64: 609–26.

Schuler, R. and Jackson, S. (1987) 'Linking Competitive Strategies with HRM Practices', *Academy of Management Executive*, 1 (3): 209–13.

Schuster, J. and Zingheim, P. (1992) *The New Pay*. New York: Lexington Books.

Schuster, J. and Zingheim, P. (2000) *Pay People Right! Pay Strategies for the New Economy*. San Franciso: Jossey-Bass.

Shenkar, O. and Zeira, Y. (1987) 'Human Resources Management in International Joint Ventures: Directions for Research', *Academy of Management Review*, 12 (3): 546–57.

Simon, H. (1957) *Models of Man*. New York: Wiley.

Simon, H. (1959) 'Theories of Decision Making in Economics and Behavioural Science', *American Economic Review*, 49: 353–83.

Sisson, K. (1995) 'Human Resource Management and the Personnel Function', in J. Storey (ed.) *Human Resource Management: A Critical Text*. London: Routledge.

Sloan, A. P. (1963) *My Life at General Motors*. New York: Free Press.

Smith, I. C. (1993) 'Reward Management: A Retrospective Assessment', *Employee Relations*, 15 (3): 45–9.

Snell, S. A. (1992) 'Control Theory in Strategic Human Resource Management: The Mediating Effect of Administrative Information', *Academy of Management Journal*, 35 (2): 292–327.

Snell, S. A., Youndt, M. A., and Wright, P. M. (1996). 'Establishing a Framework for Research in Strategic Human Resource Management. Merging Resource Theory and Organizational Learning', in G. Ferris (ed.) *Research in Personnel and Human Resource Management*. 14: 61–90.

Stacey, R. (1993) *Strategic Management and Organisational Dynamics*. London: Pitman.

Stiles, P and Kulvisaechana, S. (2003) 'Human Capital and Performance' [Online] www.accountingforpeople.gov.uk.

Storey, J. (1995) 'Human Resource Management: Still Marching On, or Marching Out?' in J. Storey (ed.) *Human Resource Management: A Critical Text*. London: Thomson Business Press.

Storey, J. (2001) 'Human Resource Management Today: An Assessment', in J. Storey (ed.) *Human Resource Management: A Critical Text*. London: Thomson Learning.

Terpstra, D. E. and Rozell, E. J. (1993) 'The Relationship of Staffing Practices to Organizational Level Measures of Performance', *Personnel Psychology*, 46: 27–48.

Truss, C., Gratton, L., Hope-Hailey, V., McGovern, P. and Stiles, P. (1997) 'Soft and Hard Models of Human Rresource Management: A Reappraisal', *Journal of Management Studies*, 34 (1): 53–73.

Ulrich, D. (1997) *Human Resource Champions: The Next Agenda for Adding Value and Delivering Results*. Boston: Harvard Business School Press.

Von Newmann, J. and Morgenstern, O. (1944) *Theory of Games and Economic Behaviour*. Princeton: Princeton University Press.

Walsh, J. (1992) *Internalisation versus Decentralisation: An Analysis of Recent Development in Pay*. Discussion paper. Leeds University Business School.

Watson Wyatt Worldwide (2006/2007) *Effectively Managing Global Compensation & Benefits*.

Weitzman, M. L. and Kruse, D. L. (1990) 'Profit Sharing and Productivity', in A. S. Blinder (ed.) *Paying for Productivity*. Washington: Brookings Institution.

Whittington, R. (1997) *What is Strategy and Does It Matter?* London: Thomson Business Press.

Williamson, O. E. (1986) 'Vertical Integration and Related Variations on a Transaction Cost Theme', in J. E. Stiglitz and G. F. Mathewson (eds) *New Developments in the Analysis of Market Structures*. London: Macmillan.

Wood, S. (1996) 'High Commitment Management and Organization in the UK', *The International Journal of Human Resource Management*, 6: 41–58.

Wright, P. and Boswell, W. (2002) 'Desegregating HRM: A Review and Synthesis of Micro and Macro Human Resource Management Research, *Journal of Management*, 28 (3): 247–76.

Wright, P. M., Dunford, B. B. and Snell, S. A. (2001) 'Human Resources and the Resource-Based View of the Firm', *Journal of Management*, 27: 701–21.

Wright, P. M. and Gardner, T. M. (2000) *Theoretical and Empirical Challenges in Studying the HR Practice-Performance Relationship*. Paper presented at the Special Workshop 'Strategic Human Resource Management', European Institute for Advance Management Studies, INSEAD, Fontainbleau, France, 30 March–1 April.

Wright, P. M. and Nishii, L. H. (2004) *Strategic HRM and Organizational Behavior: Integrating Multiple Levels of Analysis*. Erasmus University Conference 'HRM: What's Next', 2004.

Wright, P. M. and Snell, S. (1998) 'Towards a Unifying Framework for Exploring Fit and Flexibility in Strategic Human Resource Management', *Academy of Management Review*, 23 (4).

Yin, R. K. (1994) *Case Study Research: Design and Methods*. London: Sage.

Youndt, M. A., Snell, S. A., Dean, J. W. and Lepak, D. P. (1996) 'Human Resource Management, Manufacturing Strategy and Firm Performance', *Academy of Management Journal*, 39: 836–66.

Zbaracki, M. (1998) 'The Rhetoric and Reality of Total Quality Management', *Administrative Science Quarterly*, 43.

Zingheim, P. K. and Schuster, J. R. (2000) *Pay People Right*. San Francisco: Jossey-Bass.

Index